D0853549

FANTASY ISLAND

ED MORALES

FANTASY ISLAND

COLONIALISM, EXPLOITATION, AND THE BETRAYAL OF PUERTO RICO

BOLD TYPE BOOKS

NEW YORK

Bold Type Books
116 East 16th Street, 8th Floor New York, NY 10003
www.boldtypebooks.org
@BoldTypeBooks

Printed in the United States of America

First Edition: September 2019

Published by Bold Type Books, an imprint of Perseus Books, LLC, a subsidiary of Hachette Book Group, Inc. Bold Type Books is a co-publishing venture of the Type Media Center and Perseus Books.

The Hachette Speakers Bureau provides a wide range of authors for speaking events. To find out more, go to www.hachettespeakersbureau.com or call (866) 376-6591.

The publisher is not responsible for websites (or their content) that are not owned by the publisher.

Editorial production by Christine Marra, Marrathon Production Services.
www.marrathoneditorial.org

Book design by Jane Raese
Set in 11.5-point Fairfield

Library of Congress Cataloging-in-Publication Data has been applied for.
ISBNs: 978-1-56858-899-5 (hardcover); 978-1-56858-898-8 (ebook); 978-1-5417-6299-2 (trade paperback, Spanish edition); 978-1-5417-3046-5 (ebook, Spanish edition)

LSC-C

Printing 3, 2021

FOR MY MOTHER AND MY SISTER

CONTENTS

INTRODUCTION

Puerto Rican flag on the beach in Piñones. © Joseph Rodríguez

When Hurricane María unleashed its devastating Category 4 hurricane winds and rains on the already-vulnerable island of Puerto Rico, I understood almost immediately that it was the inevitable disaster that I'd dreaded for years. The colonial government had been accumulating accelerated amounts of debt for ten years and had defaulted on it, prompting a bipartisan Congress to impose a fiscal oversight and management board. The island's electrical infrastructure had begun to collapse, and I'd already been caught in traffic snarls with no stoplights and driven up the winding, dark roads into the island's mountainous interior feeling the encroachment of a dystopian future for myself, my family, and all Puerto Ricans.

I was born in New York and consider myself a die-hard city kid, having grown up in the East Bronx, lived through the downtown years of art explosion and gentrification of the East Village, resettled in brownstone Brooklyn, and returned like a prodigal son to the Bronx's southern tip in Mott Haven. But like most "Nuyoricans," I consider Puerto Rico my mecca, the repository of my spiritual self and the endless story of my extended family, who came from two adjacent areas of the island's mountainous central region. During my childhood visits I immersed myself in those hillside *fincas*, or subsistence farms; watched as my grandfather milked his cows and chased his roosters; and picked up mangos ripe enough to eat that had fallen from the trees. When I go for a swim at the Balneario de Luqillo, our local beach, I feel myself embraced by the Yoruban spirit of Yemayá and ask to be healed from all the times I missed subway trains pulling out of stations and editors who spiked my stories from publication.

For Puerto Ricans living on the island and in the United States, the twin crises of debt and hurricane recovery present a fundamental reassessment of how they view themselves. After more than a hundred years since the United States granted Puerto Ricans US citizenship, that identity's value is being questioned and the fantasy of its promise is being exposed. Puerto Rico is now revealed to be what it always was: a colonial satellite, a dumping ground for US manufactured goods, and a tax shelter/investment casino in a land of temptation for tourists: white-sand beaches, exotic cocktails, and polyrhythmic hedonism. It had already been threatened with decades of economic contraction, an emptying of its population, and the transformation into something wasting away but undying, a hollowed-out shell of itself, a site for speculative profit—an island no longer resembling the nationalist dreams of a proud people.[1] Post–Hurricane María, all of these factors will be exacerbated, and the challenges facing Puerto Rico's reinvention are staggering.

The time-stopping, hope-shattering moment of María, which can be extended into the weeks and months immediately following the storm, was the final straw that exposed the illusion of US citizenship that islanders had been granted in 1917. This is how our wannabe American fantasy balloon burst: despite being denied the right to vote in presidential elections and lacking voting representation in Congress, many Puerto Ricans had long felt that their citizenship, which was realized more fully when they migrated to the United States, included equal protection under the law. The cries of dismay heard over and over again in the weeks after María—"We're US citizens, aren't we?"—revealed the poignant nature of our delusion.

Despite these fantasies, the US response to Hurricane María proved beyond the shadow of a doubt that residents of Puerto Rico have never really been first-class citizens. The Trump administration's sluggish and neglectful deployment of FEMA and military assistance, coupled with its brazen willingness to privatize any and all relief efforts, laid bare the racist colonialism with which the United States has often administered Puerto Rico, the largest of its five major inhabited "unincorporated territories." A *Politico* investigation published in March 2018 made this stunningly clear: of the individual assistance aid approved in the nine days after each hurricane, $141.8 million went to Houston, whereas Puerto Rico received only $6.2 million.[2] The amount of personnel and food and water distribution as well as the number of temporary roof tarps were at least two or three times higher for Texas than for Puerto Rico. Although these numbers came out months after the storm, Puerto Ricans could sense the ugly truth that they were being deprioritized, and it was having fatal results.

The callous indifference of the Trump administration and several officials from FEMA and the military was demonstrated in so many ways—from employing the talking point that there is "a really big ocean" separating Puerto Rico from Washington and that the electrical grid was "dead before the storms ever hit" to tossing paper towels to a handpicked throng of evangelicals in a church in a well-off suburb, believing that constituted compassion. Trump's oblivious condescension stood as stark proof that the citizenship granted to Puerto Ricans in 1917 has always been second class.

Puerto Ricans have been excluded from first-class citizenship through a legal process that demonstrates the inseparable tie between colonialism and racism. This process goes back as far as the 1901 case *Downes v. Bidwell*, decided by some of the judges who ruled on *Plessy v. Ferguson*, when a new colonial turn of phrase entered the American vocabulary. According to *Downes*, Puerto Rico should not be considered fit for becoming a state in the Union but would be instead an "unincorporated territory" "belonging to, but not part of" the United States. Belonging to, but not part of. Separate, but also not equal. Sort of.

Although most Puerto Ricans grow up not knowing much about this tawdry history, the 1900 debate in Congress about the possibility of Puerto Rico becoming a state was littered with epithets about Puerto Ricans being "mongrels" and an "alien race" unfit to govern themselves.[3] We were bodies, then, that should not mix with the body of white America, for we were already stained with mixture, through both our fraught tropical sweatbox of consensual and nonconsensual unions as well as the legacy of our Iberian antecedents, who had already been festooned in Moorish veils of uncertain North African origin. Unwashed bodies, unworthy bodies, and—like the body of Homer Plessy, the Louisiana Creole passenger booted from the whites-only section of the train—bodies marked for exclusion/destruction, the objects of violence, both literally and figuratively.

María came just weeks after Charlottesville and the many other spectacles of implied and literal racial conflict that had marked the first year of the Trump reign, with the mainstream media apoplectically ping-ponging between the Colin Kaepernick–inspired national anthem–kneeling protests and the tragedy of tens of thousands of Puerto Ricans. They were traumatized, root-shocked, and *desesperados* by a landscape of twigs where Ceiba trees grew, zinc roofs shattered into shards, and a simmering, rising tide of noxious, contaminated water flowing through what were once quaint Caribbean towns. African American athletes' kneeling protests were a silent rejection of internal colonialism, while the shock doctrine military-P3 complex that was about to overtake Puerto Rico was the endgame of a century or so of external colonialism.

Even well-meaning, proud Puerto Ricans who had served in the US military complained about Trump's slow-motion doddering on María, insisting that their sacrifice deserved respect. But they seemed to forget that when African American and Mexican soldiers returned home to Jim Crow segregation and dehumanization after fighting the "Good War" of Tom Brokaw's "Greatest Generation," their angry disappointment significantly motivated the Civil Rights Movement. The language of "belonging to, but not a part of" and "separate but equal" has never been formally written out of America's narrative.

So here we were, vulnerable in our beautiful brown bodies, at the intersection of mainland and island, of diaspora and *isleñidad*, and of what is perhaps the ruling dialectic of the late-capitalist world system, *debt* and *crisis*. The debt, all $72 or so billion of it plus $49 billion in unfunded pension obligations, is a kind of fiction, but the crisis is all too real. The privatization frenzy promised by PROMESA, the congressional debt collection agency, has already begun to accelerate as the spin of Trump's casino-government roulette wheel picks out the winning bids. Planeloads of desperate *Boricuas* will evacuate to

Central Florida, Texas, and beyond, while billionaires like John Paulson gobble up prime beach real estate as they seek the latest in chic tax havens.

In the ancient world, Middle Ages, and early Modern Europe, there were debt jubilees, where the slate of obligations was wiped clean and the collective citizenry could start over again. But aside from some progressive proposals by Bernie Sanders and Elizabeth Warren, most Democrats have focused on investigating the Trump administration's unacceptable handling of María while virtually ignoring the machinations of the Fiscal Oversight and Management Board (FOMB)—known in Puerto Rico as "La Junta"—as it imposes austerity policies. With its local government officials rendered powerless by the FOMB, Puerto Rico remains stuck in the powerlessness of its colonial status and can't find a path to economic self-determination.

Although it is the only possible humanitarian solution, rescinding the debt—or even a vast reduction of the debt—seems highly unlikely, and the US government seems poised to use the debt's nagging accumulated weight to institute a permanent state of crisis. The indebting of Puerto Rico was accomplished through a systematic policy intertwined with colonialism. After the end of the slave economies in the nineteenth century, the United States and European countries have intervened in Caribbean economies by overwhelming local currencies and leveraging control of agricultural production, creating the conditions for debt accumulation. In the second half of the twentieth century the US financial sector offered indebtedness as a solution to Puerto Rico's inability to weather the 1970s recession, creating the conditions for speculation on its rising obligations.

The debt crisis represents a normalized scenario for a colony—or "unincorporated territory"—to be able to operate when its economy is no longer creating jobs or retaining profits made by outside investors. A major motif of this crisis is the infrastructure that—like our bodies, subjected to violence—was exposed and poorly maintained. Electrical cables running along haphazardly installed posts crisscrossing the island, constantly failing for years before the storm, now lay fallen like the mass casualties of war. Collapsed like the stick-figure balloons that advertise car washes, Puerto Rico's infrastructure is in a grand mal seizure.

The state of the electrical infrastructure is directly related to the way the island territory got caught in a web of borrowing in the form of municipal bonds just to pay government expenditures. As payroll and pension payouts for its hundreds of thousands of workers as well as minimum operating costs swallowed up most of the liquid funds available, maintaining the infrastructure—including roads, public buildings, and so on—was neglected. Hurricane María merely made visible what had already been apparent to Puerto Ricans: the island as a whole was deteriorating, and the merciless path of destruction created by the endgame of Puerto Rico's debt crisis could no longer be covered up.

So how did we get here? For me it all started when I went to visit my mother in the house she and my late father built in the 1980s for their retirement. It was the end of June in 2015, and I found myself watching, along with millions of television viewers, Governor Alejandro García Padilla declare that the island territory's $72 billion debt to a staggering array of bondholders was unpayable. The warning sirens of the debt crisis had been sounding for a year, but now we were all facing a watershed moment in our—and America's—history: the life we had lived as the people of Puerto Rico, the Caribbean's Great Democratic Experiment, was a fantasy, and now it was over.

For many Puerto Ricans on the island, hoping to live a sustainable life with a steady job in a viable profession or to start and grow a small business and raise some children, the looming debt crisis and the hurricane's aftermath had created a tremendous amount of doubt. An exodus of both skilled professionals and unskilled workers had already been underway since the island had gone into a recession in 2006, and the seeming inevitability of prolonged economic contraction was creating a sustained feeling of anxiety about the future. Talk show hosts who once focused on political gossip with manic intensity began to lapse into a kind of somber monotone, a fully realized voice of *ay bendito* resignation, recalling the lament of songwriter Rafael Hernández's suddenly impoverished mountain peasant *jíbaro*.[4]

Yet all those folks whose hopes were dashed by the default had never fully acknowledged that they were based on a fantasy that the island was a "commonwealth" with a position in the US orbit that *almost* made it one of the "states." Over the last four years—since Alejandro García Padilla's 2015 announcement through the September 2017 nightmare of María—I saw over a hundred years of America's failed colonial experiment flash before my eyes. The 1898 landing of American troops in the southern port of Guánica, the imposition of the English language in schools and in the courts, the massacre of nationalists in Ponce, the false hope of the 1952 Constitution and commonwealth status, the Great Migration of the 1950s and 1960s, *West Side Story*, Freddie Prinze, the Young Lords, the Nuyorican Poets, Rita Moreno, the South Bronx's Fort Apache, Roberto Clemente, Raúl Julia, Rosie Pérez, Ricky Martin, Jennifer Lopez, Marc Anthony, and Daddy Yankee. All of it spinning before us, evading our grasp like the snow globe that slips from the hands of a flagging Citizen Kane.

Clearly this was the beginning of an end, yet the whole story, from its very prologue, had never been adequately explained. Few Puerto Ricans—let alone mainland US citizens—had really come to grips with the reality that Puerto Rico is the world's longest-held colony, tracing back to its seizure by the Spanish in 1493, and that its history is emblematic of how a dark side of colonizer behavior has always tainted America's founding story—its noble declaration of independence from a colonial power. At various points in its history Puerto Rico has served as a military outpost, laboratory for birth control experiments, and dry run for free-trade policies like the North American Free Trade Agreement (NAFTA). Now it would become a testing ground for how far a fiscal control board could go to impose austerity on a subservient government to extract as much as possible from the Puerto Rican people and its public institutions to pay debts generated by Wall Street speculation.

It's also crucial to understand how Puerto Rico's cycle of debt is part of a long-established set of economic relationships between Europe and the Americas. The common knowledge about this part of world history focuses on the origin story of industrial capitalism in Europe and how that dynamic played out in the United States. However, the expansion of trade and finance capital, coupled with the massive exploitation of slavery, is key to understanding the underdevelopment of the Caribbean and Latin America. The late-nineteenth- and early twentieth-century period was not just playing out the final stages of Manifest Destiny; it was when the United States took control of Latin American economic activity to its advantage.

This takeover entailed not only penetrating and controlling the productive sectors of those newly acquired possessions and economies but also enforcing a new debt-collection regime on the Caribbean, including the islands of Dominican Republic and Cuba. In the early twentieth century Wall Street investment banks like the City Bank, J.P. Morgan, Speyer, and Kuhn, Loeb & Co. began lending money to Caribbean nations and the colony of Puerto Rico, epitomizing what economist Peter James Hudson calls the confluence of "finance capitalism with racial capitalism."[5] Almost a century earlier, in 1825, France demanded a 150-million-franc payment from Haiti to compensate for its loss of slaves and land after their late-eighteenth-century revolution. This helped set up a model that other European powers quickly emulated: indenturing Latin American countries through debt. The United States merely decided to assume the debt collector role as a way to eliminate European influence.

After it came under US control in 1898, Puerto Rico evolved from being a site of domination by US-based sugar manufacturers to a midcentury showcase for the success of US industrial capitalism in the Caribbean. The latter phase came about as a reaction to pressures from the postwar UN for world decolonization, the threat of a militant Puerto Rican nationalist

movement that called for independence, and a Western desire
to blunt any optimism about Cuba's socialist experiment. But
as the optimism generated by the industrialization of the island
in the 1950s faded with the 1970s recession, the turn to globalization and free trade became the key to Puerto Rico's modern
demise.

As part of the industrialization effort, euphemistically called
"Operation Bootstrap," the United States allowed corporations
to set up tax-free on the island, employ workers for below minimum wage, and corner the market on selling to Puerto Rican
consumers. But when the NAFTA era began in 1994, American
businesses flocked to Mexico, Central America, and beyond,
where the wages and operating costs were a fraction of those
in Puerto Rico, which no longer held a competitive advantage.
When a provision of the IRS tax code giving tax breaks to American corporations operating in Puerto Rico was phased out between 1996 and 2006, the exodus of US corporations accelerated,
and a deep recession set in. The island's government, which had
been already borrowing to cover essential services, engaged in
a shadowy partnership with Wall Street municipal bond market
speculators, exacerbating the accumulation of the debt, which
eventually grew into the current $72 billion debt crisis.

The crisis was highly abstract, and at first almost no one
seemed to understand or care much about it. Its intricacies were
couched in the exotic language of finance: interest rate swaps,
complex financial instruments, triple-tax exemptions. The island's political discourse was wrapped up in its never-ending
status debate and a continual back and forth between its two
main political parties, which favored either a continuance of
the commonwealth status or petitioning for US statehood. Media coverage was limited to local San Juan newspapers and business press outlets like the *Wall Street Journal* and *Bloomberg
Business*, emphasizing at first the plight of the mom-and-pop
investor and, as the crisis worsened, the threat to the municipal
bond market itself. The accumulation of debt had an ambivalent morality to it—bond selling was irresponsible and reckless,

but from the Puerto Rico government's perspective, it could at least be justified with keeping public services afloat and saving the jobs of tens of thousands of Puerto Ricans. As the private sector began to struggle, the government became one of the most reliable employers on the island, propping up its tenuous middle class.

The slow erosion of the island's quality of life, infrastructure, and essential services was a constant theme after the US corporate tax breaks were phased out from 1996 to 2006. Private-sector jobs were evaporating at a record pace, and the government implemented job cuts by the tens of thousands. Hundreds of thousands of Puerto Ricans were migrating to the mainland, as US citizenship allowed them to do so without restriction. When Governor García Padilla determined that the debt was unpayable, Congress rushed to pass a bill called PROMESA—the Spanish word for "promise"—which President Barack Obama signed into law in June 2016. It imposed an unelected fiscal oversight and management board with the power to control all aspects of public policy on the island. PROMESA was ostensibly installed as a federal mechanism to restore fiscal responsibility, with a moral mission to cut back on expenses and impose on the US territory a sense of shared sacrifice. But islanders saw it as a very expensive debt collection agency, one whose $1.5 billion cost over its initial five-year term would even have to be covered by the island's government coffers.

Appointed by former president Barack Obama from nominations made by both Republicans and Democrats, the original PROMESA board had seven members, only two of whom were residents of Puerto Rico, and all were from the financial sector. The use of fiscal oversight boards goes back to New York's financial crisis of the 1970s and such boards were more recently used for public budget crises in Detroit and Washington, DC. But this oversight board—which includes a former executive of Santander Bank and a member of the island's Government Development Bank, both institutions that were players in the formation of the crisis—is widely perceived as a group of self-interested outsiders, an obvious imposition of colonial authority. What's more, as Puerto Ricans increasingly suspect their elected officials of corruption, many are not willing to accept guilt for the accumulation of the island's debt.

Beyond the national trauma that Puerto Ricans are experiencing, the present cataclysms may also provoke a pernicious blowback into the United States' municipal bond market. While one of the narratives about Puerto Rico's accumulation of debt places blame on the Puerto Rico government for excessive borrowing, seeking to instill a sense of guilt on the island as a whole, the financial crisis may inevitably send market headwinds crashing beyond the island's borders. The fiscal oversight and management board is partially meant to forestall any rippling effects from Puerto Rico's crisis that could unmoor looming debt crises for some US states—like California, New Jersey, and Illinois—that, like Puerto Rico, don't have access to bankruptcy protection. Many economists predict that the slow recovery from the 2008 crash most likely means there is another financial crisis in the future, brought on by failing states and their foundational positions in the bond market.

The debtor relationship between the United States and Puerto Rico, though always present, has exploded as a product of the neoliberal free-trade era. Straddling the border between being treated as a US state and an international territorial entity, the island became sucked into a rapidly expanding municipal bond market, an arena that could quickly shift from "safe," low-risk investment to the distressed debt favored by vulture investors. All of this activity was cloaked in the mysterious language and practices of high finance, with the average Puerto Rican only able to measure their standing through their status as consumers of US products or their ability to escape the island to live as fully entitled citizens in one of the fifty states.

Although Puerto Rico's debt crisis situation, as a result of its use as a laboratory for bond speculation and offshore banking for tax avoidance, seems remote in its far-off Caribbean location, it could serve as a preview for the trouble brewing in the United States. In 2018, as Congress rolled back the Dodd-Frank measures designed to regulate banking institutions after the 2008 financial crisis, it became increasingly clear that Puerto Rico–like municipal debt crises may become more common in the US. The debt that Puerto Rico had accumulated by borrowing for decades just to cover governmental expenses has been portrayed as irresponsible, but it was the same public-sector spending strategy that New York City used in the 1970s, that had caused bankruptcy-like procedures in Detroit and Washington, DC, and currently threatens Illinois and other troubled states.

In many ways imposing austerity on Puerto Rico is a way for the United States to externalize its own shaky financing and create its own "exceptionalism" by asking its colony to pay for its own sins. With the Trump administration driving up the national debt to $22 trillion, it's hard to argue that the United States is a paragon of financial responsibility. Puerto Ricans increasingly use slogans like "esa deuda es inmoral" (that debt is immoral) that absolve them from a debt created by a government and elite banking sector unchecked by Washington and Wall Street, reflecting that all this trouble may yet come home to roost in the United States.

Ringing out faintly over the howling of natural disasters, alarm bells have sounded in Puerto Rico. Its government is reeling from being perceived as corrupt and powerless, plunging its civil society into uncertainty, with many islanders girding for active resistance in the form of street protests and general strikes. Puerto Ricans' collective spirit may soon shift from passive guilt over their government's ineffectiveness to hardened regret that they weren't quicker to identify and counter the true authors of their home's decay. The battle lines have already been drawn in the fight to save the island's university and public-school system, the surface road infrastructure is rapidly crumbling, and the electrical grid, particularly after Hurricane María, has been shown vulnerable to complete collapse. There is an imminent healthcare crisis as hundreds of doctors flee daily from a system struggling to serve an aging population. This societal precarity, in addition to vulnerability to new ecological disasters, will make any recovery long, tortuous, and prone to setbacks.

But across the water how soon will it be before mainland Americans realize that Puerto Rico's fall may greatly erode the American Dream from within? How long will it take before it becomes obvious that the original dream of American emancipation from European colonial control is inevitably connected to the US subjugation of a multiracial, "foreign" people? The more the bad news about this unincorporated tropical paradise is exposed under the media microscope, the more it threatens to subvert the best-laid plans of a nation that sees itself as the light of the world. The imposition of PROMESA—its program of austerity and the tension this will create between the Puerto Rican people and vulture- and hedge-fund bondholders—may further fracture US global financial primacy if the municipal bond market, a linchpin of finance capital worldwide, is called into question.

Even before María the drama stirred by the imposition of the FOMB, which took power in January 2017, had been building in intensity. Tensions between La Junta and the government, headed by pro-statehood governor Ricardo Rosselló, were already being felt in the process of creating a budget and fiscal plan. To complicate matters further, when the government and La Junta filed for a modified bankruptcy procedure facilitated by PROMESA in May 2017, a circuit court judge from Brooklyn, Laura Taylor Swain, became a third major player controlling the island's destiny.

As the PROMESA process plays out, the central conflict is among representatives of the Puerto Rico government, which administrates various services and institutions; La Junta, which has authority over all budget proposals and expenditure allocations; and bondholders, who want the most return on their defaulted debt. The FOMB wields the final approval of all budgetary decisions and represents the island's government in bankruptcy court. The key decisions made by the board will be around which services are deemed "essential" and need to be left largely intact and which are not and can be cut drastically. The tricky business of prioritizing which bondholders get paid and at what rate, will be decided by Judge Taylor Swain. Complicating matters further, debates over which services and jobs to cut will only intensify, and which government authorities will be privatized will also be contested—at stake may be the island's cherished university, vast public land holdings, and even its museum's art collections.

Two main constituencies have emerged to provide long-term solutions on behalf of Puerto Ricans themselves. First, there is the pro-statehood government and its voters, who continue to put pressure on the US Congress to accept Puerto Rico's petition for statehood. Second, there is what I would call Puerto Rico's civil society—a coalition of university student activists, labor unions, and various political parties on the left who advocate for progressive solutions. These would include an audit of the debt to potentially reduce it by altering negotiations with creditors as well as increasingly advocating for independence from the United States. This second constituency tends to argue that the blame for the debt is extraneous to Puerto Ricans themselves and sees freeing the island of its debt as a form of social justice.

These two constituencies are somewhat parallel to the political landscape of the United States right now, representing conservative and liberal forces that have moved more and more to political extremes in the current global political climate. Yet they are both driven by a similarly stated goal—the decolonization of Puerto Rico, either by its full acceptance into the Union or by some form of autonomy from the United States, whether it be full independence or some variation of the current status. The lack of sovereignty that the island has lived under since Columbus's explorers seized it in 1493 has created a nationalist passion that in some senses transcends divisions between right and left. So even when the center-right pro-statehood party,

NPP, embraces Republican benefactors, they still call for the island's decolonization.

This rapidly accelerating conflict takes place in the context of a hot, humid, densely populated island with decaying infrastructure and a consumer landscape of American-style malls, fast food, suburban tract housing, and car culture. The expectation of a pseudo-American lifestyle has been eroding for years, and a high-rolling new-money billionaire crowd along with widespread urban and rural poverty is about to eviscerate the fragile middle class. Politics, however, is Puerto Rico's number-one spectator sport, so rather than the nihilist escapism that has infected middle America, the new clashes and tensions are intensely debated on local broadcast media, several competing newspapers, and a growing social media free-for-all that involves everyone's voice.

In the aftermath of Hurricane María an entirely new tableau confronts Puerto Ricans. Whereas PROMESA fomented a kind of slow deterioration, the catastrophic hurricane accelerated the crisis into an immediately life-threatening one. Emigration will most likely double or triple in the coming years, and intense debates will occur over how much debt, if any, can be collected until the island returns to a semblance of normalcy. The growing threat of quickly organized, large-scale privatization that would benefit so-called disaster capitalists will be constantly debated in the media and public life.

While many Puerto Ricans fear a massive gentrification project—in which wealthy Americans buy up beach land that was once a low-rent dance-shack paradise, perfect for fried plantains and roast pork fetes highlighting local music and drink—others point to a rush of new, innovative initiatives, such as micro-agriculture, and new green businesses, including solar and wind energy as well as food cooperatives. Still others look to increase ties with the rest of the Caribbean and Latin America. It's impossible to say how this will end, but Puerto Rico is coming to grips with the end of its fantasy status as the Capitalist Showcase of the Caribbean, with the hopeful possibility of a kind of progressive futurism beginning. Still, the specter of a new authoritarianism to repress dissent imposed by a rightist element in the pro-statehood party is looming.

In the pages of this book I want to take you on a journey that begins and ends with questions about the American Dream, about what being an American means, and what it means to be an "other" from within that world. That ambiguous, ambivalent sense of Caribbean national energy is essentially where Puerto Rico is and where Puerto Ricans start from, whether they are living on the island or elsewhere. The flowering and disintegration of that dream is something I've lived through in my lifetime, which began in a post–World War II moment of optimism, when my parents strived for inclusion, only to fade slowly in the bitter reality that the fate of our homeland and, possibly, even our culture and tradition was to die in slow bankruptcy.

I am the child of a generation who came to New York during the so-called Great Migration of Puerto Ricans, as part of the escape valve of a displaced rural countryside in order to realize Operation Bootstrap's modest industrialization goals. Our family lived through the turmoil of the Civil Rights Era and White Flight in the Bronx, inhabiting racialized working-class Catholic identities, transitioning from *West Side Story* to the Decade of the Hispanic, but never losing touch with the island we left behind. My parents fared moderately well as blue-collar and government workers. They invested in building a house back on the island and returned after they retired, only to watch uneasily as the fantasy of Puerto Rico as a middle-class US outpost in the Caribbean slipped into uncertainty. Their struggle informed my own as I tried to hold onto my bicultural Nuyorican identity, one that never fully embraced "Americanness" in a country that desperately resisted racial difference, increasingly seeing it as a sign of disloyalty.

As Puerto Rico sits in tatters and both the neoliberal agenda that created the FOMB and Trump's neo-authoritarianism cruelly double down on the cycle of neglect, I find myself tracing the narrative arc of my own life and in some ways feel grateful that the truth has been exposed. We Puerto Ricans have never really been Americans, despite being citizens for a century and often as authentic as any American could be. Puerto Ricans' suffering and struggle are colossal evidence of both the colonial wound the United States has inflicted on most of Latin America and a nagging harbinger of the potential fate of the fifty so-called states.

CHAPTER 1

A BRIEF HISTORY OF US COLONIALISM IN PUERTO RICO

Statue of Puerto Rico governor Luis Muñoz-Marín in Mayaguez.
© Joseph Rodríguez

There was never any doubt that the United States "wanted" Puerto Rico for its own use when it began a war with Spain near the turn of the twentieth century. Cuba had been in the throes of independence wars with Spain off and on since 1868, and the conflict that began in 1895 seemed ripe for the United States to capitalize on. The sinking of the USS *Maine*, an American naval ship destroyed by an explosion while moored just outside Havana, fueled American entry into the war. Although there are conflicting theories about the source of the explosion, including the likelihood that it was caused by a spontaneous internal fire, William Randolph Hearst's newspaper chain blew the incident up into the perfect catalyst for the United States to enter the conflict.[1]

When Theodore Roosevelt entered the fray with his army of Rough Riders, the whole affair came as no surprise to anyone who had been paying attention to the lust US government leaders and military had long expressed to expand southward and westward. And although the idea of Manifest Destiny was at the forefront of the political discourse of this period, it's less often observed that the United States' expansionist gaze was saturated with racial language and attitudes, at once desirous of and repelled by Latin America's mestizo/mulatto social dynamic. The Haitian Revolution at the end of the nineteenth century and into the twentieth created a US obsession with both Cuba and Puerto Rico because of the potential of a similar black-led revolt on those islands. In 1826 Virginia senator John Randolph feared that such a revolt would render the southern United States vulnerable to invasion from Cubans on rowboats. For this reason he objected to the United States participating in the 1826 Panama Congress because American diplomats would have to endure the horror of a US diplomat taking his seat in the Congress "beside the native African, their American descendants, the mixed breeds, the Indians, and the half breeds, without any offense or scandal at so motley a mixture."[2]

The logic driving this perspective underlined not only the importance of slavery to the emergence of capitalism in the nineteenth century but also, as Matthew Karp points out in *This Vast Southern Empire*, the extent to which slaveowners and their elected representatives disproportionately shaped US foreign policy. Going back as far as the Haitian Revolution, fear of a successful slave rebellion in the newly formed United States strongly motivated southern politicians. As Karp mentions, to that end Presidents Madison and Monroe "used overwhelming force to destroy black Maroon settlements in Spanish Florida." Fear of slave rebellions also briefly united the interests of American slaveholders and Cuban elites who wanted independence from Spain, but in the late nineteenth century—after abolition—Roosevelt's forces fought in conjunction with Afro-Cuban armies against their common Spanish foe.

The move to wrest Cuba and Puerto Rico from Spain came just as Spain had finally relented to end slavery as a concession to black rebel Cuban armies that had formed to push for independence. In a further move to placate continuing unrest on the island, in November 1897 Spain signed "Autonomic Charters for Cuba and Puerto Rico," which gave limited home-rule governments to both islands. Puerto Rico would gain full representation in the *Cortés*, the Spanish parliament, and could veto Spanish commercial treaties unfavorable to them while also retaining the right to set tariffs on imports and exports. In this way Puerto Ricans were granted a kind of citizenship that allowed self-government, grafted onto what was left of their Spanish subjecthood.

Yet on July 25, 1898, eight days after the first meeting of the newly formed Puerto Rican Parliament, US troops arrived in the southern port of Guánica and replaced the Spanish flag with the Stars and Stripes. This date would be remembered over fifty years later when the United States finally followed through on a project to allow Puerto Ricans to have limited autonomy and self-government, but at the time it was both the end of Teddy Roosevelt's "splendid little war" and the beginning of the current quandary over what exactly Puerto Rico's new colonial master would do with the island. Although historians agree that there was no preexisting plan for designating Puerto Rico's status, there was a general belief that Puerto Rico would be incorporated as a US territory. This led many to assume that it would follow a similar path to statehood as had former territories like Florida and Louisiana. At the very least it would, by acceding to military control, receive "the advantages and blessings of enlightened civilization," as Puerto Rico's first military governor, Nelson A. Miles, declared three days after the landing at Guánica.

Because Cuba was so militarized during its wars for independence, the United States decided to allow it national sovereignty, thinking it could still exert considerable control over the economy because of existing business interests and a ready-made set of Cuban consumers, who were already buying Ford Model Ts. But although Puerto Rico had experienced anti-Spanish uprisings in the mid-nineteenth century, in 1898 they did not have nearly the same level of armed mobilization present. So the United States held on to it, particularly because of its geographic location, which would provide the United States with a stronghold on the easternmost tip of the Caribbean archipelago. Yet the practical results that accompanied the United States including Puerto Rico in its "orbit" were that, as José Ayala and Rafael Bernabe write in their book, *Puerto Rico in the American Century*, "the island was thus pushed and pulled in opposite directions: increasingly tied to the United States and insistently defined as not part of it."

The acquisition of Puerto Rico, Cuba, and the Philippines presented new problems for the United States, which had a history of ultimately accepting previously acquired territories as states and subsequently granting their inhabitants full citizenship rights. For the first time in US history the acquisition of new territories did not come with any commitment to extend citizenship. Beginning with the Treaty of Paris, which was signed at the end of the War with Spain, continuing through the Foraker Act of 1900, and climaxing with the so-called Insular Cases of 1901, a series of legal decisions would create a

new identity for Puerto Ricans and other colonized subjects acquired during the creation of a new American Empire.

> "The question here is as to the legal status of a great coher-
> ent mass of civilized people, who cannot and of course will
> not be exterminated, and who can not be assimilated."
>   —**Frederic Coudert,** Solicitor General, during a hearing
>   before the Court, *Gonzales v. Williams,* December 4, 1903

How could the United States solve the problem of suddenly
absorbing a great mass of colonial subjects who were racially
unfit for inclusion in the rights granted to American citizens?
By creating a new identity that set them apart somehow. The
roots of this new identity could be found in both the way blacks
were redefined during the transition from slavery to the Jim
Crow Era, when newly freed slaves were denied rights, and the
way Asians were prevented from immigrating through the Chinese Exclusion Act. The *Gonzales v. Williams* decision asserted
that because of their acquisition through the War with Spain,
Puerto Ricans had acquired the nationality of the United States
and would not be "foreigners," according to the Immigration
Act of 1891. But that also meant that "Citizens of Porto [*sic*]
Rico, whose permanent allegiance is due to the United States;
who live in the peace of the dominion of the United States . . .
are not 'alien immigrants.'"[3]

The idea that Puerto Ricans were "alien in culture" seemed
to selectively employ the concept of "alien exclusion," which
defined certain ethnic or racial groups as "alien" and, thus, not
deserving of full citizenship rights. But viewing Puerto Ricans
as "alien nationals" was a necessary legal premise that allowed
the United States to absorb new "unincorporated" territories
for economic exploitation by creating a free-trade opportunity
within its territory while at the same time not violating its own
constitution regarding the rights of citizens. The US Department of War created the Bureau of Insular Affairs to administer
issues having to do with new territories, taking the term *insular*

from a designation Spain had given to its island colonies and territories to which it had granted autonomous rule prior to the 1898 war. *Insular* in Spanish means "being from an island or having to do with an island."

Applying alien exclusion to Puerto Rico was, according to legal scholar Edgardo Meléndez, a "notion that the peoples of the newly conquered territories were 'alien' in nature and character to the United States and should be excluded from the American polity."[4] Meléndez notes that the debate about what to do with the new territories came out of the debates between Americans in favor of imperialism and American anti-imperialists. "Although imperialists and anti-imperialists differed on many issues," he wrote, "they shared the belief that the inhabitants of the conquered territories were racially inferior and lacked the capacity for self-government, and thus that they should not become U.S. citizens."

During these first years of a new American century, the rulings made by the Foraker Act, which denied citizenship, as well as the Insular Cases established that citizenship would be "detached" from the right of political participation. The Foraker Act, largely authored by Secretary of War Elihu Root, established a form of government in Puerto Rico that was ostensibly democratic yet was top-heavy with colonial overseers at the executive level. The US-appointed governor and executive council comprised the upper body of the legislature and exercised both executive and legislative duties. Only five of its eleven members could be natives of Puerto Rico—a requirement that, over a hundred years later, was almost exactly replicated in the FOMB created by the PROMESA Act, which intended to restructure Puerto Rico's $72 billion debt.

The new idea of citizenship and "Americanness" was created by making a distinction between "incorporated territories," which were acknowledged to be somehow on the path toward statehood, and "unincorporated territories," which were not because they were considered to be populated by people of an inferior race and culture. A previous penetration and organizational takeover of a territory's government and infrastructure by Anglo-Saxons or other Europeans seemed to be a prerequisite for being designated as an incorporated territory. This was demonstrated by the fact that although territories like Alaska and Hawaii were not exactly Anglo-Saxon in origin, they had both experienced a takeover of sorts by European immigrants who established "Western" governments in lieu of indigenous ones and, thus, were not seen as a threat to America's racial order.

When *Downes v. Bidwell* of 1901 asserted that Puerto Rico belonged to but was not part of the United States, the nature of unincorporated citizenship was codified. The United States did not want to have colonial "subjects" like Europe did and so felt compelled to extend a certain kind of citizenship in which it referred to Puerto Ricans (and Filipinos) as "nationals." The United States thus retained what it called a "plenary" or absolute power over islanders while also extending certain privileges of US citizenship. These included the ability to freely travel to the United States and at home to be, in general, protected by the US Constitution and its laws, including enjoying the rights provided by the federal court system. Puerto Rican nationals could enter the United States as "legal aliens," but they were not full citizens. The United States, through its rulings in the Insular Cases, exercised what legal scholar Efraín Rivera Ramos called "the power of naming" to "generate new understandings, and therefore, new realities."

These new understandings were made necessary by the shift the United States made, as a country and an economy, from one where capital accumulation was derived from the profits from slavery and the investment in industrial capitalism that slavery made possible, to its entrance on the world stage as an imperial power. Two centuries of exterminating and displacing indigenous people and enslaving African Americans, whose racial character made them unfit for American freedom, made clear the separateness of othered bodies in America. But with the turn of the century's fixation on race science—whose practitioners measured human skulls to demonstrate a hierarchy of "races"—this narrative found more subtle and ambiguous ways to exclude bodies and cultures in a way that at least partially obscured the apparent genocidal excesses of its previous expansions.

THE JONES ACT: AMERICAN CITIZENSHIP GRANTED TO PUERTO RICO

"The Puerto Ricans neither yearned for United States citizenship nor did Congress intend to impose it on them. As is often the case, the truth lies somewhere between contradictory historical theses."

—José A. Cabranes, *Citizenship and the American Empire:*
Notes on the Legislative History of the
United States Citizenship of Puerto Ricans

As a child growing up, I had a clear sense that I was an American citizen. As part of a rapidly growing population of Puerto Rican migrants, I was living in New York among European ethnics and African Americans, all of whom felt sure about their citizenship. I remember when I first became aware of world maps and found Puerto Rico in the Caribbean Sea. But underneath the words "Puerto Rico" was a parenthesis that read "(U.S.)". I asked my father what it meant that United States was below the name Puerto Rico, and he said, "Puerto Rico is part of the US, but we are a nation." Somehow I knew that being a "possession" denied our national sovereignty, but he vehemently disagreed, insisting, "Puerto Rico is my country." Thus began my peculiar relationship with US citizenship: I had a strong sense of the meaning of the Puerto Rican nation from the passion in my father's voice, yet was clear that the dominant culture I was targeted for assimilation into considered the island's sovereignty a fairly meaningless afterthought.

The extension of US citizenship to Puerto Rico is a controversial issue, one that is often used to support two opposed rhetorical positions about the moral nature of the United States' involvement in Puerto Rico: either it was immoral to impose citizenship on a people or it was an act that afforded a vast array of legal and military protections. The idea that citizenship was imposed on Puerto Rico without the consent of Puerto Ricans is, on face value, true, but there are extenuating circumstances. There were many Puerto Ricans who preferred independence and would not want US citizenship, there were those who wanted to be annexed as a state and had mixed opinions about how that would happen, and there was the vast majority of the islanders who did not favor the policies the United States imposed, which required most educational and legal institutions to perform their functions in English, but they otherwise remained ambivalent about the island's territorial status.

Several times the US Congress attempted to extend citizenship to Puerto Ricans in the first two decades after Guánica, and on the island they were usually opposed. In 1914 the Puerto Rican House of Delegates declared that it "firmly and loyally maintain[ed] opposition to being declared, in defiance of our express wish or without our express consent, citizens of any country whatsoever than our own." Those against annexation even seemed to embrace Anglo stereotypes by claiming that because they were "Porto Ricans, Spanish-Americans, of Latin soul, imaginative, high-strung, ardorous by reason of the sun of our climate and by the blood in our veins, separated from you by over four hundred years and by more than four hundred leagues, with a different historic process, diverse language, different customs," they did not consent to citizenship.[5]

One of the island's major political voices, Luis Muñoz Rivera of the Unionist Party—which favored confederation with the United States as a state but, failing that, wanted independence with the protection of the United States—objected to citizenship not because he was against citizenship in principle but because he knew that the citizenship America was offering was a token gesture because America was still uninterested in accepting Puerto Rico as a state of the Union. But the debate in Puerto Rico, though nuanced and thoughtful, was always hypothetical, with the United States fully in control. In 1917, three years after the Puerto Rico House of Delegates demanded independence, the Jones Act conferred citizenship on all Puerto Ricans. It established a resident commissioner and a nonvoting representative of Congress, and it subjected the island to its shipping laws, which permanently raised the prices of goods shipped to the island.

The Jones Act represented an evolution of the US involvement with Puerto Rico. When the United States granted citizenship, it immediately exposed Puerto Rican residents to military conscription. This has been used as an argument for those who favor independence, but authors like Cabranes and Harry Fraqui-Rivera have pointed out that even noncitizens in territories could be conscripted.[6] The timing of this sudden granting of citizenship, however, will always arouse suspicion among not only nationalists, who favor independence, but also the majority of Puerto Ricans, who desperately crave some sense of national sovereignty.

Several members of my extended family have served in the armed forces, from my maternal grandfather, who was stationed in the Panama Canal Zone during World War I, to several of my uncles, who served in places like Surinam during World War II as well as various bases in the continental United States during and after the Korean War. Although none of them saw significant action in combat, their time in the military served to create a kind of dual allegiance, with the benefits of the military safety net and its legitimizing stamp on the one hand and Puerto Rico's national identity and culture on the other. Serving in the military and being denied full citizenship has historically been a driving force for those seeking civil rights, just as it was for African American and Mexican American soldiers who returned from World War II only to find the same Jim Crow and other segregation laws facing them and their families.

The celebrated Borinqeneers unit that served in the Korean War had their exploits memorialized in a PBS documentary that described how they played a key role during the Battle of the Chosin Reservoir. There, after apparently being deployed as cannon fodder to buy time for the arrival of more troops, they put up a decisive resistance that played a role in changing the course of the war. For my family members it served to reinforce their feelings that, having played by the rules, they deserved some respected status as "Americans," even though they simultaneously saw themselves as essentially Puerto Rican, aligned with the national culture, language, and fertile tropical soil.

Edgardo Meléndez argues that citizenship was less "about the narrow strategic interests generated by the war or the military recruitment of Puerto Ricans" than it was about rewarding Puerto Ricans' loyalty and making the island "a bridge to the Latin race and the improvement of U.S. relations with Latin America." Franqui-Rivera argues that the extension of citizenship for loyalty helped deter potential German interference in the Caribbean and provided President Woodrow Wilson cover for his openly declared sentiments that Europe should decolonize its possessions.[7] Most likely there's truth to both of these perspectives, as the US involvement in Puerto Rico, just as it is in other parts of the world, has often been a mix of condescending paternalism and controlling exploitation that can have mixed results. But even if you view the United States' intentions in their most benevolent light, they can't escape the context that Spain had held Puerto Rico as a colony for over four hundred years and the island had still not experienced national sovereignty. Thus, part of Puerto Rico's "national" character was an ambivalent mix of extracting concessions from colonial powers while maintaining an ethos grounded in words, culture, sensations, and interactions with physical surroundings: a strong feeling of nationhood.

It's useful to see the relationship between the United States and Puerto Rico as both reciprocal and unbalanced, with several interests intersecting as the United States became an actor in worlds outside its original Manifest Destiny borders. Then, as today, American involvement included outright racist and exploitative actions toward Puerto Rico while putting forth a kind of warped moral justification for its presence there. It also involved looking for new ways to create zones of economic opportunity, and in Puerto Rico the United States found a way to enjoy the economic benefits of incorporating new territories while formally denying political or territorial incorporation.

With Puerto Rico the United States created a new kind of free-trade zone where it could avoid import duties while also imposing tariffs on its nonincorporated territory. The Jones Act forbid Puerto Rico from allowing any commercial ships to dock at its ports that were not constructed in the United States and flying the US flag. All imports to the United States from Puerto Rico became duty-free, which benefited American consumers. However, although Puerto Ricans, in order to justify their lack of voting representation in Congress, would not pay federal income tax, US tax officials experimented with alternate, exploitative methods of taxation on the island. During the first stage of the US occupation of Puerto Rico, existing Spanish colonial tax laws, which used indirect taxation through stamps and embargoes, were overhauled to include more direct taxation and create a more favorable climate for the operation of American corporate sugar industry interests. The Jones Act also provided for the triple-tax exemption from the sale of government bonds that helped create the current debt crisis. This was the crucial moment that presaged the future debt crisis: the exemption meant that no federal, local, or state taxes could be collected on the bonds, making them more attractive than those issued by the vast majority of US municipalities.

In many ways the ambiguous status of Puerto Rico that the Jones Act cemented set the stage for the island's unstable future. The United States' unwillingness to make Puerto Rico an incorporated territory was a strong signal that the US government thought the island had a racial and cultural incompatibility with the mainland. At the same time, it wanted to prove itself a benevolent colonial master, one that, through linguistic wizardry, tried to create the illusion that it was not a colonizer at all. From the beginning Puerto Rico was an American fantasy.

The United States' treatment of Puerto Rico was beginning to resemble the assessment that Spanish friar Bartolomé de las Casas made in the sixteenth century in his famous debate with Ginés Sepulveda. De las Casas argued that indigenous people should not be considered less than human and not be condemned to chattel slavery but merely indoctrinated as Christians and made to work in the regimented encomienda system of agricultural labor. Rather than being condemned to servitude, as Spain originally imposed on the New World's indigenous people, Puerto Ricans were somehow fit to become pseudo-Americans and could aspire to full citizenship if they migrated to the mainland and passed their final exams in assimilation and acculturation. The Puerto Rican experiment would succeed to the extent that Americanization did.

There were some indisputable benefits that arose from America's intervention on the island. Indirectly, it represented a check on the ruling, lighter-skinned, creole class of Puerto Ricans left over from the Spanish regime, who were not necessarily interested in the expansion of opportunities or redistribution of wealth to its darker-skinned peasant majority. Early US visitors to the island included US labor giant Samuel Gompers, who established a chapter of the American Federation of Labor on the island that had the positive effect of encouraging Puerto Rican labor to organize. Later, from the 1970s on, return migrants to Puerto Rico reimplemented ideas gleaned from the Civil Rights Movement in the United States.

Along with cementing loyalty, as Congress and the Executive Branch desired when they extended limited self-government, Puerto Rico's conditional citizenship renewed efforts to strongly discourage—if not prohibit—any discourse about or promotion of the island's independence. The US-appointed governor E. Montgomery Reilly rejected some residents' attempts to display the flag—which was created through a joint effort between Puerto Rican and Cuban revolutionaries in New York in 1895 during the struggle with Spain—referring to it in 1921 as a "dirty rag." Although it's true that Puerto Rico was not as virulent as Cuba in its attempts to gain independence from Spain, there was still considerable resistance growing, as the United States was determined to stay. The key to its ability to do so was by promoting an Americanization program that threatened the island's national identity.

One of those nationalists in Puerto Rico who had argued that citizenship had come to Puerto Ricans for *razones de guerra*—or "reasons of war," specifically World War I—was Pedro Albizu Campos. A charismatic, African-descended Harvard graduate, Albizu Campos was the definition of a firebrand, often exhorting crowds with speeches that were part oratory, part sermon, and always relentlessly unforgiving of the US presence in his homeland. Albizu Campos was enigmatic in that, on the one hand, he came to embody the heart and soul of Puerto Rico's nationalist movement, unflinching in his opposition to any and all forms of control the United States exercised in Puerto Rico, and, on the other, because he spent twenty-six years—one-third of his life—in prison, he was ultimately detached from the people he intended to liberate. For me Albizu Campos is the ultimate symbol of our displeasure with being "possessed." As someone who identifies as part Afro-Caribbean, of unprivileged social status and having gotten my university education in a liberal arts New England university, I connected with his journey into the belly of the beast. He was at once our MLK and Malcolm X, and he endured a life of struggle and met an untimely death as a result of his activism.

The contradictions of Albizu Campos's life reflected his circumstances. As a colonial subject in the Caribbean, affected by the way such societies masked racial and sexual power inequalities—where whiteness was a relatively unspoken privilege, and caste-like societies placed citizens in racial and sexual hierarchies that often determined their career opportunities—he was also acutely aware of the imperializing project of US banks and industrial interests and the way all those forms of social and economic control serve to render such a life in an indistinguishable blur. Albizu Campos's message was crystal clear: the US presence in Puerto Rico was at the root of all the island's evils; it was the "assassin" of everyday citizens on all levels, and it did this by greatly limiting islanders' self-determination. Authorities always target true revolutionaries to be silenced, exiled, or imprisoned; in Albizu Campos's case, this occurred relatively early in his career, with his first arrest in 1936.

The legend of Albizu Campos's early life is well documented: he was the illegitimate son of a Spanish-descended, well-off, and married customs collector who refused to acknowledge him as his own child, and his mother was a local Ponce mestiza who lost her wits and died while Campos was still young. His mother's sanity was clearly affected by the way Puerto Rican society condoned extra-marital sexual relationships between light-skinned Creoles and lower-class dark-skinned women without any social consequences for the father and much to the detriment of women. Yet Albizu Campos became an outstanding student in his hometown and was given a scholarship to the University of Vermont, from which he transferred to Harvard, went to the law school, and became one of its early Puerto Rican graduates.

He volunteered for the Army during World War I and witnessed the racism in the American South firsthand. This "belly of the beast" trope is familiar to many Puerto Rican scholars, intellectuals, and, of course, members of the popular classes who spend some part of their youth in the United States. When they sense discrimination against them, they don't feel the need to swallow their experience of the dark side of America because they are not in search of permanent resident or citizenship status. They take in the immigrant experience without the legal pitfalls of being an immigrant and enjoy the luxury of being able to mount a critique of the hypocrisy of the country that claimed it was spreading democracy through the world.

In a way this narrative was replayed in my own life, with my father having served in the Army in Louisiana and Missouri, and I attending Brandeis University, a private university just outside of Boston that allowed me to mingle with the Harvard and MIT elite. Although my father was brought up in a family who lionized Puerto Rico's Liberal Party—which had consolidated its power through Albizu Campos's lifetime political rival, Luis Muñoz Marín—he was, like most Puerto Ricans, riveted by Albizu Campos's messianic speaking talents and his call to demand freedom. When I was in my teens my father brought home a copy of a 1971 book by Federico Ribes Tovar about Albizu Campos and, with some reservation, impressed on me that his voice was an essential distillation of our identity as Puerto Ricans. I held on to that book like a trophy, despite its having been tattered through my university years. Yet for my father, who had always been in the thrall of the pragmatic moderate Muñoz Marín, Albizu Campos was a dark figure whose message was limited by his intransigence.

My father was not alone. Albizu Campos still retains a venerated status in Puerto Rico and even more so among the mainland diaspora, regardless of political orientation in US or Puerto Rican politics. His great strength—perhaps to a fault—was his intense nationalism. Having been denied national sovereignty since the arrival of the Spanish colonists, Puerto Rico craves its national identity in many ways more than countries and islands with national sovereignty. The desire for nation status in Puerto Rico is so strong that even the parties that identify themselves with a desire for statehood or commonwealth—a vague proposition of a continually evolving version of the current status—use symbols of the nation in their political campaigns and advertisements, such as the flag; "La Borinqueña," the unofficial national anthem; and the sports teams the island is allowed to send to the Olympic Games every four years.

Albizu Campos's oratory skills and self-sacrificing dedication to independence cemented his legacy, which of course likewise has its contradictions. Even as he was unfailing in his fight with the United States, he embodied some of the same patriarchal ideas held by those he wanted to displace. Although he made common cause with Irish nationalists, the National Cadets he helped create wore black shirts with white crosses that resembled the "cross potent" used by both the Crusades forces and the Austrofascists, an authoritarian Catholic government of Austria that was, ultimately, overthrown by Germany's National Socialists. In his book on Albizu Campos, Ribes Tovar says that the black shirts symbolized a state of mourning over Puerto Rico's colonial captivity, a symbolism that would be used after Hurricane María in a rendering of the Puerto Rican flag in all black.

Albizu Campos was concerned about women's rights, despite his strong affiliation with Roman Catholic morals. Although he strongly opposed birth control and abortion, he and his Nationalist Party encouraged women to be a part of the struggle.[8] "Puerto Rico will be sovereign and independent when Puerto Rican women feel free, feel sovereign, feel independent," he insisted in a 1933 speech.[9] Albizu Campos was most concerned with allegiance to Roman Catholicism as a building block for nationalism similar to the way it was used in the movement for Irish independence, in the way Catholicism could be viewed to protect local tradition against the universalizing force of Protestantism. His recruitment of women was not nearly as radical as the anarchist/socialist tendencies of labor union organizer Luisa Capetillo, who died in 1922, and his intolerance of gays was apparent when he said, "Sex is a biological accident for the propagation of the species, but the people that have to be reminded of its sex deserve not sympathy but punishment."[10] Then again, despite his intense focus on the nation, his political activism was clearly in line with a class-based left/Marxism, but he never acknowledged it as such. Although Albizu's nationalist vision focused more on symbols, tradition, and religious ethics, his involvement in labor activism underlined his awareness of class struggle, and the way he demonized the United States' presence in Puerto Rico most often emphasized the way it effected economic hegemony.

Ironically, Albizu Campos attempted to use the same mechanism that the United States had participated in to engage Puerto Rico and the Caribbean in a debt relationship—the selling of bonds—to strengthen the nationalist cause. The party began to issue bonds from a proposed Treasury of the Republic of Puerto Rico to "establish the Republic of Puerto Rico . . . educate Puerto Ricans about their history, and encourage people to make a financial and political commitment to independence."

The bonds were issued decorated with images of nationalist figures like Mariana Bracetti and Francisco Ramírez, leaders of the
Grito de Lares revolt; José de Diego; Emerio Ramón Betances;
and Eugenio María de Hostos, all late-nineteenth-century independence movement leaders. When the bonds showed up on
Wall Street trading floors, they were the first motivation the US
government considered to bring charges against him.[11]

Yet the most significant threat Albizu Campos and the nationalists posed to the United States was their ability to harness
the discontent of workers, particularly in the sugar industry,
who were bearing the most significant costs of Puerto Rico's
annexation for profit. Some nationalist accounts of American
economic intervention are overly simplistic, blaming the concentration of capital in the sugar industry solely on the United
States and not recognizing how existing island sugar barons also
benefited from monocrop consolidation. Yet it's undeniable that
dismantling any possibility for autonomous economic growth
began almost immediately after the US Navy arrived in Guánica.

One immediate impact was that the Puerto Rican economy
was severed from its two largest trading partners, Spain and
Cuba. The 1900 Foraker Act blocked the growth of an indigenous entrepreneurial class who had emerged during the final
years of Spanish rule and engaged in sugar production, coffee
farming, and other forms of small-scale industry as well as replaced the peso with the US dollar, creating a huge advantage
for outside investors.

The devaluation of the local currency, an inevitable result of
a dominant economy coming into contact with a weaker one,
quickly spurred US investors to buy up large pieces of land.
This particularly impacted the island's profitable sugar industry,
whose sprawling interconnected system of larger *ingenios* and
smaller *cañaverales* was quickly consolidated. In the period between 1898 and 1920 only four US firms owned more than half
of all Puerto Rican sugar production.[12]

Increasing US control over agriculture on the island also de-
railed coffee production. Puerto Rico's coffee had historically

sold well in Cuba and Spain because of its darker quality and more robust flavor, but the United States' involvement interrupted those export markets. And because US coffee drinkers were more accustomed to lighter brews like those originating from Brazil, Puerto Rican coffee was not favored as a US import. The final blow was Hurricane San Ciriaco, which caused so much widespread damage to coffee cultivation that local, independent coffee production never recovered.

The relationship between the United States and Puerto Rico in the first part of the twentieth century took on a character that could best be described as imperial, in which a metropolitan economy, possessing a superior currency as well as a production and distribution apparatus, asserted domination over an inferior, peripheral economy. This created a model where almost all production in Puerto Rico was steered toward exporting to the United States, to the point that food and other necessities for local consumption had to then be imported from the United States. This situation remains in effect today, where it can be difficult to find avocados, pineapples, and other locally grown fruit in Puerto Rican supermarkets, which are stocked with meat and frozen fish flown in from the mainland.

As part of its colonial policy, the United States engaged in a form of "tax imperialism," in which it rewrote old Spanish tax laws "to provide an ideal environment for large US corporations to do business on the island," writes legal scholar Dianne Lourdes Dick. The painful irony here is that Puerto Rico's Spanish taxation system was part of a slowly growing economy that not only had no external debt when the United States arrived on the island but actually had been lending money to Spain to help finance the repression of the Cuban independence movement. "Considering that the Founding Fathers' chief grievance with Great Britain concerned the imposition of tax laws that were detrimental to the interests of the American colonies," Dick wrote, "our subsequent interventions in Puerto Rico—whether driven by malice, greed, neglect, or indifference—are especially disquieting."[13]

It was the Foraker Act that allowed the United States to exempt nonincorporated territories from strictly complying with the Internal Revenue Service, thereby relieving Puerto Ricans from paying federal taxes while imposing, as it saw fit to protect US companies, tariffs that would have been unconstitutional between states. The famously ambiguous phrase in *Downes v. Bidwell*, claiming that Puerto Rico would be "Foreign in a domestic sense," was at the root of this policy, which sought to make Puerto Rico a free-trade zone for US imports while finding other ways to charge duties for goods imported to Puerto Rico from the United States.

Albizu Campos most likely grasped much of this structural injustice and, coupled with his personal discomfort with what he experienced in New England in the 1920s, refused to remain in the belly of the beast, preferring instead to make it his life goal to free Puerto Rico from the United States' grasp. When he returned to Ponce he maintained a law practice, staying in close contact with local struggles. From that vantage point he began to see the effects of how the United States dealt with the major crisis of the 1930s Depression. In this way Albizu Campos began to see clearly the connection between global finance capital, represented by Wall Street banks such as the City Bank of New York, and the sugar cane industry it controlled. In a not-unsurprising precedent for the actions that the FOMB would impose in 2017, the major companies began to cut sugar cane workers' wages almost in half.

The chain of events resulting from the formation of the Nationalist Party was decisive as Puerto Rico transitioned from near-total US domination to its semiautonomous "Showcase of the Caribbean" period, which America found particularly useful during its Cold War with the Soviet Union. According to Nelson Denis, author of *War Against All Puerto Ricans*, Albizu Campos had lunch with E. Francis Riggs, the chief of the Puerto Rico Police and heir to the Washington, DC-based Riggs Bank fortune. According to Denis, Riggs offered Albizu Campos the backing necessary to become Puerto Rico's first native

governor—if he backed off from his leadership role in the growing momentum of strikes, which had spread from agricultural
workers to tobacco, needlework, and other laborers.

According to Denis, Albizu Campos responded by saying,
"Puerto Rico is not for sale, at least by me"—in Spanish, "no
se vende"—a slogan activists still use today when protesting
the government's potential sell-off of Puerto Rican–owned land
and resources to private investors in the aftermath of Hurricane
María. This refusal to compromise led to a series of violent confrontations that resulted in Riggs's death at the hands of nationalists, Albizu Campos's imprisonment, and the infamous Ponce
Massacre of 1937, during which seventeen civilians and two police officers were killed. The photographs from Albizu Campos's
prison confinement as well as his numerous hospitalizations,
where he was allegedly subject to radiation treatments, would
go on to dominate the way Albizu Campos maintains a public
presence. His legacy was permanently intertwined with the violence of the nationalist movement, including the two famous
1950s shootings in Washington, DC—an assassination attempt
on President Truman at Blair House and a shooting attack on
Congress itself by nationalists like Lolita Lebrón.

Albizu Campos also famously weighed in on another US intervention in Puerto Rico, one whose deleterious effects were
clouded in debate. In 1937 a sterilization law favored by American eugenicist Clarence Gamble (of Proctor and Gamble fame)
and Planned Parenthood founder Margaret Sanger went into
effect. Albizu Campos saw the increased availability of birth
control and the at-times coerced sterilization of women as an
example of the United States "trying to invade the very insides of
nationality." The law established a eugenics board, and scholar
Laura Briggs claims that although there were many involuntary
sterilizations of women in Puerto Rico, most were not ordered
by the Eugenics Board created by the 1937 law.

The roots of mass sterilization in Puerto Rico can be found
in Thomas Malthus's pronouncements about the poor and over-
population. Some writers, like Iris Ofelia López, have theorized

that Margaret Sanger saw the eugenics movement as an opportunity to support women's birth control while also creating a racial and class divide between privileged white women, who had the option to use birth control, and poorer and nonwhite women as well as some who were "feeble," who would all be encouraged to use it.[14]

The ambivalence about how much of this was a pernicious genocidal plot and how many Puerto Rican women actually wanted to take advantage of birth control does cloud the issue: What is the role of "Americanization" here? *La Operación*, a chilling 1982 documentary by Puerto Rican filmmaker Ana María García, appears to show evidence of women being steered toward being used as guinea pigs for previously untested birth control pills. There is considerable documentation of verifiable sterilization campaigns against African American and Mexican women in California, which passed eugenics-friendly Asexualization Acts in the early twentieth century, with Virginia and North Carolina following suit. Awareness of this agenda may have intersected with Catholicism in Puerto Rico and the patriarchal essence of Latin American administration to create a militant narrative that the Sanger/Gamble campaign was genocidal in nature. Nationalist Puerto Rican groups as well as the US-based Young Lords Party helped build the momentum to condemn sterilization practices as attempts to "erase" Puerto Ricans.[15] The data documenting the unusually high sterilization rates and the fact that many of the birth control pills had not passed FDA tests are evidence of the abuse of Puerto Rican women.

What became clear to the US government as the militant nationalism in Puerto Rico grew through the late 1930s and 1940s is that the United States was losing its grip on the hearts and minds of Puerto Ricans. US-appointed governors like Robert H. Gore and Blanton Winship were the objects of scorn and derision for their various heavy-handed tactics as they sought to Americanize Puerto Ricans and repress labor strikes. As a result, President Franklin D. Roosevelt and Secretary of the

Interior Harold Ickes planted the seeds of a new transition for Puerto Rico's sociopolitical future.

In 1941 Roosevelt appointed as governor of Puerto Rico Rexford Tugwell, who had worked in the Department of Agriculture under the ultra-liberal Henry Wallace. With his more liberal and reformist ideas gaining favor, Tugwell also worked to get Jesús T. Piñero appointed as the first-ever Puerto Rico governor in 1946.

But Piñero's appointment carried with it an antinationalist "Gag Law" that was in part inspired by a new insidious development in the United States: McCarthyism. According to this law—"La Mordaza," as it was known—advocating for violent action against the Puerto Rico government in speech or writing became a felony, echoing the United States' Smith Act (a.k.a. the Alien Registration Act) of 1940, which set criminal penalties for anyone advocating for the overthrow of the US government by force or violence and also required all noncitizen adult residents to register with the federal government. The Smith/Alien Registration Act was one of McCarthy's many tools during the infamous hearings with which he exposed and delegitimized members or sympathizers of the Communist Party at the dawn of the Cold War.

Although the text of the law makes it a felony to "print, publish, edit, circulate, sell, distribute, or publicly exhibit any writing which encourages, pleads, advises, or preaches the necessity, desirability or suitability of overthrowing the insular government," officials also used it to intimidate Puerto Ricans from playing "La Borinqueña," the unofficial anthem that was played in Ponce right before the massacre, or displaying the single-star Puerto Rican flag that had been conceived as a symbol of anti-Spanish colonialism at the end of the nineteenth century.

Reviled as it has become, La Mordaza was part of a strategy that attempted to enact something other than the pseudo-fascist trappings of McCarthyism. Fueled by the progress of liberal FDR/Ickes interventionism, the United States was intent on putting a human face on its colonial experiment. With the cooperation of Luis Muñoz Marín—a privileged member of the Puerto Rican elite, sometimes referred to as "café poet" because of his bohemian tenure in New York's Greenwich Village in the 1930s—a new political party called the Popular Democratic Party (PDP) was created. It fused elements of socialist, *independentista*, and liberal politics to create a different narrative that would put a beneficent gloss on the United States' continuing possession of the island while also permanently demonizing militant nationalism.

In Mexico Spanish colonialists built their churches directly on top of Aztec and Mayan temples, erasing their spiritual power while at the same time promoting the creation of new sacred objects of worship that fused Catholicism with indigenous religion. La Virgen de Guadalupe, a mestiza version of Virgin Mary, became one of the most powerful religious symbols in Mexico because she so successfully commanded a sense of Mexican national pride. So was the case when the FDR and Truman administrations orchestrated the emergence of Luis Muñoz Marín, the son of Luis Muñoz Rivera, the third resident commissioner of Puerto Rico. An unimpressive orator with connections to the United States' governmental and literary elite, Muñoz Marín became the perfect moderate spokesman for a Puerto Rico that rejected the nationalist violence of Albizu Campos, who had been in prison since 1936.

Co-opting the Mexican Revolution's slogan of "Pan, Tierra y Libertad" (Bread, Land, and Freedom), the old Nationalist single-star flag (which had been overshadowed by Albizu Campos's Nationalists' use of the black-and-white "cross" flag) and the straw hat (*pava*) of the rural jíbaro, Muñoz Marín constructed a Virgen de Guadalupe–like symbol for a new Puerto Rico that believed in an economic coexistence with the United States that would eventually lead to independence. To accomplish this, he worked with the Truman administration to create a meaningless new status for Puerto Rico that would change nothing regarding the US Constitution's "Territorial Clause," through which Congress would continue to have complete authority over territories.

Through the efforts of Antonio Fernós Isern, who took office with Piñero as resident commissioner in 1946, the Puerto Rican Congress drew up Public Law 600. This law would allow Puerto Ricans to elect a Constitutional Assembly that would then draft a constitution. Fernós and Muñoz Marín believed that language used in PL 600 indicated that the relationship between the United States and Puerto Rico would be substantially changed. In fact, the PDP placed pretty much all of its political stock in this notion until recent Supreme Court rulings regarding Puerto Rico's ability to write its own bankruptcy law to renegotiate its debt.[16]

In reality, the language of PL 600 did nothing to change anything about the Territorial Clause of the Constitution, which allows Congress complete control over territories. The creation of the Puerto Rican Commonwealth, or ELA (Estado Libre Asociado, or Free Associated State), was always a kind of fantasy whose main purpose was to solve the nationalist problem in Puerto Rico and satisfy the newly formed UN requirements for decolonization. This fantasy was essential to help Puerto Ricans avoid the cognitive dissonance between their view of their cultural and national identity and their legal status as colonial subjects with second-class citizenship.

There were, however, some positive aspects of the creation of the Puerto Rican Constitution. Unlike the US Constitution, it was written after the International Declaration of Human Rights and, thus, included some of its provisions, such as a ban on the death penalty and an explicit provision against discrimination on the basis of race, color, sex, birth, social origin or condition, or political or religious ideas. When Puerto Ricans elected Muñoz Marín as governor, the island seemed to have more autonomy and the illusion of self-determination. But, unsurprisingly, there was considerable backlash from the Nationalist Party.

In October 1950 there was what many have described as a "revolution" but is perhaps more accurately termed an "insurrection" in Puerto Rico. With the passage of PL 600, the Nationalist Party began to ramp up its rhetoric, amass arms, and plan for armed conflict. Sporadic incidents like a prison break in Oso Blanco, the island's largest prison located in Rio Piedras just outside of San Juan, and the bombing of the house of a nationalist leader, Blanca Canales, in the mountain town of Jayuya became legendary for their level of violence. But the Nationalists never intended to win an armed struggle with Puerto Rico's police, national guard, or the US military; rather, they hoped to create a political crisis that would discourage the UN from recognizing the process PL 600 had put in motion.

Then, when the Puerto Rico National Guard and the Puerto Rico police attacked towns like Arecibo, Jayuya, and Utuado—all west of San Juan—the center of the struggle moved away from the metropolitan area. Campos had designated these western areas, particularly Utuado, as potential strongholds because their agricultural base was intact and productive and because once the mountainous roads between these towns were secured, an uprising could effectively control movement across the western half of the island. In Jayuya the Nationalists declared an independent Republic of Puerto Rico, prompting the National Guard to aerial bomb the town and, subsequently, occupy it.

For most Puerto Ricans these events, which resulted in twenty-eight mortalities, are almost completely forgotten. There are no national holidays in memory of them, no well-funded historical revisitings of this period, no stadiums or street corners named after the protagonists. An independent 2018 documentary about it, *1950: La Insurrección Nacionalista* does not have distribution in the US. Yet there is an undeniable sense among the people that there were those who sacrificed for some idea about national honor, something that is not attainable under commonwealth or statehood. It's a kind of unfocused collective memory that was reactivated when an FBI squadron gunned down radical independentista Filiberto Ojeda Ríos of the FALN (Fuerzas Armadas de Liberación Nacional, or National Armed Forces of Liberation) in 2005 or when Oscar López Rivera, another FALN member whose sentence was commuted by President Obama in 2016, was released. The political ends or consequences—militant resistance and a desire for national autonomy—seem extreme or unattainable, but the desire for a national spirit remains strong. On the western half of the island in particular, its relative independence from colonial control still resonates today when Puerto Ricans talk about having roots in the area or buying property there. When someone suggests they are from Utuado; or Lares, the site of the 1868 rebellion against Spain; or San Sebastián; or Cabo Rojo, they either make a subtle coded gesture or openly discuss that their town has strong independentista roots. Sadly, these towns were among the most badly hit during Hurricane María, dealing a severe blow to the potential for the revolutionary roots in the western soil to reactivate political action.

The new commonwealth's constitution was put into effect on July 25, 1952, which also happened to be the fifty-fourth anniversary of when the US Navy landed in Guánica—the beginning of the US occupation and territorial control. On that day Luis Muñoz Marín raised the once-prohibited single-star Puerto Rican flag during a speech and effectively erased the symbolic power of that US landing, which Nationalists had used as a rallying cry for at times violent protests. When the remnants of the Nationalist Party or disaffected independentistas rally at Guánica to commemorate the invasion, ceremonies held to celebrate the 1952 Constitution and Commonwealth in San Juan distract most of the island's attention. Although the new commonwealth was granted a considerable degree of autonomous self-government, Muñoz Marín oversaw its creation, declaring it a means for Puerto Rico to build the kind of economy that would make independence possible. The label "commonwealth" was intended to erase "colony," but it effectively assured that the island would remain a US colony indefinitely. The economy that the Muñoz-Marín/US partnership would create would become a bonanza for US corporations, but little was reinvested locally to ensure the island's stability and growth.

Part of the creation of the new Commonwealth of Puerto Rico was the implementation of Operation Bootstrap (Manos a la Obra, or "Let's Get to Work"), which transformed the island's agricultural economy into an industrial one. Muñoz Marín led the effort to attract US corporate investment to the island so as to establish textile, clothing, and other manufacturing operations. This economic transformation also included a long process of consolidating agricultural production, which eliminated jobs and land for rural residents, who were tied to it through wage labor and subsistence farming.

While living standards for many improved, Bootstrap's success depended on exporting surplus labor to the United States, and this created a wave of migrant Puerto Rican workers to the mainland. Earlier migrations had seen thousands migrating to Hawaii to be employed by the California and Hawaii Sugar Corporation as well as to New York and Tampa, Florida, to work as *tabaqueros*, or cigar-factory workers. But the Great Migration of the post–World War II era was a definitive one for Puerto Ricans because it firmly established them as a growing population in urban centers like New York, Boston, Philadelphia, and Cleveland.

The Great Migration to the North for Puerto Ricans closely paralleled that of African Americans, as Puerto Ricans came to live in large urban centers in the North just a few years after African Americans began their migration to escape Jim Crow laws. Puerto Ricans and African Americans became neighbors in the same segregated areas. Because many—if not most—of the Puerto Ricans forced to flee northward were darker skinned and not part of the island's white-ish elite, there was some cultural crossover between the two groups: they faced parallel forms of race discrimination, lived in the same or bordering neighborhoods, and began to influence each other's culture. In addition, because Puerto Ricans were already American citizens, their experience aligned more with the established African American status of second-class citizenship than that of Latin American immigrants from other countries.

While there was considerable exchange between Puerto Ricans and African Americans, racist attitudes from the island created a kind of ambivalence that placed Puerto Ricans in a kind of nether-ground between black and white. Earlier Cuban immigrants like jazz musician Mario Bauzá had begun to fuse African American jazz techniques with Afro-Cuban ones, so when Puerto Ricans arrived they heard music that allowed them to build bridges with American blacks. Fusion music like *bugalú* combined Afro-Cuban music with R&B and was promoted by mostly Puerto Rican groups. But the variations in Puerto Rican skin tones and appearance had a tendency to be something "other" than African American while also clearly racially distinct from white Americans.

My parents were part of this migration, arriving in New York within years of each other in the early 1950s. They had come from different corners of the Luquillo Mountain Range in the northeastern part of the island, both children of rural farmers with somewhat different levels of accumulated wealth. My father's family owned a large, prosperous finca in a mountainous region south of the municipality now known as Canóvanas, until a disgruntled suitor of one of my aunts, as my family members describe him, murdered my grandfather. Without my grandfather, the farm collapsed and had to be sold off, forcing my father, one of fourteen children spread over two marriages, to live in difficult conditions in a poor barrio of San Juan called Buen Consejo. My mother was one of nine children and grew up in a mountainside finca a short distance from what would become the only tropical rain forest in the US National Forest System, the El Yunque National Rain Forest. Her parents' finca operated more on the subsistence level, and my mother grew up in near-poverty conditions during the Great Depression, which gravely impacted rural Puerto Ricans. My mother did well in high school and attended the University of Puerto Rico on a scholarship, where she trained to be a schoolteacher. Yet economic conditions on the island remained desperate, so both my parents decided to take advantage of the low airfares Operation Bootstrap provided to look for work in New York City.

Migrating or immigrating to the United States from Europe, Asia, Africa, and Latin America has been a constant thread in

American history, a compelling narrative through which American exceptionalism is manufactured and celebrated. Unfortunately, although this narrative speaks to many and encourages them to feel hopeful and proud, it fails to acknowledge the narratives of African Americans and Native Americans: one group was forcibly brought here to be enslaved and the other driven from their land and decimated by genocidal practices and policies. The case of the Puerto Rican migrant is somewhat unique in that it contains a little bit of all of these narratives, with an important twist: Puerto Rico's Great Migration grew out of an anticipated problem with Operation Bootstrap: there would be too many laborers on the island as it transitioned from an agricultural to an industrial economy.

Just as eugenicists tried to solve the problem of "overpopulation" in Puerto Rico by increasing access to birth control and sterilizing women, the *guagua aérea* or "aerial bus" pattern created to ship islanders to the mainland to prevent the increases in landless and unemployed "peasants" was part of a plan to impose on a group of subjected people the illusion of US citizenship. Flights from San Juan to New York were very inexpensive—as cheap as $25—and Puerto Ricans quickly became the first set of migrants to the United States who arrived mostly via airplane. Further, because Puerto Ricans were already US citizens, there was no restriction on their travel. This fostered a pattern of circular migration unheard of among other groups, who would do everything they could to stay permanently. Because of this nomadic uncertainty, I've always felt profound ambivalence about my parents' journey here, although in their eyes it was just as difficult and uncertain as it was for other migrants and immigrants. They were part of a process that, in a few short decades, would see the Puerto Rican population in the United States surpass that on the island. And with that came an awareness of a Puerto Rican nation that didn't need accoutrements like national sovereignty or even national territory to flourish and prosper.

CHAPTER 2

CLEAR AND PRESENT DANGER

Prelude to the Crisis

A well-known street mural of Nationalist Party Leader Pedro Albizu Campos in Old San Juan. © Ed Morales

By the mid-twentieth century Puerto Rico had been firmly in the United States' grasp for fifty years, with the relationship experiencing modifications designed to at once further US interests while also exerting a kind of social control that would substitute true sovereignty with limited autonomous government and a "protective" military presence. The island's economy was remade from one based on family-owned agricultural industry and subsistence farming to a US-imposed consolidation of agriculture of monocrop farming, mostly owned by large corporations, then transformed by Operation Bootstrap into a manufacturing and tourist/service economy.

This restructuring caused labor turmoil, which led to working-class strife infused with renewed nationalist militancy. Puerto Rico's upswing in nationalist fervor then prompted the Roosevelt administration to create a fantasized version of "local" democracy on the island that gave the illusion of national sovereignty without changing anything about its legal status. The United States' so-called plenary powers over everything that happened in Puerto Rico, in addition to all its future goals, remained in effect and unchallenged. The transition from the first fifty years of "unincorporated territory" with limited citizenship to that of the Commonwealth of Puerto Rico, an imaginary nation whose territorial status remained unchanged, was a new thread in the Fantasy of Puerto Rico.

This postwar manufactured consensus made a "national hero" out of Roosevelt favorite Luis Muñoz Marín while all but burying the legacy of nationalist leader Pedro Albizu Campos. It allowed Puerto Ricans to resume flying their national flag without any threat to the US economy as long as the idea of an autonomous Puerto Rican nation remained buried. It also created both a kind of modernist double consciousness of national identity that both islanders and mainlanders still maintain, for better or worse, as well as a circular migration of the labor force. This circular migration would come to predict not only patterns that other Latinx immigrants, most notably Mexicans and citizens of the Dominican Republic, would later utilize but also the nomadic nature of work in the era of globalization.

My parents arrived in New York City in the early 1950s to escape the grim conditions in Puerto Rico that were in part created by Operation Bootstrap, the US-initiated plan for reorganizing Puerto Rico's economy. Conditions of severe poverty and lack of employment persisted despite Tugwell and Muñoz Marín's reform efforts, and the gravitational pull northward was an intended effect of the Bootstrap industrialization project. Both of my parents arrived in local airports, thanks to cheap plane fares and money borrowed from relatives already in New York. They immediately settled in apartments crowded with family members living in poor conditions, like no heat or hot water. My mother was able to find a job as a seamstress, my father behind the counter of numerous midtown coffee shops.

My father's sisters worked at the same sewing factory as my mother and soon invited her to a party held at my paternal grandmother's, where their fateful meeting took place. Their courtship played out as Puerto Rican migrants began to make their imprint on New York's cultural and political fabric. Lolita Lebrón and the nationalists' attack on the Blair House stunned most of my extended family, and like many Puerto Ricans in New York at the time, they felt they should maintain a low profile to avoid the increasing climate of fear mongering and suspicion fueled by the McCarthy era. They were part of the manufacturing job force that was still expanding, making it possible to at least work toward social advancement, which was their goal. Their migration to New York was part of a planned escape valve of Operation Bootstrap and helped create the conditions for the growth of a new postwar middle class in Puerto Rico who would live in suburban communities that paralleled those in the United States. Some of the names for these new communities were taken from those on Long Island: Levittown and Floral Park.

Operation Bootstrap succeeded in the way that mainstream US economists like to measure success. With its focus on outside investment leading to job creation, the numbers showed that profit rates in Puerto Rico averaged two to three times the profit rates in the United States between 1951 and 1984. This meant there was sizable job creation, and many workers were able to take advantage of that. However, unemployment rates remained higher than in the United States, and the manufacturing sector was highly volatile, depending on how efficiently corporations were taking advantage of tax breaks. Early investments in manufacturing paperboard and glass bottles gave way to the petrochemical experiment and the relatively stable pharmaceutical industry. Rising wages for workers often caused US businesses to abruptly withdraw from Puerto Rico, as they were only in it for short-term investment. There was almost no focus on indigenous economic development, and economic planning was nonexistent outside of feeding the external investment model, with the occasional major government infrastructure project providing for some homegrown dynamism, albeit while also fostering major boondoggles.

The two-pronged methodology of Operation Bootstrap—a shift to industrialization at the expense of subsistence agriculture and accompanied by encouraging mass migration—largely succeeded in creating the illusion that Puerto Rico had become a thriving economy in the Caribbean. The new industrial economy, fueled by the growth of the manufacturing sector, would favor US interests by continuing various kinds of exemptions from federal taxes, a wage scale that was somewhat lower than in the United States, and the creation of exports almost exclusively for the US market. As large chunks of the rural peasantry—relatively lacking in education and often without the white privilege afforded to mestizos in Puerto Rico and Latin America's curiously stratified racial hierarchy—fled northward, those who remained experienced a consumer-driven modernization of their lifestyle that paralleled America's transformation to a suburban-driven nation whose culture and politics were increasingly defined by suburbanites.

The society that US intervention created in postwar Puerto Rico was one where old-standing morals were somewhat loosened, despite the island's relatively conservative Catholic tradition; consumerism was woven into the fabric of everyday life, fueled by the availability of American products; and a small professional and skilled middle class emerged from the remnants of the metropolitan elite and suburban influx of migrants, whose roots were often in the traditional cultures of peasants called *jíbaros*. The food jíbaros had once produced on small plots was now, for the most part, only available via import from the United States. By 1956, for the first time in the island's history, the income from the manufacturing sector outpaced agricultural production. Puerto Rico's countryside, once dotted with subsistence farms, began to lose population, with poorer, non-landowning unskilled people either taking the guagua aérea to New York or resettling in poorer barrios on the margins of San Juan and Ponce.

Yet the kind of problems that would continue in Puerto Rico—high unemployment at around 10 percent, overdependence on external investment searching for the lowest wages, clustering industrial employment in limited urban areas—were largely unacknowledged, nagging symptoms of the island's long-term collision course with economic disaster. "What was troubling" about Operation Bootstrap's transition, say César Ayala and Rafael Bernabe in *Puerto Rico in the American Century*, "was the missed chance of creating a more diversified agriculture and a healthier link between rural and urban development on the island."

Economist James Dietz grants that "the shift to foreign capital promotion and export-led industrialization created stupendous growth—GNP increased at an annual rate of 8.3% in the 1950s and 10.8% in the 1960s."[1] And although this led to large increases in disposable income for Puerto Ricans, even this was, by design, wholly favorable to the United States. Because consumers had more money available to buy US-made products, corporations could dump on the island much of what could not be sold on the mainland, and the lack of any plan for economic growth based on locally based business and industry was telling. The increase in GNP benefited the US investors, with the GDP falling behind and creating one of the largest gaps between profits generated in a location and profits retained there. According to Ayala and Bernabe, by 1990 "the flow of profits and dividends out of the island stood at almost $11 billion or 35 per cent of the insular GDP," which made the GDP figure misleading, as Puerto Rico's economy was designed to create profit for external investment and interests, not to retain the percentage of wealth creation typical for sovereign nations. What this boils down to is that Puerto Rico's economic model was designed to increase production and profits for American corporations, but markedly lower percentages of that profit would remain on the island to reinvest in the local economy.

As a result of Operation Bootstrap, between 1950 and 1959 the total number of jobs in Puerto Rico decreased by sixty thousand. This compelled about 27 percent of the island's population to migrate between 1950 and 1970. This migration overlapped with the decline of the industrial sector of the northeastern United States, where most of the migrants settled. Their early optimism soon became a kind of shellshock as Puerto Ricans in cities like New York and Philadelphia began to realize that, for the most part, as industrial jobs dried up, they would be assigned to the urban underclass, once called the surplus labor pool, frequently un- or underemployed and increasingly dependent on SSI entitlements like welfare and food stamps.

I was raised at the tail end of a period when Puerto Ricans were emerging from obscurity—only to be immediately typecast as societal problems. In a misguided attempt to make sense of us, the news media and Hollywood began constructing stereotypes that depicted us as juvenile delinquents and street criminals. Many people point to the beginning of this trend in films like *Blackboard Jungle*, *The Young Savages*, and, of course, *West Side Story*. The real-life slaying of two white teenagers in a Hell's Kitchen park by Salvador Agrón gave birth to the legend of the Capeman, which decades later became a Broadway play written by singer Paul Simon and poet Derek Walcott. Agrón's case in particular was extraordinary in the way he used news media to glamorize his dysfunctional alienation and brag about murders that he would later claim not to have committed. Less well known was his prison-time involvement with a cult-like pseudo-Marxist group called the New Alliance Party and the reams of unpublished poetry that captured his transnational trauma, underlining it with a surprising optimism.

The acculturation of Puerto Rican migrants to New York was accompanied by the uncertain status of their ability to stay on the mainland. This was usually determined by the cold logic of maintaining a surplus labor army in large cities. As the economies of most of the major urban centers in the United States began to shift from the industrial to the service sector, jobs for relatively unskilled and undereducated workers quickly disappeared. After struggling for many years as a food service worker, my father managed to land a civil service job with the Transit Authority, and my mother went back and forth from working in department stores and staying at home with their children. Yet by the 1970s the majority of Puerto Ricans in the United States were largely relegated to low-wage jobs or, even worse, unemployment and a growing dependency on government assistance and long-term residence in crumbling public housing. And all of this happened as disinvestment in government programs under increasingly conservative economic regimes accelerated.

During the 1970s the postwar economic boom began to subside as major cities in the United States underwent a kind of deindustrialization process. Cities like New York, which was home to all manner of manufacturing, from Swingline Staplers to Silvercup Bread, began to transition to an economy based strictly on service jobs and, of course, the emergence of the finance sector as the principal driver of its economic engine. This era was a turning point in the shift from the FDR era's Keynesian approach to a government-investment-led economy to what became "neoliberalism," an ideology that favored cutting spending on social programs and looking to the private sector to create societal wealth. But at the same time, the neoliberal era defined the way the United States' relationship with Puerto Rico was not only changing but also, in a strange way, merging. It wasn't only Puerto Ricans who were facing a crisis in New York—New York itself was in crisis.

By the mid-1970s, when Democratic mayor Abraham Beame replaced the last of the Republican liberals, John Lindsay, New York found itself facing a serious fiscal crisis caused by shrinking revenue from the city's tax base as the white middle class moved out in droves. The growth of this aforementioned financial sector was in many ways exemplified by the emergence of Donald J. Trump, a once-obscure Queens middle-class housing mogul, because of the way he took advantage of New York City's desperate desire to promote business investment by offering tax breaks—not unlike the business model imposed on Puerto Rico. In Kim Phillips-Fein's exhaustive study of New York's 1970s debt crisis, *Fear City: New York's Fiscal Crisis and the Rise of Austerity Politics*, she notes that "New York expanded its borrowing at a time when public debt was growing across the country, when bankers were enthusiastically marketing its bonds and notes." She also describes a similar dynamic between what happened in New York in the mid-seventies and in Puerto Rico forty years later: the financial sector played a huge role in encouraging the accumulation of debt, and those emerging technocrats who favored the push toward privileging business interests would then place the blame on the "irresponsible" politicians who incurred the debt.

Although the parallels between New York's fiscal crisis and Puerto Rico are numerous, there are also significant differences. Most obvious was New York's position as the financial capital of the United States, its previously very healthy manufacturing economy, and its access to a tax base that included some of the wealthiest families and family-owned businesses in America. Yet the quick erosion of its industrial base made it more vulnerable than one would imagine for the city of Rockefellers, Vanderbilts, and Astors. The collapse of the industrial economy led to a situation in which, predicting the actions of Puerto Rico's government when faced with its erratic economy, New York compensated for lost blue-collar jobs by employing a massive number of New Yorkers. By the early 1970s the city employed seven times as many workers as the New York Telephone Company.[2]

The city's tax base was also eroding drastically as a result of not only the closure of factories and other businesses but also the flight of middle- to upper-middle-class professionals, wage earners, and small business owners who were abandoning New York for the same suburban lifestyle that had drawn Puerto Ricans from rural areas. The city's decision to go into more debt through bond issuance was less motivated by mere survival, as in Puerto Rico's case, than by maintaining the social contract that the New Deal had established with its urban working class: public education, cultural institutions, parks, and government-funded social programs were maintained at all costs to allow the fantasy of a fully entitled working and middle class to flourish.

By 1973 some pundits were forecasting eventual bankruptcy, but the ascendance of Mayor Abraham Beame, replacing the "limousine liberal" Republican John Lindsay, would mark a period of renewed and more desperate borrowing, analogous to the early 2010s in Puerto Rico. When President Gerald Ford refused to offer the city a federal bailout, resulting in the infamously "misquoted" *Daily News* headline "Ford to City: Drop Dead," the long neoliberal process of shifting funds and investment away from government and toward the private sector—particularly real estate—began.[3] The eventual gutting of the public sector and investment in public institutions and spaces while handing tax breaks to real estate entrepreneurs hit with full force just as a growing majority of Puerto Ricans in major urban areas found themselves in a hard-to-break spiral of downward mobility.

The growth of the municipal bond market was one of the spectacular growth spurts of the finance sector–driven economy that took off in the 1970s and 1980s. As new bipartisan economic policies drove interest rates down, favoring supply-side investors, the volume of municipal bonds issued grew from $14 billion in 1971 to $222 billion in 1985. A *New York Times* article described how municipalities rushed to replace high-yielding bonds with lower-interest ones because they were uncertain about potential tax law changes. Municipalities were beginning to see bonds as volatile yet influential paths to securing funding—instead of the old-fashioned sensible investments that played unglamorous roles in infrastructure financing. "Scores of investment firms and banks entered the field," the article said. "Mayors of towns and heads of power authorities could no longer find room on their calendars for all the bond brokers dying to treat them to lunch."[4]

The events in New York and Puerto Rico set off a new moment of radical politics, which emerged to counter the onset of the new austerity as well as the contradictions inherent in US foreign policy around the world. The period of 1970s recession in New York was marked on some fronts by the decline of leftist political and cultural groups, which were at times harassed by FBI undercover informants while others were the victims of the confusing evolution of radical Maoist factions that dominated left discourse. But this time also saw the flowering of a bilingual and bicultural identity that adopted the name *Nuyorican* to describe a new kind of American citizen, a hybrid identity that embraced both worlds. Nuyoricans operated in three spheres: the radical politics of the Young Lords, who represented the contemporary moment; the ethnomusical outburst of salsa music, which prioritized the use of Spanish language in an attempt to reformulate the past; and the futurist bilingual Nuyorican poets whose work anticipated not only hip-hop and spoken-word performance but also Spanglish code-switching flourishes.

In this way Puerto Ricans in New York and on the island were living out a kind of modernist cultural explosion at the dawn of postmodernism and globalization/transnationalism, but these two groups would soon take different tracks. As political activism began to intensify on the island, the movement on the mainland turned to more conventional electoral politics. The 1970s saw the growth of new networks of professionals, elected officials, and "social justice warriors" in New York, Boston, Philadelphia, and Chicago, while on the island an intensified form of militant nationalism took place as the Bootstrap Dream began to deteriorate under the aftereffects of the US recession.

In the 1960s and 1970s a new pro-independence movement on the island gained strength, organizing protest actions among student and labor groups. As documented in Nelson Denis's *War Against All Puerto Ricans*, the FBI worked closely with the Puerto Rico Police Department to keep files on anyone with pro-independence sympathies. These infamous files, known as *carpetas*, were an early form of widespread civilian surveillance by the government and functioned as an unspoken restraint on political thinking. But at the University of Puerto Rico, activism intensified, on several occasions leading to acts of violence by police on protestors. In 1978 an FBI informer infiltrated a group of pro-independence activists who planned to protest and disrupt business as usual, but Puerto Rico police killed two of them during an aborted attempt to sabotage a TV tower on Cerro Maravilla. During the 1980s the case became a cause célèbre, and a series of hearings connected to an investigation into possible wrongdoing in the murders became a major pop-cultural event in Puerto Rico. The Watergate-style hearings featured a dramatic performance by the lead prosecutor Héctor Rivera Cruz and became daily must-see TV, a kind of real-life spectacle that combined elements of *Judge Judy* or *Caso Cerrado* with soap opera and tabloid TV crime coverage. It also damaged the pro-statehood New Progressive Party (NPP) for many years, as Carlos Romero Barceló, the sitting governor during the events in question, became associated with the classic Latin American archetype of the anti-communist *caudillo*, or strongman.

Meanwhile, in New York and Chicago a new militant group, FALN (Fuerzas Armadas de Liberación Nacional, or Armed Forces of National Liberation), began a campaign of bombings to force dialog on independence. One of its initial demands was for the release of Lolita Lebrón and her fellow prisoners who were arrested as a result of the 1954 Washington, DC, attacks. FALN, which was active both in Puerto Rico and in the mainland United States, symbolized a different kind of nationalist militancy, one forged by the experience of Puerto Rican migrants directly impacted by racism, segregation, and social injustice as well as the antiracist activism of the Civil Rights Movement and protest against the Vietnam War. Another contemporary group, Los Macheteros, also active on the island and New York, were equally radical and at times even more violent, attacking military bases and occasionally planting bombs in the financial district known as the Milla de Oro, or the Golden Mile, in the surreal glass-box-filled financial district of Hato Rey.

Like the Weathermen, an offshoot of the new left organization Students for a Democratic Society (SDS), FALN believed in armed confrontation with the US government and multinational corporations. And like the Irish Republican Army, FALN viewed its members as having the right to militarily struggle for national sovereignty, distinguishing them from the nihilist pursuits of so-called terrorist groups. Their first action—coordinated bombings of Exxon, Union Carbide, and Federal Reserve Bank buildings, among other targets—came the day before a pro-independence rally to be held at Madison Square Garden by a coalition of pro-independence and left-leaning groups and three days before hearings about Puerto Rico's colonial status at the UN Special Committee on Decolonization. Although at first the Puerto Rican Socialist Party objected to FALN's use of violence even though most of it was "symbolic" and focused on property rather than people as targets, there was a strategic shift among Puerto Rican nationalist movements toward the idea that imprisoned FALN members were "freedom fighters" and "patriots," and they began to garner sympathy from a more unified New York Puerto Rican constituency.

This shift created an unusual public consensus that, in a sense, could only happen in a colonial setting. Despite the fact that most of the militant activists had engaged in activities that would at least be questionable in terms of promoting violence and terrorist philosophies, a large swath—if not a majority—of Puerto Ricans supported them in their quest for freedom from US imprisonment. Even members of the usually right-wing NPP pro-statehood party have found it necessary to nominally support the cause of imprisoned political prisoners, if only to point out that if Puerto Rico were accepted as a state and, thereby, attained full citizenship and political rights, such movements would be unnecessary.

As the 1970s wore on, the sluggish and at times declining nature of Puerto Rico's economy had a strong effect on its internal politics. The long period of dominance that Luis Muñoz Marín's Popular Democratic Party (PDP) enjoyed began to wane, essentially because the ultimate resolution of Puerto Rico's status remained clouded. The narrative Muñoz Marín created in 1952 was that, with the help of Operation Bootstrap, Puerto Rico's economy would evolve to the point at which it would be robust and independent enough for the island to finally consider independence. The political dynamic that Operation Bootstrap created, however, favored the growth of the newly organized New Progressive Party (NPP). The NPP preferred statehood, and despite its use of the word *progressive*, it leaned toward the center-right tendencies of the United States' Republican Party.

There were many factors leading up to the emergence of the NPP: the PDP's message was beginning to sound stale; Muñoz-Marín's replacement, Roberto Sánchez Vilella, was seen as too whimsical and left leaning; and there was increasing uneasiness among Puerto Rico's new middle class that paralleled the unease of the American middle class of the late 1960s—as the largely Catholic voting constituency feared political radicalism and the rise of women's rights and sexual liberation movements, many were motivated to seek a more socially conservative party platform. Perhaps most importantly, at the level of basic economics and wages, some of Puerto Rico's workers feared independence because of their Caribbean neighbors' relative poverty. Instead, they wanted full-citizenship entitlement because Puerto Rico's economy was still far behind the mainland's and codependent with the United States—there was no way of being sure they could improve it after gaining independence.

By the mid-1970s an economic stagnation that led to recession threatened the era of US global dominance, and just like during the 1930s Great Depression, Puerto Rico's economy endured crippling effects. By 1974 the strategy to attract outside investment and reduce unemployment at all costs had resulted in external investors owning 70 percent of all productive wealth in Puerto Rico, according to economist James Dietz.[5] The US recession had strongly impacted the Puerto Rican economy, causing precipitous drops in the GNP, a rise in unemployment to almost 20 percent, and a large increase in federal transfer payments in the form of food stamps and other government-assistance entitlements.

In 1974 PDP governor Rafael Hernández Colón appointed a commission to be led by Professor James Tobin of Yale University, who had been a member of President Kennedy's Council of Economic Advisers, to assemble a report with recommendations for the Puerto Rican economy. Like many progressive economists, Tobin was concerned that Puerto Rico was in a state of dependence, as external investors owned most of the island's financial assets and profits generated were not reinvested locally. He even made reference to the glaring gap between the GDP and GNP. Yet Tobin's recommendations seemed to belie his liberal stance and were among the first evidence of an emerging neoliberal solution to depressed economies with negative growth and high unemployment.

Tobin was a devout Keynesian, which meant he strongly believed that government investment in public works projects and social programs would sustain economic growth. He had spent much of his career battling with the infamous Milton Friedman and his supply-side University of Chicago bad boys, whose place in economic history was secured by their harsh privatization of Chile's economy following the CIA-sponsored replacement of socialist president Salvador Allende with militarist authoritarian General Augusto Pinochet on September 11, 1973. Yet Tobin felt that one of Puerto Rico's main problems was that the United States' minimum wage applied there—at the time $2.30 an hour—was too high to attract US investment. Although it was true that Puerto Rico was no longer the only game in town for offshore manufacturers and that other neighboring islands and nations had begun to attract investment through the promise of lower wages, Tobin's analysis did not take into account the impact that depressing wages would have on Puerto Ricans, who were still nominally US citizens; instead, he focused more on potential impacts on investors.

Tobin's recommendation to lower wages would later be echoed in the Krueger Report of 2015, released as the swirling winds of debt crisis began to blow through Puerto Rico. It symbolized once again the distinctions the United States makes when it deals with the territory: "belonging to, but not a part of" means that in some ways it is under federal laws and protections, but in other ways distinctions between Puerto Rico and the mainland United States can be drawn according to the federal government's particular needs at particular times. His recommendations reflect the bottom line of how the United States externalizes Puerto Rico: economic solutions must first consider the stability of US capital investment, and Puerto Ricans' right to economic prosperity is secondary.

In response, however, Puerto Rican elected officials need to attend to the bottom line, which is their re-election, and, beyond that, the ultimate goals of the three main parties: a continuation of the commonwealth, or colony with limited self-rule; petitioning Congress for statehood; or independence, ostensibly with some form of friendly relationship to the United States.

In 1976, an election year, Governor Hernández Colón pushed Congress to reassess its tax policies toward Puerto Rico in a way that would stabilize the island's economy. Congress reacted by creating Section 936 of the Internal Revenue Tax Code, which allowed corporations to shift profits to mainland banks at any time. Under the previous system, defined by Section 931, transfers were only allowed to be made to other territories or upon liquidation of a company. In addition, according to Ayala and Bernabe, "936 corporations could and did shift income generated elsewhere to Puerto Rico, thus avoiding the payment of federal corporate taxes," which allowed companies like Pepsi, Union Carbide, and Abbott Laboratories to register anywhere from 25 to 71 percent of their incomes in the territory without having to invest in Puerto Rican workers or the broader community.[6]

The Puerto Rican economy was now completely immersed in a model that was greatly distanced from the governmental ideal of limited autonomous government. Whereas the "commonwealth" was a faintly realized fantasy of "free association," the economic policies implemented entailed almost absolute subjugation and dependence. The thriving areas of the economy gradually became centered on pharmaceutical companies, which could transfer profits from intellectual property and patents to the island and would hire relatively few workers; tourism; and an array of banking and real estate businesses that essentially acted as go-betweens for US investors interested in the island, analogous to the creole classes who managed the interests of the Spanish empire.

An experiment with petrochemical industrial development failed disastrously after the consolidation of the Organization of Petroleum Exporting Countries (OPEC) raised oil prices. The rusted vestiges of petrochemical plants along the southern coast of the island are grim reminders of that. Perhaps not ironically, they mar the horizon near the town of Guánica, which once housed a major sugar refinery and was also the site of the landing of the US Navy in 1898.

THE STRANGE CASE OF THE REMOVAL OF PUERTO RICO'S RIGHT TO BANKRUPTCY

"Why would Congress put Puerto Rico in this never-never land? Why in the world? What explains Congress wanting to put Puerto Rico in this anomalous position of not being able to restructure its debt?"

—**Justice Ruth Bader Ginsburg,** speaking at a Supreme Court Hearing considering a ruling on *Franklin California v. Commonwealth of Puerto Rico et al.*, July 2015

Another curious episode, in 1984, would come to spell trouble for Puerto Rico and its finances. Most likely owing to neoliberal shifts in economic policy, Congress became obsessed with reforming tax laws in the early 1980s. According to legal scholar Stephen J. Lubben, the new reforms resulted in Puerto Rico (and the District of Columbia), which had previously not been defined as states for the purposes of tax law, being suddenly excluded from bankruptcy protection by being considered a state, which is not covered by Chapter 9 bankruptcy law. "The reasons are uncertain," he wrote, "as the new definition was added as part of a wealth of new additions."[7]

A vague conspiracy theory of sorts invokes Strom Thurmond, the legendary conservative and, some might say, white supremacist senator from South Carolina, whose name was brought up in a Supreme Court hearing to decide the fate of *Puerto Rico v. Franklin California Tax-Free Trust*, which challenged the island's attempt to write its own bankruptcy law in 2015. Thurmond was said to have introduced the change in language precluding Puerto Rico from being considered a state for the purposes of Chapter 9 bankruptcy (among many other changes). *Hamilton* playwright and performer Lin-Manuel Miranda, who was born in New York to Puerto Rican parents, even alluded to this in an April 2016 episode of John Oliver's show, *Last Week Tonight*.

Many respected commentators, such as Juan González and Nelson Denis, have mentioned Thurmond's segregationist history as a motivating factor, yet the fact that DC was included convolutes this argument. The record also shows that Thurmond formally introduced the changes along with Bob Dole and Howell Heflin, who, although Republican, don't fit Thurmond's more extremist profile. But this seemingly arbitrary change was made in the midst of the Reagan Revolution, with Republican control of Congress bent on reducing regulation of the financial sector and freeing up capital from taxation so it could be used to speculate in markets like the rapidly expanding municipal bond market. Regardless of whether the change was intentional, it certainly served a purpose by increasing speculative interest in

Puerto Rico bonds, as it was now legally impossible for the territory to seek bankruptcy relief.

Excluding the District of Columbia from Chapter 9 would make sense if it was due to a desire for "reining in debt" and imposing strict financial-control measures on DC by denying it access to bankruptcy procedures. Puerto Rico had already been established as an offshore haven to hide profits, so the reforms meant that its municipal bonds, which were already tax exempt, could be sold to the investor as foolproof. Not only did the Puerto Rican constitution—like that of some states—cap the rate of borrowing to "responsible" levels, without bankruptcy protection, Puerto Rico could never default on the bonds—they would always be required to be paid back in full.

The change in the bankruptcy law meant that Puerto Rico was set up to become a fearsome bond-issuing machine. The combination of its triple-tax exemption from city, state, and federal taxes and its inability to declare bankruptcy basically guaranteed that investors would be happy to buy any bonds on offer, and the government's increasing role as one of its main employers provided a strong incentive to issue the bonds. Like Hernández Colón, successive Puerto Rico governors would increasingly resort to borrowing in the form of debt issuance to guarantee not only essential operations but also the illusion that Puerto Rico was a stable and viable place to live and work. Just as the island had been propped up as an illusory middle-class workers' paradise so as to favorably compare it with outcomes achieved by the Cuban Revolution, the economy of postrecession Puerto Rico was an artifice, an offshore haven for stashing profits, and a dumping ground for US consumer products. And it was about to receive another blow to its stability.

Over the next decade the resulting combination of the bloated assets held in island banks and the revenue losses to the US Treasury, which increased the federal deficit without doing anything to help Puerto Rico, made continuing Section 936 almost untenable. As a tax scheme, 936 had turned more into a way to avoid taxes than to create a self-sustaining economy. The

Clinton administration, with all of its neoliberal focus on budget balancing and cutting back on federal expenditures, seized on the opportunity and decided to eliminate the corporate tax-break provision.

In his 1993 State of the Union Address, Clinton made it clear that he was eager to boost revenues to reduce the US deficit. The Clinton administration's slow creep to the right was increasingly about favoring entrepreneurialism and demonizing the growing masses of jobless or underemployed poor. Even though his decision to cut was motivated by disciplining corporations who avoided taxes, it would ultimately have the effect of setting up Puerto Rico to be demonized as a poor, nonwhite population dependent on government entitlement programs. The ten-year phaseout of Section 936 was fittingly folded into the Small Business Job Protection Act of 1996, and the stage was set for the final decline of Puerto Rico's economy.

The phaseout of 936 is often associated with a conspiracy theory of sorts involving Bill Clinton and the then governor of Puerto Rico, Pedro Rosselló, the father of the current Puerto Rico governor. The logic behind this theory is that by ending Section 936, the farce of the Puerto Rican economy under the commonwealth would be exposed as the sham that it was, causing Puerto Rican voters to abandon the PDP, permanently embrace the NPP, and pass a referendum petitioning Congress to add it as a state. Objectively, however, NPP governors from Luis Ferré to Barceló to Rosselló had all supported Section 936 as a way to keep money flowing into the Government Development Bank as well as the island's main banks, such as Banco Popular, Scotia Bank, and Doral Bank, all of whom counted eventual members of NPP administrations as employees.

It seemed suicidal for statehooders to promote the end of 936, even if there were a possibility that its elimination would force the United States' hand on Puerto Rico's status. But Congress was never going to grant Puerto Rico statehood status. The federal taxes Puerto Ricans would newly be required to pay as residents of the fifty-first state would not match the massive increase in federal spending that would result. Bob Woodward's book *The Agenda: Inside the Clinton White House* discusses how Clinton fretted with Daniel Moynihan over doomsday scenarios around the elimination of Section 936. The senator warned that doing so would double unemployment and increase migration to New York and that the resulting strain on social-service costs would render revenues gained from eliminating 936 moot. There is yet another theory that Clinton finally agreed to sign the bill requiring its elimination as a compromise with Newt Gingrich and the Republican Contract with America's agenda to balance the budget.

Whatever the reason, Clinton did sign into law the elimination of 936 over a ten-year phaseout, and it happened in an almost synergistic relationship with one of the most important events of the twentieth century: the implementation of the North American Free Trade Agreement, which was signed into law two years prior. NAFTA signaled a new direction for the world economy by eroding economic nationalism in favor of globalist free-trade policy. The implication for Puerto Rico was that it would no longer enjoy an exclusive free-trade relationship with the United States, and therefore, it would lose its competitive advantage with Caribbean and Latin American neighbors.

From the beginning of Puerto Rico's relationship with the United States, the United States protected its own exports to the island through the shipping requirements of the Jones Act while at the same time importing freely from Puerto Rico through its own corporations. After World War II, however, through Operation Bootstrap, Puerto Rico was used as a laboratory for US corporations wanting to directly employ a civilian labor force from a place that did not share the mainland's territory and culture. Department store chains, fast food restaurants, and car rental companies that had rarely directly employed workers who were not acculturated as "Americans" began to see how this was possible outside the fifty states.

The postwar economic relationship between the United States and Puerto Rico was basically a dry run for what was to come with liberal free-trade zone export-led development. During the Reagan era, policies like the Caribbean Basin Initiative, which extended free-trade and tariff exemptions to Caribbean and Central American countries, clearly predicted NAFTA. At the same time, the expansion of these policies to areas like Mexico was already beginning to seriously undermine the attractiveness of Puerto Rican labor to US corporations. Yet, ironically, the very 936 tax policy that accompanied this style of development and exploitation was clearly incompatible with future free-trade-zone initiatives.

The deadly combination of phasing out Section 936 and implementing NAFTA was devastating to Puerto Rico as the end of the millennium approached. While Puerto Rico enjoyed the presence of major US labor unions, the right to collective bargaining, and the ability to litigate within the framework of the regulatory mechanisms of the Environmental Protection Agency (EPA), other countries in the region were becoming the top choices for investment from US corporations and effectively destroying the demand for Puerto Rican labor. The insular logic behind instruments like Section 936 was contrary to the neoliberal commitment to free-trade zones and unfettered circulation of investment capital. While pharmaceutical and tech companies like Microsoft continued to stash profits from intellectual property in Puerto Rico, most investors sought areas with lower wages and fewer labor and environmental protections.

In 1996 Puerto Rico found itself doomed to a long, slow descent into fiscal crisis, what Governor Alejandro García Padilla would call a "death spiral" in 2015 when he announced that the island's debt was unpayable. But Puerto Ricans on the island who were not economists, by and large did not grasp the reality of this impending doom. Mainland Puerto Ricans understood it even less, and it was absolutely off the radar for mainstream Americans.

When Clinton signed the bill to eliminate Section 936, my parents had already moved back to Puerto Rico, having forgone the American dream by not buying a house in the New York area in favor of enjoying a relatively comfortable life on the island. They had reasonably good access to health care and were able to shop at most of the US chain department stores scattered around the island in dreary strip malls as well as more ambitious shopping centers like Plaza Carolina and Plaza Las Américas, a sprawling mall—the largest in the Caribbean—indistinguishable from one in the San Fernando Valley near Los Angeles or New York's Westchester County. They went to see movies at one of the Caribbean Cinemas chain of theaters, and my father played golf at hotel resorts as well as a less expensive one operated and maintained by the Roosevelt Roads Naval Station in a town called Ceiba on the east coast of the island.

When I went to visit my parents they had become just as consumer obsessed and Home Depot driven as any suburban American. They subscribed to a cable television company that eventually provided high-speed internet, yet they were still able to eat indigenous *criollo* cuisine and go to salsa dances in small halls designed for the over-fifty set. Their new life in the northeast corner of the island provided all the suburban comforts they never had while living in Bronx apartments. They encouraged me to visit often so they could indulge me in a kind of fantasy suburban tropical life that would allow me to offset the hassles of living in the overcrowded, grime-covered streetscape of highly competitive New York.

But they had no idea about the increasing and seemingly out-of-control pattern of debt issuance, aside from warnings from pessimistic radio commentaries—which were extremely high profile and part of the island's late-twentieth-century zeitgeist. They didn't realize that their easy access to Lacoste golf shirts and exotic new varieties of ice cream would soon become severely threatened. Radio commentary on the island had become increasingly important, as US Spanish-language chains like Univision and Telemundo had taken over locally run television stations. Hosts like Luis Fernando Ojeda were acerbic skeptics who harangued politicians whose actions were exposed by the island's declining fate as ineffectual—their backwoods preaching style capturing the energy of the vast majority who were not members of the San Juan elite.

Despite the fact that it was obvious to everyone that Puerto Rico was a dependent colony that could not develop its own economy, the eccentric fantasy that was the Commonwealth of Puerto Rico had buried the old idea of poor, backward semifeudal Puerto Rico. People believed that the island would continue to survive just the way New York had after the 1975 fiscal crisis. There would always be government money and borrowing and infrastructure projects and new companies hoping to make a quick buck by paying lower wages and using existing laws to stash profits.

There was also, of course, tourism and the pristine beaches that were still protected against competition from Cuba's through the embargo-based travel restrictions as well as the naval bases on Roosevelt Roads and Vieques, which also provided huge consumer capital for large and small businesses, particularly in the northeast corner where they lived. The Fajardo strip-mall supermarket was stocking all the latest American and European magazines and top-shelf liquor, while auto dealerships were still making sale after sale of the new sports utility vehicles, Jeeps, and, of course, Chevy and Ford sedans.

Despite the fact that my father often felt discriminated against in New York and the United States and made sure I learned to read and write perfect English to protect me from that, he was not able to see that the fate of Puerto Rico was tied to "the racial logic of global capitalism," as professors Paula Chakravartty and Denise Ferreira da Silva would put it.[8] It should have been obvious from the beginning—following from the racial logic of exclusion implicit in the Insular Cases—that Puerto Rico was a state when it needed to be and was not a state when that was more convenient. And it was clear that Wall Street debt vultures preyed on the island the same way subprime loans from US banks targeted poor black and brown people in the early 2000s.

Nor would the rest of the manufactured Puerto Rican middle class recognize what Vijay Prashad called the "assassination of the Third World" through debt or, even further down the line, the imposition of austerity measures that had been pioneered in Argentina in the early 1980s and were resurrected in Puerto Rico in 2017.[9] The rule of the finance capital game determines how loss would be shared among societies, and those chosen to bear its burden are mostly people of color. "Why . . . should the holders of the 'subprime mortgage' pay the exorbitant interest rates attached to their loans?" ask Chakravartty and Ferreira da Silva. "Why should the economically dispossessed be expected to take on the risk assumed by those who, enabled by the privatization of public housing and the deregulation of financial markets, bet against them?"

Racial difference has always determined Puerto Rico's relationship to the United States, and the island's history is written by liberal and conservative policies to ease the burden or forcefully reimpose it. When the autocratic control of military governors and sugar corporations became too unsightly, the commonwealth was born to create a semblance of autonomous rule and hope for a positive economic future. The downturn that postrecession economies took in the 1970s had set into motion the irreversible effects of what some would call *neoliberalism* and others *late capitalism*. When the financial sector's speculative bubble burst in the form of default on Puerto Rico's municipal bonds, austerity was mandated to provide investor remedy. In the end it was about who was controlling profits and losses and how certain moments in history allow racially differentiated people to temporarily share in surplus while saddling them with the losses when the economy inevitably sputters.

As Puerto Rico headed into an uncertain future, the United States was also in the process of assigning responsibility for economic losses to its own people and setting up battles between finance capital and indebted municipalities and states. In many ways these stories would parallel and mirror each other. The subprime mortgage crisis of 2008 was a harbinger of what would happen in Puerto Rico, but the dumping of debt and imposition of austerity pioneered in Greece and Argentina would affect the discourse about Puerto Rico greatly, though these practices did not, ultimately, impact Puerto Rico's chosen legal and political strategies.

Even as the real crisis began to snowball in Puerto Rico, it would not become apparent in the United States largely because there has traditionally been almost no media coverage of the island outside of the occasional crime wave or hurricane. In fact, awareness of the crisis would become widespread at first only through the business press, which saw a threat to not only American investors but also the municipal debt market itself. But the mainstream awareness of Puerto Ricans as a people and a nation has created a formidable discourse, one that would emerge suddenly to disrupt the stark silences and to directly or indirectly remind America that the loss Wall Street and Congress had worked so hard to externalize will not be shed so easily when the people who must pay for it are not as "separate" as has been thought. Through the debt crisis, as much as the United States tried to maintain its distance, Puerto Rico would finally become a permanent, internal problem.

CHAPTER 3

THE *DIABLO* IN DERIVATIVES

Borrowing to Meet Basic Needs

Banco Popular headquarters in San Juan. © Joseph Rodríguez

"If all debts are guaranteed, why should lenders lend responsibly?"

> —**Yanis Varoufakis**, *Adults in the Room: My Battle with the European and American Deep Establishment*

"The very fact that we don't know what debt is, the very flexibility of the concept, is the basis of its power."

> **David Graeber**, *Debt: The First 5000 Years*

In the early 2000s—after years of experiencing Puerto Rico either as a tourist or a prodigal son, visiting only to see family and without making any serious effort to engage in a culture I had claimed as part of a subaltern, "minority" identity in New York and the vast empire of mainland America—I tried to change things up a bit. I arranged for an appearance to promote *Living in Spanglish,* a book I'd written with a broad swath of US Latinos in mind, at the Borders bookstore in Plaza Las Américas, the largest shopping mall in the entire Caribbean basin. I knew there would not be much of a reception for a book written in English by a Nuyorican who seemed to have more affinity with a bilingual US-based cultural movement than *la cultura de la isla,* but I hadn't come to sell books—I came to reconnect with something I'd lost long ago, a mystery buried deep in my childhood.

Soon after the sparsely attended Borders event, I followed up with people I'd met during the week of the event—local reporters for the government-run TV station, WIPR, and *plena* musicians and their friends—stopping at local spots like El Boricua, a raucous college bar with $2 bottles of Medalla, the island's lightweight beer. I began to visit frequently, staying in a San Juan–area apartment and making more and more friends and acquaintances—journalists, musicians, theater people, political activists—while the weeks turned to months. With great difficulty and maximum effort, I expanded my "Puerto Rican Spanish" vocabulary and local cliché toolset and refined my pronunciation and diction to the point where I began to approximate an authentic Boricua. I went to plays, lingered at art openings, and began to hang out at joints like El Balcón del Zumbador, an unpretentious shack-like tavern on a strip in a rustic area near San Juan called Piñones, where *bomba* and plena were played live for fevered dancers until the wee hours of the morning.

Despite my newly revived connection, there was always some low-intensity buzz I was picking up on that seemed to pervade the island—a neighbor losing their job and getting behind on their mortgage, the sudden closing of a promising local restaurant, the slow deterioration of the University of Puerto Rico's main campus in Rio Piedras, the inescapable spread of enormous potholes, and the increasing numbers of panhandlers with the washed-out faces of substance abuse and addiction. I felt all of these as part of an anxious feeling of precarity that had been growing on the island. It was as if the island was beginning to awaken from its delusion of being the Showcase of the Caribbean to realize neoliberalism's unleashing of a debt trap. Puerto Ricans were being ensnared by what David Harvey calls the neoliberal era of "accumulation by dispossession," generally understood as centralizing wealth and power in fewer hands by taking away land and property from the public sector. This strategy is accomplished by forcing localities to privatize publicly held resources like nationalized oil, financializing local economies by ensnaring them in a cycle of debt, and capitalizing on the management of extreme weather event crises such as Hurricane María.[1]

Harvey believes "accumulation by dispossession" is a logical progression of a capitalist world system whose reaction to crises in manufacturing, which no longer produced reliably profitable rates of return, should be remedied by privatizing public resources and increasingly financializing local and global economies. These are among the basic tenets of neoliberalism. High labor costs achieved through organized labor are increasingly remedied by using lower-wage labor in developing countries through free-trade policies, transforming US and European economies into finance-sector and service industries. This pit the wealthy metropolitan regions (i.e., the United States, Europe, and parts of Asia) against what many have called the Global South (Latin America, Africa, and South Asia).

The Global South is almost entirely made up of people of color, living in countries that were decolonized in the nineteenth and twentieth centuries. Their raw materials were extracted before and after their colonization, and their economies have long been considered "dependent" on developed countries' economies. The idea of the Global South is powerful because it reminds us of the forces of colonization and imperialism that created an economic advantage for Western countries and mired "southern" countries in a cycle of underdevelopment. As an unincorporated territory adrift in the Caribbean, Puerto Rico had always effectively been part of the Global South, although the temporary illusion of commonwealth shielded it from that reality. But at the dawn of the new millennium the island was returning to its true status with a measured uneasiness.

It's impossible to talk about what has happened in Puerto Rico without addressing neoliberalism, which can simply be described as the abandonment of New Deal–era economic principles—anchored by the government-led investment strategies outlined by John Maynard Keynes—in favor of eroding public investment, breaking up organized labor, and promoting the unchecked growth of the financial sector. Neoliberalism maintains that economic growth can be driven by eliminating barriers to export manufacturing while also requiring massive expansion of "unsecured" private individual consumer debt due to cuts to government programs and the stagnation of what economists call "real wages"—wages adjusted for inflation. As we saw in the last chapter, neoliberalism took off in New York as a series of policy reforms that would solve an intractable debt crisis, but the New York it created was an almost unrecognizable breeding ground for financialization where workers in low-rise neighborhoods were physically replaced by the land-owning rich and their ever-expanding high-rise buildings that housed not only the 1 percent but also the banks and investment houses that created them.

Puerto Rico had generally lived a political-economic reality that was an unfaithful simulacrum of a capitalist democracy. It had also been somewhat detached from the debates surrounding mainland political reform, largely because of its insular nature, which was characterized by the fact that it operates in a decidedly different language and culture than the United States. Without representation in Congress and a public intellectual class that produced work in English, Puerto Ricans remained outside the conversation as their economic system pretended to be dynamic enough to support a middle class with stable jobs but was actually a mechanism for sucking profit out of the island while providing little local reinvestment.

But the debates centering on status change engaged islanders in a zero-sum quarrel over the possibilities of something that could only be granted by an indifferent Congress in Washington. Despite fairly clear divisions based on liberal and conservative politics, the question had devolved into a perfect arena for lobbyists intent on selling something that would never come to pass. Republicans, some of whom were disingenuously involved in supporting the pro-statehood movement, would never vote for Puerto Rican statehood because it would increase federal spending on social programs—Puerto Rico's entitlements are currently subject to a spending cap due to its territorial status— and also because its population, which would be the poorest state in the Union, would likely lean Democratic, automatically adding two senators and perhaps four to five representatives to Congress at the expense of other states, whose Representatives would decrease, most likely replacing Republicans.

At the beginning of the millennium one constant remained in postmodern life in Puerto Rico: its economy was rapidly shrinking because of a steep decline in the manufacturing sector, attributable to both the end of Section 936 and the general decline of manufacturing globally. The only thing that was holding up the economy was government employment and borrowing to assure the continuance of essential services, such as police, firefighters, municipal hospitals, and the electrical grid.

The many dilemmas Puerto Rico faces point again to the profoundly undemocratic way Congress defined Puerto Rico as a state for some purposes and a territory for others, using it as a laboratory for imposing undemocratic practices on US citizens. Economist James Dietz sums up Puerto Rico's economic dysfunction: "Puerto Rico's strategy of development lacked a focus on the systematic support or fostering of local entrepreneurs and local sources of finance," which led to the inevitable result that the Puerto Rican entrepreneurs, skilled workers, and technological advancements that might otherwise have led to consistent economic progress had been stifled, preventing the island from creating growth.[2] Moreover, the decisions around government investment were much more focused on short-term concerns—paying salaries and pension contributions, businesses set up just to export capital to the mainland—leading to the deterioration of public schools and universities, cultural institutions, the healthcare system, and infrastructure such as roads, sewage, and, perhaps most significantly, electricity. Although it seems illogical for Puerto Rico's government to prop up businesses that encouraged capital flight, the jobs they provided were crucial for ensuring the government wouldn't need to absorb more of the labor force and support a growing population dependent on social entitlements like SSI and food stamps.

Up until the advent of NAFTA and other free-trade agreements, the relationship between the United States and Puerto Rico had been based on an unequal economic exchange, with Puerto Rico's lower salaried workers forced to provide both cheap labor and consumer dollars to mainland US businesses, leading to rising GDP/GNP differentials. This means that the wealth created by Puerto Ricans was not staying on the island. As neoliberalism blossomed, the United States' method of exploitation shifted to extending credit.[3] However, the sheer volume of federal government transfer payments was not enough to keep the ship afloat, so the exploitive debt relationship expanded exponentially. This differed from the way dominant global capital was able to exploit weak states like Argentina and Greece, who could adjust their currency rates and borrow from the IMF, because Puerto Rico had no state sovereignty or IMF to bail them out, which signaled a catastrophic outcome.

The signs that Puerto Rico might be lurching toward a crisis point began to proliferate in the early 2000s. As the economy shrunk and disappeared as a result of being a dependent economy, the phaseout of Section 936 then made it all worse. A public perception began to emerge of a society with little opportunity, and a series of crime waves that ranged from carjackings to increasing violence around drug-sale points stirred up old-school racist attitudes in Puerto Rico. On top of this, pro-statehood governor Pedro Rosselló and President Bill Clinton began the experimental use of police mini-stations as part of a Mano Dura Contra Crimen (Hard Hand Against Crime) initiative within the island's many public housing developments, called *caseríos*. These mini-stations would play a role in the subsequent development of a resistant Afro-Caribbean music explosion.[4]

The full brunt of the impending crisis was yet to be felt in Puerto Rico as the second decade of the 2000s began, but it was clear that the commonwealth governing model, which had held its own against pro-statehood challenges over the years, was losing credibility in the eyes of Puerto Rican voters. Job loss began to staggeringly increase, and the federal government became the island's largest employer.

From the beginning of this particular downturn—brought on by the phaseout of Section 936, as US corporations pulled out of Puerto Rico in search of cheaper wages—even Wall Street expressed concern. Even before the phaseout bill was passed, an August 1996 article in *Bond Buyer* quoted Moody's bond rater Steve Hochman as saying that the phaseout would create "a long-term negative impact. This action will hurt the island's economic growth potential."[5] Ratings agencies and bond-buying investment institutions, which consistently left ratings acceptable despite disturbing signs in the bond-issuing economies, displayed pervasive myopia in the lead-up to the debt crisis—arguably to the point of being a prominent factor in debt accumulation. Yet the business and government class in Puerto Rico had no problem playing along.

In the years leading up to the crisis, after each new wrinkle was announced in the business press, there was an explosion in the use of financial instruments and developing new ways to avoid constitutional requirements for debt ceilings, in turn creating new optimism in the bond markets. In the ten years between 1996, when the 936 phaseout began, and 2006, when the government passed a law that allowed the issuing of bonds to be backed by a sales and use tax (under the infamous acronym COFINA—Corporación del Fondo de Interés Apremiante, or Sales Tax Financing Corporation), the Puerto Rico economy morphed from that of a failing welfare state to one wholly absorbed by advanced Wall Street risk-avoidance mechanisms. By financing its growing debt with a sales tax, Puerto Rico would directly pass the debt burden on to the average consumer, who would be paying an increasing rate for an undetermined amount of time. Yet in the media and even academic analysis of the reasons for the debt crisis, the narrative was delineated by the special-case scenario of a Caribbean unincorporated territory, with the island government framed as an overextended if not irresponsible borrower, in over its head in a legitimate activity that is an essential part of financing municipalities and states within the mainland United States.

The idea that Puerto Rico was "irresponsible" in managing its finances is legitimate in the sense that its governmental apparatus acted in a short-sighted way to secure its operations' viability and keep intact a system of patronage and, at times, corruption that has always been part of the mainland American landscape. But the way that the narrative is constructed around how and why Puerto Rico came to owe $72 billion in debt plus about $50 billion in pension liabilities is strongly framed through racist and classist tropes, such as the ones concocted in the Reagan era about the profligate spending of welfare queens as well as the late-2000s stigmatization of people who took out high-risk mortgages, which were targeted to mostly people of color. When those risky debts were packaged together with others that varied in risk, the resulting collapse in prices was one of the central causes of the 2008 recession.

The financialization of Western economies, a central feature of neoliberalism, was a crucial part of solving the recessions of the 1970s. These economies struggled with conditions in which manufactured products outstripped effective demand, creating falling profit margins, job losses, and inflationary trends exacerbated by the increasing power of the Organization of Petroleum Exporting Countries (OPEC) and the resulting rise in fossil fuel prices. Marxist or neo-Marxist economists would explain those recessions as inevitable crises generated by the very nature of capitalism—it strives to expand by exhausting markets until their profitability is tapped and also concentrates wealth and, in that way, limits its own circulation.

Sources ranging from Oxfam to *Forbes* magazine estimate anywhere from $7 to $32 trillion are held in offshore tax havens, money that could be used to repair infrastructure, hire workers, and allow consumers to keep economies dynamic. Regardless of whether you believe in Marxist economic analysis, it is clear that a group of economists led by Friedrich Hayek and Milton Friedman of the University of Chicago successfully advanced the idea that the Keynesian policies of government-led investment and financial regulation—which allowed the US economy to revitalize itself after the Great Depression of the 1930s—were to blame for the 1970s stagnation and that the answer to this problem was to promote and clear the way for unfettered capitalism. That shift from the liberalism of the New Deal, in which government financing and institutions would be the bedrock of society, to identifying it as the source of everything that held progress back was the Chicago school's greatest achievement.

These ideological developments created a new push to deregulate industry and finance, a pattern championed by Ronald Reagan and British prime minister Margaret Thatcher, who both hired Friedman as a chief economic adviser. This created a brave new world where economies would not only no longer be dependent on industrial manufacturing but would also, in an increasingly abstract way, begin to shift the risk of capital accumulation and profit away from physical production and enterprise and onto consumers. Employer-financed pensions were replaced by private retirement plans such as IRAs and 401(k)s, whose growth was linked to the rise and fall of stocks, bonds, and commodity markets, and wages remained stagnant, which fueled the growth of personal credit, whose interest rates were at the whim of how the Federal Reserve reacted to international financial capital.

From there it was a swift joyride from the subtle shift to corporate avarice personified by Charlie Sheen and Michael Douglas in *Wall Street* to the manic excess of Leonardo DiCaprio in *The Wolf of Wall Street*. Although these pop-culture clichés are effective in painting a cinematic portrait of the moving of productive activity from the manufacturing to the financial sector, they don't illuminate much about the specific practices that allowed for the creation of such wealth. In many ways that's the point. The world of speculative finance was invented in part to conceal the mechanisms of financial gain and loss. Increasingly the creation of profit shifted from something that was tangible and could be measured into a rarified air of esoteric profit-making devices—essentially a jumble of fluctuating interest rates and profit margins. This gave profit making a kind of added value to financialization that was itself an allure. Only those who were specially trained or hired by elite banking institutions—themselves the products of elite business school training—really understood how to navigate the system.

One of the key instruments Wall Street used to expand the appeal of investing was what became known as the *financial derivative*. The essential concept behind the creation of complex financial instruments is something everyone seems to know yet almost automatically shies away from, as it seems to imply knowledge of calculus. A financial derivative is a contract between two parties that protects them against the risk of price changes—in a sense it's related in meaning to the calculus derivative, which measures changes in the relationship between mathematical functions.

The original derivative practice was used to protect farmers and investors against inconsistent harvest yields. In the long run this helped depress commodity prices in the Global South and increased the dominant powers' competitive advantage in the world economy. Displacing risk onto Latin American agriculture weakened those economies and made them vulnerable to being drawn into debt traps themselves. Their positioning in the commodity markets gave them some of the competitive advantage gained during the recession years, but the collapse of prices in those markets quickly eroded that advantage.

The form of derivatives involved in Puerto Rico's debt crisis was used in banking rather than commodity markets. A group of J.P. Morgan investment bankers invented these "financial instruments" in 1994 on a working weekend in Boca Raton, Florida, as a way to share major corporate investments' risk with other banks.[6] The first derivatives deal came later that year, when Exxon asked for a new line of credit to cover damages of up to $5 billion from the *Valdez* spill. J.P. Morgan team member Blythe Masters proposed that Morgan package the risk from the Exxon line of credit to the European Bank of Reconstruction and Development (EBRD), which would owe if Exxon defaulted. In return, EBRD would receive a fee from J.P. Morgan. They called it a "credit-default swap."

Morgan's credit-default swap was the first time that debt or risk had been traded as a commodity, and it opened the floodgates on speculation. It was now possible to invest in both a company's or other entity's success and failure. Banks were able disassociate themselves from risk by writing swaps on bundles of debt, thus developing portfolios of credit risks, which were categorized at different levels. This created an entirely new marketplace of commodity exchange, where riskier credit was

packaged with less-risky loans as "collateralized debt obligations" and were rewarded with higher payoffs.

As the demand for complex financial products grew, banking
institutions saw the potential to not only allow the accumulation of escalating profits but also seize control of the dominant
mechanisms of the emerging global economy. They began resisting regulation of swaps and derivatives, as derivatives' very
nature was designed to avoid disclosure of real-time finances
by delaying debt obligations further into the future. As financial capital increasingly flooded the derivatives market, pressure
mounted on lawmakers in Washington to ease restriction further, which resulted in the repeal of the Glass-Steagall Act. This
allowed banks to no longer restrict themselves to individual and
corporate banking; they could now fully engage with the new
frontier of complex financial instruments. By undoing the sep-
aration between investment and commercial banking, "super-
bank" institutions were created that engaged in increased risk
taking by packaging and securing bundles of borrowed money
and charging underwriting fees at every stage of this financial-
instrument marketing process.[7]

As Americans began to adapt to the new scenario of neoliberalism and globalization—which, as I've noted, also benefited greatly from free-trade zones that depressed the value of
labor in the Global South and set off a mass migration that is
still in effect—they began to develop a different idea of what
middle-class stability looked like. Although the dynamics of this
new narrative were somewhat hidden, it became clear to most
Americans that they could no longer depend on long-term job
security and old-school pension plans—which are still a feature
of some federal, state, and local government jobs. Middle-class
Americans began to understand that their interests had become more closely aligned with "asset markets" than their actual income, transforming them, as Robert Reich noted, from
"citizens" in a society defined by capitalism and democracy to
"investors" concerned with asset prices and shareholder value.[8]

By 1997 the US municipal bond market was the largest in the world, with $1.2 trillion in outstanding debt.

This new direction for mainland Americans had a kind of perverse fit with the way Puerto Rico's economic situation had been evolving since the 1917 Jones Act. Individually or through those in charge of their pensions, American investors were increasingly looking for places to invest their money, but only local municipal bonds offered tax exemptions, and in many cases the local bonds were not as competitive as those offered by outside municipalities. Puerto Rico's bonds were exempt from all taxes, and Puerto Rico's government was desperate for buyers, as the economy was structurally dependent and unlikely to generate growth without outrageously generous tax subsidies.

The debt relationship between the United States and Puerto Rico, as explored in Chapter 1, had followed the pattern that Wall Street banks had begun since the onset of the era of US interventionism in Latin American economies that took off after the Spanish-American War. In order to contain excessive speculation, some nominal rules were put in place, as they were with several states and municipalities in the United States. The Jones Act stated, "No appropriation of government expenditure should be made that would exceed the total revenue provided for such appropriation or expenditure, unless the legislature instituted a tax to pay for it within a given fiscal year." Similar to laws that govern the states, these limits were intended to prevent irresponsible borrowing, but because Puerto Rico was, by law, less than a state, a place where the American Constitution could be applied differently to suit US interests, it was vulnerable to abuse by financial manipulation.

Thirty-five years later the Puerto Rico Constitution similarly said, "The appropriations made for any fiscal year shall not exceed the total revenues, including available surplus, estimated for said fiscal year unless the imposition of taxes sufficient to cover said appropriations is provided by law." Yet as the years went on, regardless of what had happened with the Puerto Rico economy—consolidating lands for agriculture, transforming industry coupled with forcing migration through Operation Bootstrap, implementing and ultimately removing Section 936 of the Internal Revenue Code—the last resort was always to find ways to avoid limits to selling bonds. This had the inevitable result of putting Puerto Rico more deeply in debt. It's hard to conceive of a different path for the island, as it lacked the ability to develop an economy independent of US corporate interests and looked to borrowing as the only way to quickly cover shortfalls.

In 1961 Congress amended a 1950 law called the Puerto Rico Federal Relations Act, ending the federally imposed debt limit pending a vote on a constitutional amendment with new debt-limitation language. The new language permitted municipalities to borrow in their own interests without exceeding commonwealth debt limits. The amendment also imposed a 15 percent ceiling on debt service, or the minimal payment required to keep interest and principal payments current, giving executive and legislative branches a green light to borrow more if they increased tax rates. Because the new borrowing limit only applied to "bonds and notes for the payment of which the full faith credit and taxing power of the Commonwealth shall be pledged," it opened a door to create the sales tax–backed bond issuance known as COFINA in 2006, which allowed bond issuances to be backed by sales tax revenues.[9]

By the time Sila Calderón, Puerto Rico's first-ever woman governor, took office in 2001, there were mixed signals about the island's future. The Pedro Rosselló administration had created a new pro-statehood style of politics by abandoning the right-wing Republicans and forging new ties with Bill Clinton and the mainstream Democratic Party. These ties had more to do with the need for interrupted federal transfer payments that would go to Supplemental Security Income, Medicare, and food stamps for eligible residents than any party's ideological commitment. The agreement between Rosselló and Clinton to eliminate Section 936—according to some an NPP tactic to force a new political-economic arrangement in the hopes that statehood would be left as the only viable choice—would begin the island's slow descent into negative economic growth. Also looming when Calderón entered office was the growing phenomenon of neonationalist resistance in Vieques, a small island off the east coast of the island. Like neighboring Culebra, Vieques is a Puerto Rican municipality and for years housed a US naval base whose relentless bombing of the island beaches during war games caused long-term environmental damage, the effects of which were still being felt.

In the spring of 1999 David Sanes Rodríguez, a civilian who worked at the Vieques naval base, was killed by a stray bomb while he was on security detail. The injustice of his death reignited protests on the island, which had been the scene of squatter encampments going back to the 1970s and 1980s (residents of the neighboring island of Culebra had managed to expel naval target practices there in 1975). This created a renaissance of nationalist activism that had been somewhat dormant since the bad old days of UPR protests and Machetero bombings in the 1980s. The encampments drew celebrity protestors, from pop singers Draco Rosa and Ricky Martin to boxer Felix Trinidad, Robert Kennedy Jr., Al Sharpton, and Jesse Jackson.

This sudden spotlight on Puerto Rico politics coincided with the end of Bill Clinton's second and final term, when he decided to acquire some political capital for his wife's run for Senate in New York by taking the Vieques issue seriously. When it came time for his final pardons, he ordered the release of twelve imprisoned nationalists—to gain points for Hillary Clinton with New York–based Puerto Ricans. One of those nationalists, Oscar López Rivera, refused the deal and insisted on remaining in prison until all fifteen were released, ultimately getting his sentence commuted by Barack Obama in 2017.

But aside from dismissing these actions as politically motivated, it's important to remember that Clinton's action was obviously welcomed by the nationalist- and independence-favoring Puerto Rican community. Although López Rivera stuck to his principles and remained in prison, activists like New York native Dylcia Pagán, who has a devoted following, and Elizam

Escobar, a noted painter, have been able to live productive lives in Puerto Rico.

Calderón came into office during a period of temporary statistical improvement of the Puerto Rican economy. The unemployment rate, at 11 percent, was three times that of the United States, but it was also down from 16.5 percent in 1992. The Rosselló administration also managed to increase tax collections significantly, from 649,000 returns filed in 1992 to 861,000 in 1998. These changes were undoubtedly tied to the economic upturn of Clinton's presidency and a perhaps inevitable modernization of Puerto Rican society, where workers in metropolitan areas were leaving behind the tax avoidance status quo that dated back to Spanish colonization. Still, per capita income remained at around $10,000 a year, about half that of Mississippi's, the poorest state in the United States.[10]

Calderón's central goal upon entering office was to try to somehow restore the 936 tax credits and salvage some of the legacy of manufacturing growth. But this would prove extremely difficult to achieve politically despite Clinton's attempts in the final years of his presidency to get the 936 phaseout extended. A central factor in this effort was the expedient connection between the NPP and the US Democratic Party that had developed during the Clinton administration. Rosselló's and Clinton's interests converged at the elimination of 936 because of the former's desire to move the needle toward statehood and the latter's interest to appear as a Democratic reformer bent on closing exotic tax loopholes even as he cut government entitlements at home.

Calderón took office with conflicting political forces at play. First, Democrats under Bill Clinton had approved the end of 936 and were unlikely to bring it back. They liked how it closed tax loopholes and didn't harm the US economy as their politics increasingly coincided with the Republican drive for government shrinkage. Second, Republicans were unlikely to do Puerto Rico any favors because of its seeming disloyalty when it rejected the presence of the Vieques US naval base. Finally, in the complex world of lobbying, the chief lobbyist for the PDP in Washington was Charles Black, a veteran lobbyist whose firm included scandal-ridden Trump associates like Roger Stone and Paul Manafort. Black and other members of the Republican Party had at various times supported the agendas of both the statehood and commonwealth parties.

Calderón's administration in many senses kept Puerto Rico afloat without changing the status quo as far as government policy and the economy. She made it a point to launch investigations to root out corruption, but ultimately she was accused of playing a part in the accumulation of government debt, which increased by almost $15 billion. Some commentators were skeptical of Calderón's association with Melba Acosta, who served as president of the Government Development Bank under Calderón and, later, Alejandro García Padilla. They also pointed to the fact that her son worked for Goldman Sachs, a firm that earned lucrative underwriting fees when existing bond debts were restructured. Although the Navy finally left Vieques in 2003, it also pulled out of the relatively large Roosevelt Roads Naval Base in the town of Ceiba on the east coast of the island, hurting the economy of the neighboring towns of Fajardo, Luquillo, and Rio Grande. The Fajardo Shopping Center, like many other businesses near my parents' house, experienced store closings as well as job and revenue loss.

In 2016, months after it was revealed that Puerto Rico's debt was unpayable, Calderón admitted in an interview with *El Nuevo Día* that her administration was responsible for adding $6.3 billion to the debt, which amounted to 8.8 percent of the $72 billion. Although history seems to prove that she did not bear the lion's share of responsibility in accumulating the debt and the corruption allegations didn't stick, in 2003 the former mayor of San Juan announced her intention not to run for a second term, choosing instead to marry one of her cabinet members and ease into retirement.

Calderón's successor, Aníbal Acevedo Vilá, was elected governor in 2004. The Harvard-educated lawyer put together an ambitious economic plan that seemed to fit right in with Clinton-esque neoliberal globalism. Many of the buzzwords of the Davos set were in the plan: he wanted to focus on "knowledge economy" areas like bioscience, technology, and computing, and he wanted to diversify the economy, buttress the growth of local enterprise, and improve public education. Foreshadowing problems that would become more salient ten years later, Acevedo Vilá wanted to streamline bureaucratic processes that were delaying things like financial reports. He also wanted to repair the infrastructure and reduce the cost of energy, already aware of the intractable problems faced by the Electrical Energy Authority, which was totally dependent on fossil fuels for creating electricity.

Acevedo Vilá, like many globalist elected officials of the United States, Europe, and Latin America, wanted to increase the use of public-private partnerships (PPPs) to move forward with partially funded projects like constructing a state-of-the-art Las Américas shipping port; building a new convention center, to be located in a drab area just south of the colonial center of San Juan; and, like Baltimore, New York, and Boston, redeveloping the waterfront area. Yet in an interview with me in his office in San Juan, he complained that his proposals were largely left unimplemented because of what he called an "obstructionist legislature."[11]

This lament, although perhaps clichéd in our era of unproductive government, did signal something important: the slow emergence of a hard-right element in the NPP that would come into power in the years ahead, taking after the Republican renaissance in the United States and perhaps given a large boost by the Cheney-Rumsfeld-Rove wing of the George W. Bush administration. After a period of relative centrism during the Pedro Rosselló reign in the 1990s, hardline figures like Tomás Rivera Schatz, the secretary general of the NPP during Acevedo Vilá's term who went on to become president of the Senate; Senator Larry Seilhamer; and Jenniffer González, current resident commissioner and ardent Trump supporter, all solidified their power at this time.

In 2005 an unexpected operation carried out by the FBI without the advance cooperation of local police resulted in the death of FALN leader Filiberto Ojeda Ríos, who had been hiding for months in the mountain town of Hormigueros on the western side of the island. Ojeda Ríos had been a fugitive for twenty years after having been on the run since 1990, when he cut off an electronic monitoring bracelet and went into hiding while awaiting trial for a 1983 Wells Fargo robbery in West Hartford, Connecticut. He had long been rumored to have been living in Cuba and was at one time a highly sought-after FBI target, but he had largely dropped out of the public eye. Although the *Macheteros*, as members of FALN were known, had not committed a violent act in over twenty years, an FBI unit based in Atlanta hatched a plan for his capture and, after a brief stakeout, suddenly surrounded his house with heavy artillery. They confronted him and his wife, finally shooting him to death in a gunfight. According to the investigation carried out by the Puerto Rico Comisíon de Derechos Civiles (Commission of Civil Rights), the FBI unit denied him medical attention, instead allowing him to bleed to death.[12]

A subsequent investigation by the Puerto Rico Comisión de Derechos Civiles determined from forensic studies that FBI agents "intended to kill" Ojeda Ríos and that their actions were illegal because of a "lack of intention to arrest" Ojeda Ríos, the nature and amount of force the federal agents used against him, the lack of availability of adequate medical attention, an effective media blackout, and the apparent compliance of the local government. One of the FBI agents in charge of the operation was José Figueroa Sancha, who would later be named head of the Puerto Rico Police Department. In the days following the incident Acevedo Vilá reacted with indignation, saying at a press conference that "the suspicion that many of us have is that this person [Ojeda Ríos] was wounded and because no one was permitted to enter the scene, he died, when if he had been given attention, he could have been saved."[13]

The report filed by the Office of the Inspector General and the Department of Justice, requested by Robert Mueller, who was at the time the director of the FBI, concluded that the three shots fired by one of their officers, one of which caused Ojeda Ríos's death, did not violate the organization's deadly force policy. "At the moment the agent fired these shots," the report concludes, "he had a reasonable belief that Ojeda posed an imminent danger of death or serious injury to himself and other agents."[14] These arguments are the ones law enforcement has used to justify a litany of deadly shootings and uses of force, and the right of reasonable suspicion is central to so many arguments about excessive use of force in police activities. Evidence that Ojeda Ríos was armed and at one point fought back is not surprising for someone who had been a leader of a group that had used violent means, albeit in the fight for self-determination. Yet intentional neglect on the part of the FBI seems to have caused his death.

The death of Ojeda Ríos became an issue that moved beyond simple crime-scene forensics and the debate over the future status of Puerto Rico or even one person's actions when engaged in a lethal struggle with FBI agents. It was, rather, an example of the Puerto Rican people's utter inability to regulate within their own boundaries the incursion of the FBI, acting seemingly outside of the consent of local residents or government. In that way it represented the impunity with which the United States wields authority over its unincorporated territory. This impunity, coupled with the lack of any respect for national sovereignty, united Puerto Ricans of all political beliefs in a sense of indignation. The violation of sovereignty in a place that has never had it—at least not since the Discovery Era of European colonization—is something that never fails to open a giant colonial wound.

A year later, during a series of FBI raids designed to gather information about possible Machetero sympathizers, agents stormed a San Juan area high-rise building to confiscate materials in the apartment of a community activist and labor organizer. When a crowd of journalists began to gather at the entrance to the building, FBI and Puerto Rico police quickly denied them access, ultimately spraying them with pepper gas and then beating some with batons while they writhed on the ground from the spray. José Figueroa Sancha, who would later become the police chief under Governor Luis Fortuño when he took office in 2009, was at the scene as FBI special agent in charge. In the following months the Puerto Rico Association of Professional Journalists filed a suit, and it seemed a new era of repression against anyone who dared question the power of US authority—even media members trying to cover an FBI raid— had begun.

The 2008 race for governor took on a new character as the Section 936 tax benefits entered their final year of phaseout. The FBI killing of Ojeda Ríos had shocked many Puerto Ricans and became polarizing as well, energizing the long-dormant right-wing aspects of the NPP. Thus, the NPP was drawn again to law-and-order "mano dura" politics as the economic system worsened. They were also energized by a Bush administration that was not only neoconservative and militaristic but also enjoyed measurable support from conservative Hispanics in the United States, from anti-Castro Cubans in Florida to moderate Mexican Americans in Texas, Bush's adopted home state. Their opposition party, the PDP, weakened from years of an inadequate response to the growing signs of recession caused by the end of 936 as well as NPP obstruction in the legislature, was reeling.

Acevedo Vilá's opponent, Resident Commissioner Luis Fortuño, had long-established ties with conservative Republicans. He had been a member of the Puerto Rico Statehood Association, a pro-statehood college group that delivered votes for the right-leaning Carlos Romero-Barceló as well as being closely associated with the Bush administration. His 2004 gubernatorial campaign chairperson, Annie Mayol, went on to work for Karl Rove in the Office of Political Affairs, the controversial propaganda/public relations bureau. Yet few eyebrows were raised outside of Puerto Rico when, at the height of the US Attorney scandal that saw former Alabama governor Don Siegelman im- prisoned because he was a "political threat," Rosa Emilia Rodrí- guez was nominated by Bush attorney general Alberto Gonzales as Puerto Rico US attorney in 2006.[15]

The US attorney scandal was a serious, if overlooked scandal during a presidential administration whose most glaring fail- ure was starting a war in Iraq when none of the 9/11 hijackers had ties to that country and none of the weapons of mass de- struction cited as the primary reason for the invasion were ulti- mately found. In 2006 the Bush administration dismissed nine US attorneys, a move widely suspected to deter investigations of Republican elected officials in various states. A 2008 Inspector General report found that most of the firings were politically motivated and inappropriate.[16] Emails released after Rove left office revealed that he, from his perch as director of the White House's Office of Public Affairs, had been involved in purging the US attorneys.[17]

In a 2011 interview with me, Puerto Rico senator Eduardo Bhatia, a product of Princeton and Stanford Law School, said he had viewed Fortuño as cozying up to right-wing Republican leaders from the start.[18] Bush attorney general Alberto González appointed Rodríguez in 2006, and after a long period when the Senate refused to confirm her, she finally took office in October 2007. "When [Rodríguez] came to Puerto Rico, a week after that, leaks started coming out on investigating the governor and it became very clear to me that there was a political agenda just like there was with Siegelman and other US attorneys through- out the United States," said Bhatia.

Five months later Governor Acevedo Vilá was indicted on nineteen criminal counts, including tax fraud and using cam- paign money to pay for family vacations in Miami, Orlando, and China as well as $57,000 worth of high-end clothing and personal credit card bills. It was the first time a sitting governor had been indicted, and it happened with just eight months to go until the election in November. The governor immediately issued a state- ment saying the charges were "politically motivated," and his attorney Thomas C. Green said, "This is an unprecedented and undeserved intrusion by the federal government into the affairs and electoral processes in the commonwealth."[19] In March 2009, four months after he lost the election, a Philadelphia jury would find Acevedo Vilá innocent of all charges, although several of his aides pleaded guilty and were sentenced. His defense team was so confident in their case that they did not even call one witness. But the damage was done, as, undoubtedly due to the fallout from the indictment, Luis Fortuño was elected governor in November. The election resulted in the NPP controlling both houses of the legislature. In a kind of reversal of what had happened in the United States with the election of Barack Obama, who took office with full Democratic control over both houses, Puerto Rico had suddenly come under the control of a right-wing government that, although focused on demanding consideration for statehood through the use of shrinking government to impress Republicans in Congress, was primarily concerned with consolidating their power.

As soon as he entered office, Fortuño formed a committee of captains of private industry called CAREF (Comité Asesor de Reconstrucción Económica y Fiscal, or Advisory Committee for Economic and Fiscal Reconstruction)—which completely excluded the public sector and unions—to formulate recommendations for a new economic policy to deal with the island's continuing recession. Then the NPP-controlled legislature passed the infamous Law 7, whose title translated to the Special Law Declaring a Fiscal State of Emergency and Establishing an Integrated Plan of Fiscal Stabilization to Save Puerto Rico's Credit Rating.

Fortuño signed Law 7 on March 9, 2009, just a few months into his term, setting the tone for his governing style. Declaring a state of emergency was a tactic that had allowed the government to set the stage for implementing severe austerity measures, including laying off twenty thousand government employees. Law enforcement could even use the language of the bill to justify more extreme actions to preserve order. Al-

though this action greatly alarmed labor unions and a large seg-
ment of the work force, which in Puerto Rico is centered in the
public sector, few noticed that because of the "emergency," the
government could reserve the use of force to "protect the life,
health and well-being of the people."

In August of 2009, three months after a massive May Day
strike to protest the impending layoffs of Puerto Rican workers, a disturbing incident of police violence occurred near the
campus of the University of Puerto Rico. After an initial scuffle
with a drunk man on a block lined with college bars, the tactical
unit of the police also known as the Fuerza de Choque, or the
riot squad, used batons to arbitrarily strike innocent bystanders.
The incident climaxed at 3 A.M. when a police officer fired a gas
canister that hit a female student, Michelle Padrón Gauthier,
standing in a fenced-in university courtyard. When other students rushed to help her, officers fired two more cannisters,
emitting noxious tear gas.[20]

In April of 2010—alarmed by the mandated layoffs of twenty
thousand government workers, heavy-handed police actions,
and the intention of the University Board of Trustees (packed
with pro-Fortuño acolytes) to privatize and sell off large parts
of the university while increasing tuition fees—a coalition of
students decided to strike. They planned a large protest action at the Capitolio building in Old San Juan, a colonial-style
building that houses the Puerto Rican legislature. The University of Puerto Rico movement had incubated a new group of
radicalized students, inspired by the indignados movement in
Spanish cities. They organized in a horizontalist structure and
were accustomed to attending various plenary meetings where
decisions on how to move forward were reached in highly de-
mocratized roll-call fashion. The Puerto Rican movement,
with veteran leaders of university protests like Xiomara Caro,
Giovanni Roberto, and Arturo Ríos Escribano emerging to help,

was an unacknowledged predecessor to the Occupy Wall Street movement, which didn't begin until the fall of 2011.

The massive demonstration at the Capitolio was held in June 2010. It began as a peaceful conglomeration of students, union members, and others objecting to the changes the Fortuño administration had planned. But the mood shifted suddenly when the police violently attacked the protestors, with the Fuerza de Choque leading the way. The violence started inside the vestibule, where independent journalists were staging a sit-in to demand access to the visitors' galleries of the legislature. Ironically, the Senate, led by Tomás Rivera Schatz, was discussing a law to ban such access. Among those staging a sit-in in the vestibule was Rachel Hiskes, originally from a suburb of Hartford, Connecticut, and a graduate of Temple University who had come to study at UPR at the urging of one of her teachers in Philadelphia. A tall, striking presence whose mainstream American looks were easily recognizable, Hiskes nonetheless integrated herself tightly into the student fabric, speaking with an impeccable Puerto Rican accent.[21]

"They were aware of me from when I showed up to protest the confirmation hearings to approve José Figueroa Sancha as chief of police," she told me in a 2011 interview, referring to security officers and police who were monitoring the protest. Hiskes along with another reporter from *Rumba Alterna*, the alternative newspaper she wrote for, formed a small group insisting on being allowed in to the hearings.[22] After several tense minutes of the protestors shouting and insisting on being let in, the Fuerza de Choque entered the area, and the group began a sit-in. An observer from Amnesty International, who had been present because of previous violent incidents involving police and student protestors, announced he was no longer an observer and decided to join the protestors in their sit-in.

Then came the spray—into their eyes, hair, bodies. And as the protestors began to move away toward the exit door, the former observer began writhing on the floor. At this point a member of the Fuerza de Choque strode up and kicked him. Hiskes later reported, "So they're kicking him, and then the guy who was behind me starts kicking me, and I lost my shoes—there's part of it that I don't even really remember because I just got so mad, and later I realized that I threw my water bottle at him."

With that, the agent pounced on Hiskes, brutally pushing her out the door and sending her flying down the Capitolio steps. Though she feared for her life during her tumble, Hiskes got off relatively lightly, with bruises and severe discomfort from the pepper spray's effects on her skin. Others, however, didn't fare so well. Omar Rodríguez, a member of the popular reggae band Cultura Profética, and student leader Giovanni Roberto both had bleeding gashes on their heads.

Carmen Yulín Cruz, the current San Juan mayor known for her strong criticism of how the Trump administration has handled Hurricane María, was then a representative in the House. Shockingly, she was also attacked. "I had been standing outside the Capitolio and then demanded the right to go in as a member of the legislature," said Cruz in a 2011 interview.[23] "I was pepper sprayed, and some students kneeled down to protect me. The Fuerza de Choque guys were pushing at me, beating students around me. I took my badge out and I was pepper sprayed all over. I started getting hit, and someone told me not to breathe. I wound up going to an orthopedist who said I had ligaments torn in my rib cage. I had a half cast for six weeks, I had bruises in my rib cage, legs, and thighs."

What was most frightening about the attack for Cruz was that it was apparently not accidental. Cruz would attest that the riot squad knew who she was: "When I was in the lobby one of the security guys said, 'This is for you, Carmen Yulín,' and they started to hit me. Later I was told by a member of the administration that they [the Fuerza de Choque] weren't going to rest until they cracked my head at the rally."

The day after the rally, with the press and most of the political establishment up in arms about the Fuerza de Choque's display of force, the local Univision station interviewed police superintendent Figueroa Sancha. He looked eerily into the camera and pointed for effect as he said, "I've always maintained the same line . . . as long as laws are obeyed, everyone has the right to demonstrate. As soon as people violate, assault, vandalize, destroy—then the police will act. And I'll say that today, tomorrow, in the past, and next month."[24]

While Governor Fortuño did not directly approve of the police's actions, in the aftermath he avoided assigning responsibility to the police and instead tried to blame students for throwing rocks and not respecting the views of others.[25] Alarmingly, he also singled out a group of "socialists"—his generalized term to describe opposition group protestors—who he accused of advertising that they wanted to take the Capitolio by force. Fortuño referred to pamphlets that one group had distributed. The Movimiento al Socialismo (Movement Toward Socialism) expressed a sentiment to *retomar*, or retake, the capitol. This reference was intended to be a call for the people to take back the legislature after Senate president Tomás Rivera Schatz had been denying them the right to enter and observe the legislative process.

Fortuño took liberties with the phrase "retomar el capitolio," changing it to "tomar por fuerza el capitolio," which implies a use of force that is closer in meaning to a mob staging a coup d'état. Both Fortuño and Chief of Police Figueroa Sancha used this phrasing to justify the Fuerza de Choque's use of force, which by all accounts was initiated by PRPD and not protestors. Free speech advocates like William Ramírez, president of Puerto Rico's ACLU chapter, insisted that the government was most interested in deterring protest through intimidation. "If you go to demonstrate," Ramírez told me, "you're going to get beat up and pepper sprayed. In constitutional law, we call that a chilling effect."[26]

Street demonstrations continued to plague the Fortuño administration, and as the violence continued to emanate from the police department, the Department of Justice appointed Tom Perez, the current head of the Democratic National Committee (DNC), to investigate the PRPD. A repeat incident of violence at the Capitolio in 2011 and on the Rio Piedras campus of the

University of Puerto Rico prompted accusations that the police were using chokeholds. A student demonstrator named Adriana Mulero told me that during the course of engaging in passive resistance adjacent to university entrance gates, a Fuerza de Choque officer applied pressure to her neck.[27] "The amount of pain surprised me, I didn't expect it to hurt so much," she told me. Members of the Puerto Rico office of the ACLU speculated that the tactic may have been learned from the NYPD, as it was implemented shortly after a visit from representatives of Ray Kelly's force.

Luis Fortuño's attempt to revive time-worn Mano Dura tactics seemed to be going nowhere. The economy in Puerto Rico continued to fail, with the only notable job growth generated by the Obama-granted stimulus funds, which were quickly running out. Puerto Rican economist José Alameda declared Law 7 a failure, saying that "the medicine has killed the patient."[28] Because of Fortuño-imposed tuition hikes, UPR enrollment had dropped by over five thousand students, fulfilling an NPP agenda of planned shrinkage to reduce government expenditures.[29]

Another ill-fated project of Fortuño's was the Gasoducto, a widely condemned ninety-two-mile natural gas pipeline that would lower the rapidly escalating electric costs. Aside from being as much a threat to the environment as the Keystone XL pipeline, which protestors had vigorously opposed, the pipeline generated additional controversy when Victor Suárez, the secretary general of the PDP, accused Fortuño's close friend, Pedro Ray Chacón, of accepting $12 million for a design for the pipeline even though he had never designed a project of that magnitude.[30] What's more, the Puerto Rico Electric Power Authority had contracted the lobbying firm of Wilmer & Hale at the cost of $1 million, presumably to lobby for necessary permits that needed to be granted by the Fish and Wildlife Service, to expedite the Gasoducto project. Emails obtained through a FOIA done by Casa Pueblo's lawyers show Fortuño clamoring for an audience with Secretary of the Interior Ken Salazar.[31]

Ultimately, committed environmental activists like the father-and-son team of Alexis and Arturo Massol, who run the self-sustaining community organization and site Casa Pueblo, helped to kill the project. The entire Gasoducto episode, however, aside from being yet another example of cronyism and government leaders' inability to envision new ways to provide Puerto Rico energy outside of gasoline-powered electrical generation, would serve as a harbinger of the disaster PREPA (Puerto Rico Electric Power Authority) faced when the debt crisis exploded in 2015. PREPA, of course, would become well known as one of the biggest debtors involved in the $72 billion debt, filing for bankruptcy in 2017 with a debt of over $9 billion.

Meanwhile, almost out of public scrutiny, Luis Fortuño's government was increasingly using the municipal bond market and Wall Street's creative solutions to money moving and risk avoidance. This was done as a way to not only finance government deficits but also keep credit rating agencies like Moody's happy and continue Puerto Rico's "access to credit markets" while it sunk further into debt and negative economic growth. After leaving office in 2013, he participated in a "revolving door" syndrome common to both San Juan and Washington, moving into a position at the law firm of Steptoe and Johnson after the firm had been rewarded with $22.8 million in contracts during his administration.[32]

Moving employees between banks like Banco Popular, Doral Bank, Santander Bank, and the Government Development Bank played a major role in the final stages of the crisis that would explode years after Fortuño left office. When an executive from a bank like Santander, for instance, moved into a position at the Government Development Bank, they would have an incentive to initiate debt issuances that could benefit their original place of work, which was also an advantage if they decided to move back to their old job. It was a period when bond raters severely overestimated the value of the continually emitted bonds. Likewise, the investors in those bonds shifted from everyday pension and individual investor-handled mutual funds to the hedge- and vulture-fund operators who would sneak almost unnoticed into position when the call to pay up was finally made in 2015.

In 2013 Fortuño was forced to leave office after losing to PDP candidate Alejandro García Padilla. In a sense the election was a huge surprise. García Padilla had begun the campaign as a relatively unpopular candidate due to his perceived lack of dynamism and ability to inspire voters. Yet Fortuño, his administration, and his cronies—typified by Police Chief Figueroa Sancha, the overbearing Senate president Thomas Rivera-Shatz, and abrasive Chief of Staff Marcos Rodríguez Ema—had created an air of authoritarianism that increasingly alienated Puerto Ricans.

Perhaps the killing blow for Fortuño was a relentless series of propaganda-style ads urging the public to support a resolution that would deny bail to those accused of violent felonies. The ads featured footage of an infamous incident in which a young drug dealer laughed in the face of police as he was being arrested. Puerto Rican voters seemed to reject the ads' blatant manipulation, and a series of anti-Fortuño demonstrations near election day as well as the perception that the island was turning into an endless battleground for clashes between protestors and police seemed to seal the deal against Fortuño.

Fortuño's defeat sparked spontaneous joy in the streets of San Juan, with many who were indignant about the cuts to the university—some graduates themselves—shouting out the idiosyncratically local epithet "Puñeta!"—"Damn!"—as their rallying cry. Yet the new administration of García Padilla was not awe inspiring, and the future was not clear. And most Puerto Ricans were not aware that, despite his ignominious defeat, Fortuño and his cronies had quietly been setting up soft landing spots that would allow them to potentially profit from and escape blame for the coming severe economic crisis.

CHAPTER 4

BOND EMISSIONS, CORRUPTION, AND BETRAYAL

How Two Governments Failed Puerto Rico

Signs protesting sales tax in front of Puerto Rico's Capitol Building in San Juan.
© Joseph Rodríguez

"Esto no es polítcia, es matemática pura." (This isn't politics, it's pure mathematics.)
—**Puerto Rico governor Alejandro García Padilla,** July 23, 2015

"Puerto Rico's problems didn't just begin recently. More than anything they were self-imposed, the result of actions by a clique of government administrators and finance capital and their intermediaries on the island. Instead of forging development they maintain a system of extracting surplus that is shared by local businessmen and global interests."
—**Puerto Rico economist Argeo Quiñones,** interview 2014

In the mid-2010s a series of events took place that revealed the depth of Puerto Rico's economic crisis and the extent to which its creation and cause had been hidden from its citizens. These events put an end to whatever remained of the fantasy islanders had about political autonomy and partial sovereignty. A pair of competing narratives emerged, one placing blame on US colonialism and the other on the corruption and inefficiency of the Puerto Rico government. But I never felt that either argument was overwhelmingly true on its own. Because I've lived my life in the mainland United States, I, like most Diaspo-Ricans, tend to place most of the blame on Washington for the reasons I've laid out in the first few chapters. But those on the island, who live the day-to-day circus of local politics while largely removed from the US media echo chamber, tend to take a harder line on the colonial government.

Still, although it's evident that the Puerto Rico government shoulders much of the blame for the debt crisis, given its colonial relationship with the United States, it's hard to imagine it acting any differently. A colonial mandate put in place the Commonwealth of Puerto Rico and its government, and even though island thinkers wrote its constitution, colonial power wholly directed its implementation. The governmental and business class the Puerto Rican Constitution created should be viewed as a necessary consequence of colonialism. Even if we were to look at the successive governments of the PDP and the NPP as corrupt, this corruption is inevitably a product of collaborating with and subjugating itself to a colonial system of government.

The government of Puerto Rico has done little to extract itself from the restrictive options it was given to develop its economy. For example, until forced to by a growing protest movement, the government did little to object to the US naval base in Vieques. In a sense even the pro-statehood movement is conditioned by colonialism, as it lacks any critique of the US acquisition of Puerto Rico in the first place, much less its continued inter- vention economically and through surveillance or FBI practices on the island. In that way the impossibility of detaching Puerto Rico's local government from its colonial masters in how we understand the situation we're in is true in reverse as well, as we consider how the mainland United States' own democracy and democratic practice is inseparable from its economic sys- tem and exploitative foreign policy.

My interest in Puerto Rico's politics and precarious sover- eign status was rekindled with Luis Fortuño's ouster in 2012. Righteous indignation about both his implementation of aus- terity measures and his use of heavy-handed mano dura po- lice enforcement tactics he employed to back them up brought about his surprise defeat. Although few on the island viewed his successor, Alejandro García Padilla, as an impressive candidate, people saw the interruption of a growing authoritarian streak in the mainstream of the NPP as a positive step forward. Still, there were some disturbing mechanisms established during the Fortuño regime that were happening unnoticed alongside the spectacles of the bad publicity created by the DOJ investiga- tion of the Puerto Rico Police Department and the government crackdown on street protest and civil disobedience.

As soon as Fortuño entered office in 2009 he named Carlos M. García as head of the Government Development Bank. The former president of Santander Bank, García staffed the GDB with current or former Santander executives and encouraged bond buyers to acquire a form of bond created in 2006 called

COFINA, which was supposed to be safer because it would be backed by payments coming directly from a sales tax.

COFINA was devised as a way to avoid constitutional requirements about the mandated debt limit that were beginning to make increased bond sales difficult. These bonds were to be funded exclusively by imposing a sales tax called the IVU, which started at 5.5 percent, with a municipal option for an additional 1.5 percent. They were put in a different category from what had come to be known as the General Obligation bonds, which were within the legal requirements of the constitution. The COFINA bonds, which amounted to $15.2 billion issued between 2006 and 2013, were often sold as capital appreciation bonds and featured interest rate swaps. A report by the independent investigative group the Hedge Clippers found that the total amount of debt issued "where Santander played an underwriting role" was as much as $61.2 billion, with more than $1 billion of that going to fees paid to Santander and other banks.[1]

It's essential to understand the destructive and exploitative nature of capital appreciation bonds (CABs) and capitalized interest, even without the compounding effects of abusive interest rate swaps. The Refund America Project has estimated, for instance, that $33.5 billion of Puerto Rico's debt is actually interest at an effective rate of 785 percent.[2] CABs are essentially a way to move debt payments into the future without eliminating the effective interest on the loan, creating a kind of economic shock when the suddenly ballooning interest rate is due. It's somewhat parallel to the practice used in adjustable rate mortgages, which allowed many unqualified borrowers to take on large debts, creating the raw material of packaged securities that would be sold as financial instruments, only to collapse when the housing bubble burst, causing the Great Recession in 2008.

Capitalized interest and bond-issuance fees are estimated to have composed $3.2 billion of the approximately $72 billion of Puerto Rico's debt.[3] This results from borrowing money to pay interest. Years earlier, when the commonwealth began to come to grips with the years of borrowing it had engaged in, it saw no choice but to continue borrowing. But its decision merely served to delay and intensify the inevitable reckoning, incurring yet more debt without any foreseeable exit plan.

As stated earlier, the first misstep of government borrowing, which extended back into the mid-1970s, was to increase borrowing to cover essential expenses rather than generating funds through capital improvement and infrastructure projects. In theory new infrastructure and capital projects might generate economic growth, but at the same time the government borrowed to avoid serious social crises. But beginning with the recession caused by the final phaseout of the Section 936 tax breaks for corporations, the Puerto Rico government began, increasingly, to borrow just to pay the costs of the borrowing done years ago.

In a sense the Fortuño administration smoothed Puerto Rico's decline by pushing it toward a governing apparatus that was rapidly becoming an economic model in the United States— shrinking government, budget cuts, militarization of the police force. The administration created a synergy between revolving-door politics, cronyism, the consolidation of social conservatism among Fortuño's religious-right base, and the final subjugation of the economy to the Wall Street financial sector. The Government Development Bank not only carried out deals to keep the government solvent and favor certain well-placed players but also obscured the details of the transactions, creating an impression that economic development was actually taking place. During his administration Fortuño handed out $9.3 billion in private contracts, largely to his allies and business associates, including expenses for publicity, training, consultancy fees, and personal services. Meanwhile he also added $16 billion to the island's debt and oversaw a budget that devoted 42 percent of its liquidity to repaying outstanding debt.

Immediately after losing the gubernatorial election, Fortuño became a partner of the Steptoe and Johnson LLP law firm, and the following year he gave a speech at a meeting for prospective bond buyers at Lazard Capital's offices in New York.[4] He followed this by making a cross-country trip to address twenty-five investors at a meeting organized by Los Angeles's Odeon Capital Group. Those meetings, like one organized previously by bankers at Morgan Stanley and Citigroup, were designed to appeal to investors who specialized in "distressed debt."[5]

That's when vulture funds, a dark variant of hedge funds, got involved in Puerto Rico's finances. They represent investors that want to leverage high-risk debt spread across financial instruments by buying municipal bonds from eighteen different governmental entities and, in the case of Puerto Rico, separately created government entities. Along with hedge funds, which are a bit more averse to taking on the extreme risk that vultures do, vulture funds slowly began buying out investments from more conventional investment banks like Franklin Templeton Funds, firms that handle retirement funds of teachers and other professionals.

Hedge and vulture funds create profit by stoking excitement around high-risk investment, teasing quick, high-yield 9 percent returns as bonds pass through several speculators' hands. The relatively high return on each transaction rouses speculators and investors. In the case of Puerto Rico investors, further attracted by the bonds' triple-tax investments and the lack of bankruptcy protection, circled like vultures, smelling "the blood and the fear," as credit and municipal bond market analyst Richard Larkin put it in a 2013 *Wall Street Journal* article.[6] All these elements converged as Puerto Rico's debt rating teetered on the edge of being declared junk. Still, there was enough time and opportunity to make a killing.

Several characters began to converge at this juncture who would play their roles in the final act of Puerto Rico's attempts to sustain itself through juggling complex financial instruments. They were Fortuño, who continued to offer investment consultancy as a partner in Steptoe and Johnson; Puerto Rico Government Development Bank officers David Chafey and his second in command, Melba Acosta; and Lazard Capital's Antonio Weiss, whose firm hosted Fortuño's October 2013 bond opportunity meeting in New York and would soon make a controversial[7] move to the US Treasury Department. These characters would be involved in successive efforts, to in some cases obscure details about debt issuances, on others promote them, and finally negotiate settlements from creditors involved in the speculative orgy that created it.

In 2013, perhaps with one eye on the restructuring of Detroit's $18 billion debt, the Puerto Rico government suspended bond sales. But by January of the following year Morgan Stanley and Barclays were both pitching bond offerings as high as $2 billion.[8] A major driver of the renewed interest was the emergence of hedge and vulture funds as players in the municipal bond market, in part because municipal bonds were outperforming treasury bonds in an era of high interest rates. The common refrain here was desperation to find a way for the government and the GDB to reestablish the ability to sell bonds, which is still the stated goal of PROMESA'S Fiscal Oversight and Management Board today.

With the help of its Wall Street enablers, Puerto Rico and its Government Development Bank were preparing what would become one of the most massive municipal bond offerings ever. At this point Moody's credit rating service was urging Puerto Rico to borrow further in the hopes that doing so would ease cash-flow pressure and avoid an inevitable downgrade of its bond rating. The business press painted an ambivalent picture of what was happening with Puerto Rico and its finances. On the one hand, there was a belief that Puerto Rico had made "progress in closing its chronic budget gap [and] . . . improved financial disclosures," and there was a "general sense of relief that the commonwealth still has access to the debt market." But, as the same article in the Deal Book section of the *New York Times* warned, the GDB had just hired Millco Advisers, an affiliate of Millstein & Company, which had several years earlier overseen the remake of AIG, the insurance company that the US government had bailed out after the 2008 crisis.[9] The hiring of a firm that specialized in restructuring raised "concerns among some

investors that Puerto Rico is weighing a revamping of its existing debt load, even as it prepares to raise fresh funds."

One would think that a government bank hiring a debt-
restructuring firm would be a deterrent to purchasing part of its
massive new $3 billion issuance, but the *Times* assured that "at
the moment, plenty of investors appear to be willing to look past
the specter of revamping as well as Puerto Rico's current liquidity issues." Maybe that was because the *Wall Street Journal* had
reported a few days earlier that a GDB spokesperson said, "We
can say clearly, we have not hired anyone to advise on restructuring."[10] The GDB had also hired the law firms Cleary Gottlieb
Steen & Hamilton and Proskaeur Rose, both debt-restructuring
experts, in January of 2014, but that was not reported until April
2014.[11] Proskaeur Rose continues to advise the PROMESA
during the Title 3 process, with its lead attorney, Martin Bienen-
stock, having invoiced $1.3 million in fees as of August 2018.[12]

Buried in the elite pages of what high-powered investors
read, much of these machinations happened outside of mainstream awareness, both in the United States and Puerto Rico.
The shift in the take on Puerto Rico's municipal bonds, from
skepticism to suddenly affected confidence, was reported in the
business press as business as usual, with little foreboding. The
reaction was completely unlike what happened three years later
when, after the news broke that the city of Hartford, Connecticut, had hired Greenberg Traurig, another firm associated with
restructuring, Standard & Poor's downgraded Hartford Stadium
Authority Bonds to junk. But even more damning evidence
about the dysfunction of the municipal bond world was evident
in the Puerto Rico bond offering itself.

In the bond-offering document dated March 11, 2014—with
the imprimatur of Barclays, Morgan Stanley, Goldman Sachs,
J.P. Morgan, Santander Securities, Merrill Lynch, and other
Wall Street firms as well as Governor García Padilla, his cabinet,
the president of the Puerto Rico Senate and the Speaker of the
Puerto Rican House, the director of Management and Budget,
and the acting president of the GDB—there is a clear statement

about the fragility of the bonds, which would come due in 2035. It began with simple statements about "risk factors."

Regarding risks related to Puerto Rico's financial state, the bond offering admits that "the Commonwealth may be unable to honor its obligation to pay debt service on the Bonds" because it faces "a number of fiscal and economic challenges that, either individually or in the aggregate, could adversely affect the Commonwealth's ability to pay debt service on the Bonds when due."[13]

The offering further concedes that although the Puerto Rico Constitution would legally protect the bonds, under "certain circumstances" the government might not be able to honor its obligation to pay back the principal and interest "in full or in a timely manner." It warns that ratings agencies' downgrading the bonds could impact the possibility of further borrowing and that if "the Commonwealth is unable to obtain sufficient funds from this and other future debt offerings, it may not have sufficient liquidity to meet its obligations as they come due."

Finally, the offering clearly states that Puerto Rico intended to continue to borrow to refinance its debts and "improve its short-term liquidity position." It committed the government to balance its budget for 2015 but that there would be "no assurance that a balanced budget will, in fact, be adopted or, if adopted, that it will be successfully implemented." There would be no assurance that any of these measures would be sustainable. In plain language the warnings in this document are more extensive and foreboding than the average listing of possible side effects in an advertisement for cutting-edge major-disease medications.

There were clear warnings in this statement that Puerto Rico might not be able to pay back the bonds, not only because of the current state of its economy but because of its future economic probabilities. The role of ratings agencies was also presented ambiguously, begging the questions: What actions might the agencies take and why? Weren't the credit agencies already aware of the state of Puerto Rico's economy, and if so, why do they continue to uphold the value of the bonds? This bond issuance happened three years after a report by a Senate subcommittee that probed the causes of the 2008 financial crisis.

According to the report, a major reason for the inaccuracy of credit ratings was an "inherent conflict of interest arising from the system used to pay for credit ratings." The major credit-rating agencies are funded by the same Wall Street firms that profit from the financial products being rated. The ratings agencies in turn depended on Wall Street firms to sustain them and were "vulnerable to threats that the firms would take their business elsewhere if they did not get the ratings they wanted." These conflicts were shown to erode the ratings agencies' standards and created a competition to keep ratings high to hold onto business and market-share volume. The result, said the report, "was a race to the bottom."[14]

With Morgan Stanley and Barclays greasing the wheels for the massive new issuance, which would eventually total $3.5 billion, the business press readied the bond-buying market with sloganeering about the hope and opportunity the new issuance provided. This created a synergy of interests in which illusory capital chases illusory profit, money flows back in the form of underwriting fees and potential paydays, and politicians avoid fiscal disaster. But there was only one problem: within a month of the sale in March, yields on Puerto Rico bonds began to plummet. A wave of uncertainty began to descend on the island's future that seemed to go beyond the typical malaise of a declining economy.

THE FOCUS OF ACTIVISM BEGINS TO SHIFT

Puerto Rican diaspora politics in mid-2014 were consumed by recurring campaigns urging the release of political prisoner Oscar López Rivera. López Rivera had refused the conditions of the deal that released many of his peers, Chicago- and New York–based FALN members in the early 1980s, as a result of a 1999 offer of clemency from Bill Clinton. I interviewed Filiberto Ojedo Ríos while he was being held at the Metropolitan

Correctional Center in Manhattan as well as Juan Segarra Palmer in his home near Hartford, Connecticut, in 1989. Because of our face-to-face contact, I had a closer understanding of who they were and what their motivations were.

Ojeda Ríos, a former trumpeter, was impressive with his apparent willingness to sacrifice himself for Puerto Rican independence, no matter what one might feel about his doctrinaire allegiance to Cuban Marxism, whereas Segarra had a thoughtful intelligence whose ambivalence about his own Ivy League experience resonated with my own about elite university education. It was clear to me that the dynamism and charisma of dissident Puerto Rican independentistas were important to the continued campaign for Puerto Rican sovereignty, painting them as freedom fighters and not merely nihilistic US antagonists.

Often the mainland Puerto Rican concern with the Puerto Rican condition had been shaped by somewhat abstract, shared feelings of frustration about second-class citizenship and colonial status. But because I had been visiting the island regularly to see my extended family, I had begun to notice a sense of uncertainty and concern as the recession deepened and once-prosperous areas—or what passed for prosperous—were beginning to lose population and business activity. The bottom-line analysis of economics—or what some might call the study of political economy—had become increasingly important in analyzing what was going on in Puerto Rico. But of course, it always had been.

I went to visit San Juan just a few weeks after the Puerto Rican Congress approved Law 71 in late June of 2014, perhaps the first strong sign that Alejandro García Padilla's government saw disaster coming. The law was called the Puerto Rico Public Corporation Debt Enforcement and Recovery Act, and it permitted certain public corporations in Puerto Rico to restructure their debt obligations. Within twenty-four hours hedge funds Franklin Templeton and Oppenheimer Funds challenged the constitutionality of the act and were soon joined by hedge-fund Blue Mountain Capital, which had heavily invested in PREPA bonds, even as rating agencies downgraded them. García Padilla was trying to implement a last-ditch strategy to keep his government afloat, insisting that Puerto Rico still had enough sovereignty or self-determination to write its own bankruptcy law despite the seemingly arbitrary quirk in 1984 that had taken that ability away.

In a cafeteria-style restaurant called Zayas, just off the Placita Roosevelt and close to San Juan's financial district, I sat for hours with Argeo Quiñones, a UMass Amherst–trained economist who had been teaching for decades at the University of Puerto Rico. "Puerto Rico's problems didn't just begin recently," he said, wrestling with his side of green plantains. "And they weren't imposed by the monsters of Wall Street. More than anything they were self-imposed, the result of actions by a clique of government administrators and finance capital and their intermediaries on the island. Instead of forging development they maintain a system of extracting surplus that is shared by local businessmen and global interests."

Quiñones's perspective was not unique, as it is not unusual for local islanders who have witnessed firsthand a litany of insular government decisions that not only reinforce neoliberalism imposed from the outside but also do so to protect their social class position. This narrative is understandable, but it also raises the question of whether the structural corruption of a political economic system determines the self-preservationist logic of local collaborators. Quiñones even went as far as to invoke G. William Domhoff's 1967 text *Who Rules America?*, which is often seen as an early influence on the notion of the "deep state," where shadow governments or corrupt processes, rather than US citizens' votes and elected officials, were actually governing America.

We talked about systemic problems that had plagued Puerto Rico since Section 936 was phased out. There was the impending housing bubble collapse, perhaps facilitated by a period of bank consolidation, where several major banks like Westernbank closed. Governor Pedro Rosselló had begun a trend of increasingly limiting workers' rights when he took the seemingly positive step of unionizing government employees but denied them the right to strike. Quiñones was also skeptical about the impact of the Jones Act's maritime restrictions, also known as cabotage laws. He blamed local businesses for lacking the initiative to use other ports of entry for the beginning of production processes, which could result in lower production costs despite Jones Act tariffs. Most importantly, he also railed against Fortuño's cuts in government jobs, not simply because of the immediate job losses but also because of the multiplier effect on the economy, where local businesses suffered from lack of disposable income that employed government workers would have otherwise spent.

García Padilla's bankruptcy law, known colloquially as La Ley de Quiebra Criolla, was also open to Quiñones's ridicule because it undercut one of the main selling points of the bonds in the first place. Talk of privatizing the electric authority had already begun, and although Quiñones didn't think it was a terrible idea overall, he saw clearly that reducing personnel costs to make the sale more attractive to potential investors was already taking its toll on the system's effectiveness. It was losing skilled personnel and the ability to provide essential maintenance and system upkeep.

"If you were to tell me that this law is part of a context where there is major reform of the political and economic system and social relations then I would say, 'this looks like Argentina's process,'" Quiñones told me. "But this looks more like Detroit. Their strategy is to drastically cut retirement funds." Puerto Rico's government, unlike Argentina's, was showing itself far less willing to confront the unfairness of the United States' economic hegemony and far more willing to follow the neoliberal model of shifting the burden onto workers. But, unlike Detroit, Puerto Rico could not declare bankruptcy.

A proposal issued that summer by Puerto Rico's philanthropic organization Fundación Francisco Carvajal suggested that the Federal Reserve Act could allow the Fed to buy up many of the bonds issued by the government and governmental entities in a way that would not be considered a bailout per se. "It would be a much-needed injection of liquidity. If they gave $85bn to AIG [a bank too big to fail], why not $4bn to Puerto Rico?" said Juan Aponte, who helped author the report.[15] This would become the seed of more progressive proposals issued later during Bernie Sanders's 2016 presidential campaign, but at the time it gained no traction because both sides feared the dreaded "bailout."

At first glance the specter of a bailout would seem to be primarily an aversion to its political implications, where Reagan-era ideas of helping undeserving "welfare queens" was not only antithetical to a balanced budget but also fed a subliminal racist narrative. But the more one digs into the bottom-line motivations of Wall Street, the municipal bond markets, and, increasingly, their indebted surrogates in Congress, it seems as if the need to preserve the fragile nature of the highly speculative financial sector was the main motivator. There are several factors that point to this: the financial sector accounts for a growing percentage of corporate products and gross domestic product; the institutions involved have been designated as "too big to fail" since the 2008 crisis; and the insurance companies that back much of the investment from default can cause a serious negative chain reaction if they are forced to pay off massive amounts to defaulted creditors.

Neoliberal prescriptions for righting Puerto Rico's economic course remained duly consistent. A 2014 Federal Reserve Bank of New York report suggested some "steps toward fiscal sustainability," including stimulating economic growth, reforming the tax collection system (Puerto Rico has a vast underground economy), cracking down on public-sector corporations, and, of course, striving for a balanced budget.[16] But these pieces of advice, as well as the Obama administration's opposition to a bailout (which would have barely scratched the surface as a form of reparations), overlooked the dangerous reality of unsustainable debt.

Quiñones suggested something different: "We have to create sustainable economic growth, intervene in evasive local and government bank practices—meaning their lack of transparency—and the preferential treatment given to the business sector, and end the revolving door between the government, its agencies, the financial world, and corporate law firms." These basic ideas about economic development and recovery seemed alien to the neoliberal agenda, which has prioritized the needs of a global financial system and its short-term agenda of maximizing profits over creating conditions for sustainable economic growth.

The way forward for the García Padilla administration was an impossible conundrum. In order for the government to keep operating, it would need to devise even more ways to shift debt obligations. Yet all the mechanisms that had been used appeared to be reaching their limit. The narrative that García Padilla was banking on was built on a circular logic that amounted to an almost total obfuscation of the many problems at hand. He issued $3.5 billion worth of bonds, openly stating that the government might have significant problems in repaying it while at the same time making public claims that payments were theoretically guaranteed because of the legal barrier to declaring bankruptcy.

He made public statements lauding the reduction in the budget deficit; these statements were intended to convey to the typical news consumer that the debt was being reduced, when it actually increased. He tried to appeal to the idea of Puerto Rican nationalism through the apparent mechanism of semi-autonomy that being a commonwealth affords. His legal attempt to establish the right to bankruptcy—a law drafted by Proskauer Rose attorneys—was a dramatic last stab at self-determination. But in reality his economy had completely submitted to the neoliberal goals of spending cuts while eroding worker's rights and allowing the infrastructure and essential services to deteriorate.

García Padilla's administration had continuously been unabashedly pro-business: at an April 2014 conference the secretary of development and commerce, Alberto Bacó, pitched Puerto Rico as a tax shelter for renegade billionaires, touting it as the "Singapore of the Caribbean." Opening the island up to more external investment capital had also been one of the

García Padilla administration's central priorities. Puerto Rico's February 2015 summit, designed to attract US investors, featured as its keynote speaker former New York City mayor Rudolph Giuliani—peddling his Giuliani Partners consultancy. Giuliani's appearance, according to Bacó, "reinforce[d] the international recognition of our government's commitment to economic growth."[17]

As the strands of Puerto Rico's debt crisis began to unravel, García Padilla would deliver perhaps the most important speech by a Puerto Rico governor since Luis Muñoz Marín's speech proclaiming the commonwealth in 1952. But this time it would not be about the start of a new, promising era for Puerto Rico; it would be about its inevitable spiral into economic ruin. Appearing on island-wide television as Puerto Ricans gathered for dinner or at a local bar and restaurant, García Padilla, using his most practiced tones of solemnity, announced that the $72 billion debt was "unpayable." The time to heal this wound, to come together as citizens and with the federal government and Wall Street to find a solution, had arrived.

Yet Puerto Rico had no access to bankruptcy court like Detroit did, no recourse to lobby the International Monetary Fund (IMF) like Argentina and Greece did, no tool of withholding payment in a game of debt-collection chicken in their back pocket. García Padilla was doing his part to establish a narrative that would try to justify some of the language being used to describe the crisis—phrases like "death spiral" and a need for "shared sacrifice." The business press likes to characterize massive municipal debt by citing per capita numbers, such as: "The island's crushing debt load, which includes $123 billion in bonds and unfunded pension liabilities . . . is worth $34,000 per person."[18] This kind of language creates an impression that all Puerto Rican residents implemented and agreed upon amassing the debt, which is kind of an easy idea to assimilate for Americans, who might compare it unfavorably to the average credit-card debt per family, which is around $8,000.[19] In his language he implied that creditors had to take "haircuts" (negotiated reductions in the debt principal) on the balances owed, but he also included citizens in that shared obligation, hitting notes familiar to a largely Catholic population primed for ideas of confessing and owning up to wrongs and embracing the concept of shared sacrifice.

Yet two very troublesome signs lurked in the background of García Padilla's public admission. First, David Chafey, the chairman of the Government Development Bank, resigned, perhaps inadvertently signaling that the bank itself was near self-implosion. Second, the failure to pay the bond payment to the Puerto Rico Electric and Power Authority, which would be due in just a few days, foreshadowed widespread default. It was as if all the forbidding ugly realities of Puerto Rico's deep debt dysfunction, as well as its teetering on the edge of disastrous infrastructure, were being exposed.

A NEOLIBERAL DOUBLE-WHAMMY

What García Padilla had put into motion was an endgame for Puerto Rico's debt crisis that threatened to be less of a solution than a path toward perpetual debt and a death sentence for any semblance of self-sustaining economic development. Though the narrative coalescing around the crisis focused on the Puerto Rico government's actions, two significant measures were being taken by US government representatives and, at least in theory, the global economic system. How these two discursive elements came together represented the growing synergy between US politics and the global financial system.

The first shoe dropped when the Krueger Report was issued.[20] Authored by Anne Krueger and former IMF collaborators, it was apparently designed to prepare Puerto Rico for a future of austerity that would be necessary to keep up with minimum debt payments, regardless of whether some form of bankruptcy was granted. Among other things, the report recommended shrinking the size of the government, lowering the minimum wage, and trimming federal entitlements—including Medicaid and Medicare, which would be a particularly dire step, as two million people, or roughly 60 percent of Puerto Rico's residents, depend on those programs. The report also recommended making it more difficult to get overtime pay. Ironically, it was issued the same week in July that President Obama expanded overtime pay for US mainland workers.

In her comments on the report, made during a public hearing in Puerto Rico, Krueger observed that the island's minimum wage, at $7.25 an hour, is 88 percent of its median wage, arguing, "Most economists conclude that half that amount would be beneficial." This statement completely ignored the already existing high levels of poverty (46.2 percent in 2014) and the unemployment rate (12 percent); a 50 percent cut in wages would be devastating in that atmosphere. The report's logic seemed like an attempt to engender a transition for Puerto Rico from privileged colonial showcase of the Caribbean with relatively high living standards to an open competition with its Caribbean neighbors. It would change Puerto Rico's wage model from one that shadowed the United States' (something comparable to how its entitlements like SSI and Medicare are capped and not full, as in the United States) to one that put the island at the mercy of lowering its minimum wage to levels near neighboring developing countries in the Caribbean region. The island's fantasy of being a pseudo-autonomous offshore "America" was to be transformed into an unprotected zone of labor exploitation, incurring all the perils of economic independence without actual sovereignty or the ability to develop its own economy.

These assessments laid bare the fading promise of Puerto Rico's status as an unincorporated star in the United States' safety-net orbit. In a way the federal entitlements provided to Puerto Ricans were part of the bargain offsetting their watered-down citizenship, at least during the postwar boom years. But now that free-trade models reigned amid a Great Recession still weighing significantly on the mainland, the United States could no longer afford to prop up the island's living standards and needed to defer to its deregulated banking system's needs, which required placing the island in its "proper" Caribbean context.

Another of the Krueger Report's arguments suggested that welfare payments were "very generous relative to per capita income," which, according to their logic, caused a disincentive to work for minimum wage. However, as the pro-statehood NPP correctly argues, such payments are capped at levels significantly lower than what residents would receive if Puerto Rico were a state; the island's lack of full entitlement is one of the reasons Puerto Ricans are second-class citizens. The report's arguments resonated with both hardcore neocon and neoliberal reasoning about entitlements like welfare transfer payments: the disenfranchised are too seduced by freeloading and have no incentive to work, so the solution is to reduce the payments rather than pressure "job creators" to increase wages.

Meanwhile the left and progressive sectors were already building a narrative that the accumulation of the debt was "premeditated" and "immoral," as Rafael Bernabe, a candidate for governor on the relatively new Working People's Party line—somewhat similar to the new US democratic socialism movement and not focused on status change—insisted. Bernabe was among the first in the political sphere to push for a citizens' debt audit, something that had been done in Greece to obtain leverage in negotiations. What's more, while restructuring Detroit's debt, legal arguments around banking institutions' abuses had also been used in limited circumstances to obtain more favorable settlements. It was also in June 2015, the same month of the "unpayable debt" announcement, when Governor García Padilla mandated a multisectoral commission to assemble a debt audit, naming labor leader Roberto Pagán as chair of a group of nonpoliticians eager to investigate the debt.

Unsurprisingly, given Puerto Rico's cash-flow problems and the government's and financial industry's unwillingness to look too closely at the house of cards they'd built, the debt commission was notoriously underfunded. In fact, it struggled in its work, completing what they called a "pre-audit" study the following spring, which revealed significant evidence of improper practices by both the government and the banking industry. Over the next six months the battle over the debt and what constituted a proper audit or analysis of it would become even more hotly contested. The way debt functions and accumulates has everything to do with time, and the insistence that time was of the essence in moving toward a solution or restructuring it became central to the debate.

In the lead-up to 2016, an election year, in part due to efforts of groups like the Hedge Clippers and the Puerto Rico Center for Investigative Journalism, it became clear how the debt had changed hands from traditional investors to high-risk hedge and vulture funds. Most of the original Puerto Rico bond buyers were traditional municipal fund houses—like Oppenheimer Funds, a "global asset manager" that did not thrive on high-risk transactions, has a philanthropic arm, and became a party in the successful legal challenge to García Padilla's bankruptcy law.[21] But the landscape changed in the aftermath of the GDB's March 2014 municipal bond issuance of an unprecedented $3.5 billion. Vulture funds like Blue Mountain Capital and Stone Lion Capital, which slowly began buying up bonds when signs of distress emerged as early as 2011, were now the major players.[22]

Under the Fortuño administration the Puerto Rico legislature passed two laws, the Export Services Act and the Individual Investors Act. These gave hedge-fund managers a flat 4 percent tax rate as an incentive to move operations to Puerto Rico and also offered investors complete tax exemptions on dividends, interest, and capital gains, provided they lived on the island for at least half the year.

The Puerto Rico Center for Investigative Journalism's investigation revealed that many of these hedge and vulture funds had dabbled in high-stakes buys in troubled places like Greece, Argentina, and Detroit. Three funds—Aurelius Capital, Monarch Alternative Capital, and Canyon Capital—had been involved in all four, while Fir Tree Partners and Marathon Asset

Management, among others, hold a trifecta of Puerto Rico, Greece, and Argentina.[23] John Paulson, who owns the most expensive hotel in San Juan's exclusive Condado district, the aptly named Vanderbilt, has also invested heavily in Greek banks.

Not only that, but Puerto Rico's symptoms were starting to look a lot like what had happened in the 2008 mortgage crisis. Double Line Capital's Jeffrey Gundlach more than doubled his holdings of junk-rated bonds in May of 2014. In an interview with *Bloomberg News*, he compared the investment potential in Puerto Rico's debt to that in US mortgage markets in 2008, evoking the perfect-storm conditions that helped set off the Great Recession.[24] Double Line Capital, Blue Mountain, and Pine River Capital, among others, organized themselves as the Ad Hoc Group, representing thirty-five investors and $4.5 billion in bonds, and the PREPA Group, which negotiated directly with PREPA.

The Puerto Rico Center for Investigative Journalism also published a bombshell article exposing that hedge- and vulture-fund representatives visited legislators' offices at the Capitol constantly. According to the report, they were sometimes accompanied by lobbyists, like pro-statehood NPP party members Kenneth McClintock and Roberto Prats; the latter also happens to be a major Democratic fundraising bundler and chair of the Democratic Party in Puerto Rico.[25] Yet the article's sources for these revelations, Commonwealth Party senator Ramón Luis Nieves and Melba Acosta, for the most part claimed to not remember or know the names of the hedge funds or their representatives.

Toward the end of the summer the *New York Times* ran a feature about President Obama's postpresidential future. It opened with a description of a dinner party at the White House that included Toni Morrison, Malcolm Gladwell, and Eva Longoria, as well as someone who was not quite of their celebrity status but certainly boasted of being in those circles: Marc Lasry, cofounder and CEO of the hedge/vulture fund Avenue Capital Group, a significant holder of PREPA debt.[26]

Lasry was perhaps more famous when, in 2014, he became the co-owner of the NBA's Milwaukee Bucks, a development that was so energizing for Wisconsin governor Scott Walker that he signed a bill in August 2015 subsidizing a new arena for the team that would cost the public twice as much as originally projected. Avenue Capital was apparently aligned with Candlewood Investment Group, Fir Tree Partners, and Perry Corp, which had formed what is known as the GDB Ad Hoc Group—a coalition of vulture funds that held bonds issued by the GDB.

The GDB Ad Hoc Group had hired the law firm of Davis, Polk & Wardwell to represent it in their battles with the Puerto Rico government, hoping to recoup its investment. This was the same law firm that helped orchestrate the US government's bailout of AIG, the bad-mortgage debt-swapping machine at the center of the 2008 recession. Obama, who favored the AIG bailout, had not hinted whether he would offer a bailout to the troubled island, instead having his office give vague declarations hinting at allowing some form of bankruptcy proceedings.

Lasry's ties to Democratic politics went back many years. A March 2010 feature in the *Wall Street Journal* described him lunching with then White House chief of staff Rahm Emanuel, in part to advise Emanuel on whether banks had begun lending again in the wake of the 2008 crisis.[27] A 2012 *New York Times* article reported that "about 50 people paid $40,000 each to crowd into an art-filled room" in Lasry's apartment to hear Obama and Bill Clinton speak.[28] Ten years ago Lasry's Avenue Capital even employed Chelsea Clinton, whose husband had famously flopped by making bad investments in Greece while heading his own hedge fund.[29]

Lasry, who had been a humble UPS driver until his parents convinced him to go to law school, came off as an investor capable of rolling the dice with anyone in the global Wall Street hedge-fund game—as well as actual casino owners, like Donald Trump. This partnership, which stretches back to Trump's Atlantic City casino bankruptcy in 2009, eventually resulted in

Lasry buying him out and becoming the chairman of Trump Entertainment Resorts in 2011, a post Lasry eventually resigned.

It seemed puzzling that someone worth $1.87 billion, according to *Forbes*, whom the business press painted as a shrewd gambler, would believe that economies that are in a "death spiral" would miraculously recover. It was unlikely that Lasry had faith in a Puerto Rican economy that had shown no signs of growth for decades and was largely driven by government employment. Instead, he likely bet that the island's inability to declare bankruptcy would yield a higher return once it defaulted, as it would be exposed to a legal proceeding without bankruptcy protections. These proceedings tend to favor the debtor, and Avenue Capital Group was one of many vultures that began hovering over Puerto Rico in late 2013, when the island's junk-leaning bonds began to tempt the vultures.

A July 2016 *Wall Street Journal* article on the Puerto Rico crisis provided a possible explanation for Lasry's interest in pushing back against bankruptcy or a debt restructuring that would provide relief to Puerto Rico and its people.[30] Low default rates in corporate debt had led such distressed-debt specialists to instead focus on high-risk, cash-strapped governments like Greece, Argentina, and Puerto Rico that would provide a higher return in the debt collection process. But while prices of Greek and Argentine bonds bottomed out at less than 20 cents on the dollar at the height of their debt crises, much of Puerto Rico's debt was still trading between 50 and 70 cents, according to MSRB (Municipal Securities Rulemaking Board) data. If a vulture fund bought a debt for $2 million that was originally $10 million, it could be satisfied with a debt restructuring that required a $6 million payback. The higher price for the Puerto Rican bonds meant that, to turn a profit, the hedge funds would need to recover more in a Puerto Rico restructuring than speculators in the Greek and Argentine defaults did.

As late as November of 2017 Lasry was still holding on to a substantial amount of Puerto Rico debt, despite having dumped about $50 million of it. Perhaps he retained his wise gambling skills, or perhaps he knew that it might be worthwhile to wait out the debt-restructuring process, the strategies of which were already being designed in Washington and on Wall Street.[31] The way PROMESA had been set up—designed to favor the best deal for investors rather than the debtors—was perhaps enough of a setup for Lasry to hang his hat on. These strategies were to be advocated for and implemented by Treasury secretary and Obama confidante Jacob Lew, whose résumé included working for the Clinton administration (as director of the Office of Management and Budget) and Citigroup and recruiting Antonio Weiss from Lazard Investment Bank to the Department of the Treasury.

OCTOBER SURPRISE

In the summer of 2015 Puerto Rico's debt crisis had begun to emerge as a serious issue rather than a nebulous danger that would be faced somewhere down the line. As Obama's lame-duck presidency went into cruise control, rumblings in Congress began to confront the issue. Obama and Jeb Bush, who was revving up his presidential campaign with an eye toward Latino voters in Florida, happened to agree that Puerto Rico should be allowed a structured form of bankruptcy, and Democratic senators Charles Schumer and Richard Blumenthal announced their support of legislation that would allow a Chapter 9 bankruptcy-like process. But as summer gave way to fall, the process became more murky, and several players' contradictory stances seemed to indicate there was a hidden agenda at play.

A teasing headline in *Politico* on October 23 set the tone for the political firestorm to come. It announced a new plan from the Obama administration calling for a "super Chapter 9" process designed to allow Puerto Rico a different kind of bankruptcy process that would allow debt restructuring.[32] The super Chapter 9 would allow Puerto Rico to go through bankruptcy proceedings as an unincorporated territory, or a state, something that had been previously unconstitutional. Suggesting that this could be a model procedure for other nonincorporated territories, the administration was proposing a work-around for Puerto Rico's mysterious 1984 disqualification from Chapter 9. Pedro Pierluisi, in his position as resident commissioner, was caught in the middle. As a Democrat and a statehooder, he wanted to go along with Obama, but he knew this super Chapter 9 undermined pro-statehooders' position.

Former governor Fortuño—who had been so active in setting up bond sales both as governor and, later, as a high-powered lawyer—was strongly against the plan. He claimed he worried that if super Chapter 9 occurred, it could set a precedent and be extended to the states themselves, who are not allowed to file for bankruptcy. However, the following year it would come out that a financial advisory firm created by Pierluisi's wife, who happens to be the sister of FOMB chair José Carrión, had been advising a hedge fund that took part in the notorious 2014 $3.5 billion bond issue. Income generated by the firm gave the couple a 2,700 percent increase in their average net worth. With Fortuño also taking part in this kind of consultancy, the prime motivator was deal making, with the actual politics of statehood seeming to shrink into irrelevance.[33]

These strangely contradictory positions shed a light on the way multiple affiliations between Democrats and Republicans and commonwealth and statehood supporters seem to paralyze common sense and reveal an agenda that looks past real politics and toward patronage politics. In many ways Puerto Rican politicians and their cross-affiliations paralleled the decline of US politics, where legislating and leadership were traded away for lobbying and influence peddling. This is further evidenced by the person who drafted the super Chapter 9 proposal, Antonio Weiss. The Treasury Department had just hired him despite strong opposition from Senator Elizabeth Warren, who was put off by the $21.2 million golden parachute Weiss received from Lazard investments upon his departure.

The language of the proposal was telling in the way it seemed to offer a kind of an ethical corporate benevolence while at the same time establishing the parameters of what was coming: a fiscal oversight board.[34] While declaring that the economic crisis in Puerto Rico was in danger of becoming a "humanitarian crisis" and using sympathetic language regarding the "3.5 million Americans living in Puerto Rico who have had to endure stagnation," the "Roadmap for Congressional Action" stresses that time was running out in a way that favored the creditors. This undercut the logic that Puerto Rico could simply continue its policy of not meeting payments and use its remaining funds to pay for essential services, betting that the United States would act to avoid the bad public relations of its colony plunged into chaos.

Further, not only was the proposed course of action in part strengthening "financial discipline," it also insisted that these solutions be carried out through "strong fiscal oversight" to "strengthen Puerto Rico's fiscal governance." Those last two phrases clearly foreshadowed the creation of the FOMB that came to be known as La Junta, although talk about a fiscal control board for Puerto Rico went back as far as 2013 in the business press. They did not, however, go so far as to anticipate that the board would "strengthen fiscal governance" by almost completely removing power from Puerto Rico's legislative and executive branches.

As the months wore on, the government's strategy of renegotiating payments about to come due continued. Congress was slow to move toward a proposal for debt relief or restructuring, but eventually hearings on the debt crisis picked up their pace, particularly in Rob Bishop's House Natural Resources Committee. By early June of 2016 most observers were convinced that the Puerto Rico government would default on an $800 million payment toward general obligation (GO) bonds, one of the two principal types of debt they held. Meanwhile the Committee on Natural Resources was working through various iterations of what had become known as the PROMESA Act. The Obama administration had announced that they were not considering a bailout. This was seen as the most logical course of action in an election year, as "bailout" had become a dirty word and a reminder of how Republican fiscal conservatism was so strong that Democrats were loath to oppose. It was that "why give Republicans something to use in their campaign?" mantra that had justified the lack of bold action among Democrats for almost a generation.

Some of the debt holders, including Koch Brothers affiliate groups that owned GO debt, still opposed PROMESA because it would require more haircuts than suited their appetites. These hardline investors have continued to noisily advocate for mercenary measures to ensure full payment even in the middle of the modified bankruptcy proceeding that the law's Title III created. The battle over PROMESA was thus framed as a conflict between the interests of debt holders and politicians, who were trying to balance the need for some kind of restructuring with any sympathy creditors might have for the plight of Puerto Ricans.

The lead negotiator in this effort—or at least the ideologue that sought to create an imagined middle path through the controversy—was Antonio Weiss. His even demeanor and plays to humanizing his agenda were accented by a kind of parental sternness when he sought to drive home a point about the need for sacrifice and compromise. His focus on the Medicare crisis, in which payments to the island were being delayed and/or eliminated, causing the departure of hundreds of doctors, was admirable, and his calls for increased funding for the Earned Income Tax Credit and Child Tax Credit for families on the island to address the problem of poverty also came across as humanitarian. Of course, his longstanding ties to the financial elite made it difficult for many to believe he was acting in the best interests of the people.

The debt issue was finally beginning to resonate outside the island, not least among the members of the Puerto Rican diaspora in the United States. Within the space of a couple of weeks in late May and early June 2016, two key gatherings were held

to discuss strategies. One, held at the headquarters of the SEIU
building in Midtown Manhattan, was geared toward progressive
responses to the crisis. These included using the legal argument
of odious debt—in which a debt could be claimed to be illegitimate because it burdens rather than benefits a people—as part
of a strategy to demand a citizen-run debt audit. The odious-
debt argument was formulated for the case of Puerto Rico by
National Lawyers Guild president Natasha Lycia Ora Bannan,
who argued that there is a possibility of attaining a "moral foundation for severing, in whole or part, the continuity of legal obligations where the debt in question was contracted and used
in ways that were not beneficial or were actually harmful to the
interests of a population."[35] Ironically, the principle of odious
debt was first raised when the United States refused to assume
the debts acquired by Spain when it gave sovereignty over Cuba,
Puerto Rico, and the Philippines to the United States after the
Spanish-American War. The United States used the concept to
legally free themselves from the debt Cuba had incurred rather
than assuming it.

In the United States there stirred the beginnings of activism
around convincing workers to divest from their pension funds
that were administered by investment houses that had bought
Puerto Rican debt. The group that organized the meeting, Va-
mos 4PR, was a coalition of unions, activist groups like nonprofit community advocacy group Make the Road, academics,
and lawyers, achieving a unique moment in diaspora collectivity.
For once the debate was not about nationalist tropes surrounding political prisoners or rhetoric for and against statehood, independence, and the commonwealth status.

Around the same time there was finally a kind of political-
economic analysis emerging that addressed the economic reality of the United States' colonial domination over Puerto Rico.
In one dramatic presentation Professor César Ayala showed a
chart that illustrated how Puerto Rico's GDP-GNP ratio was
among the lowest in the world—at one point in the mid-2000s
only US-occupied Iraq had a lower ratio. Placing the colonial

economic relationship between the United States and Puerto Rico center stage also created a groundswell around issues like the Jones Act, which limited maritime activity in a way that created considerable additional costs to Puerto Rican consumers. The Jones Act issue resonated with activists because it was easy to raise consciousness with it because it was passed in 1917, the same year US citizenship was foisted onto residents of Puerto Rico—and it was coming up on its centennial.

Although there was much discussion of the Jones Act and its deleterious effect on Puerto Rico's ability to sustain a developing economy, its impact was often exaggerated, particularly claims that it made all consumer items more expensive. Whereas on average, prices were about 21 percent greater in Puerto Rico than in the United States, they compared favorably with major metropolitan areas like New York and Miami, whose poverty rates are 19 percent and 24 percent, respectively. Still, the island's 41 percent poverty rate (compared to the United States' average of 14.3 percent) represented a much higher percentage of the population that has a difficult time just grocery shopping.[36] This high rate reflects the concentration of poverty you'd expect to see in peripheral areas of US cities, showing how "American" socioeconomic problems are reproduced in an isolated island territory.

Just as unscrupulous mortgage lenders had visited ruin on poor people of color by exploiting their dreams of home ownership and issuing mortgages doomed to fail, Puerto Rico's debt had been pushed by the ravenous hunger of speculative capital. But through the Jones Act, the unexplained change in bankruptcy law, the triple-tax exemption, and the corruption of an ineffectual-by-design political class, Puerto Rico's colonial status exacerbated the damage. This should have led to a strong movement to press for a debt audit, as had been done in sovereign nations like Greece and Argentina. But instead what emerged was rhetoric about Puerto Rico being "saved" by a benevolent collaboration between the federal government and the banking establishment, who together had the ultimate goal of regaining Puerto Rico's access to credit markets—never mind that what Puerto Rico needed were conditions to build a stable economy. This was typical of the Democratic Party's policy: previous attempts at extending bankruptcy protection to Puerto Rico had been aimed primarily at getting the colony back on its feet just enough so it could borrow more money. Access to credit markets was the mantra, with no sense that borrowing should be reserved for major capital projects like infrastructure and not used to keep essential services going. All that mattered was for investors to be able to recoup investments that were largely driven by the knowledge that Puerto Rico's bonds were triple-tax exempt and that it had no bankruptcy protection.

The independent investigative group the Hedge Clippers issued a report on Weiss in September 2015 that contained several accusations against him—some cases of guilt by association but many based on clear conflicts of interest. First, his former firm, Lazard, had been involved in marketing Puerto Rico's debt to hedge funds in 2013. Second, Lazard Asset Management was strongly invested in Blue Mountain Capital, which owned GO bonds, and Pine River Capital Management, which owned COFINA bonds. Finally, as far back as 1993 a top Lazard banker, Richard Poirier, made large campaign contributions to then Governor Pedro Rosselló in exchange for preference on municipal underwriting deals. Poirier was later convicted of wire fraud and conspiracy for similar bribery activity in Fulton County, Georgia.[37]

Weiss urged people to think of the legislation that was being conceived in Congress as emergency legislation—"necessary, but not sufficient." He was intent on establishing an "independent" oversight board that would "protect essential services" through the stay on litigation, which would suspend all pending legal action to collect debts and would be enforced with the passage of what would become the PROMESA bill. Yet he seemed to have little interest in determining whether debt relief could be achieved through a thorough audit. When questioned at a forum held at New York's Hunter College of Social Work in the spring of 2016 by journalist Juan González about whether the debt was legal, Weiss refused to give a straight answer. "There are legal theories about the legality of the debt, and the legal theories can play out in a court of law, and it is possible that one could pursue legal cases that would not provide any protection for essential services," he said. "Cases need to be decided, and appealed, they are often reversed. They often end up . . . in the Supreme Court. We are out of time. There is no time left. If Congress is prepared to enact legislation which allows the debt to be reduced to an amount that the economy can sustain, we need to pursue that because anything that plays out in a court of law will take, in our judgment, a decade."[38]

Invoking a time limit was telling. Weiss was threatening that time had run out for Puerto Rico and its ability to continue with minimum payments. Failing to make those payments would mean going into default, which would trigger an endless flood of lawsuits from bondholders. Similar situations had played out in Greece and Argentina, countries that at various moments suspended payments, renegotiated, had austerity imposed on them, went to trials held in lower Manhattan, and used their sovereignty to continue to hold off total disaster. But the reason Puerto Rico was out of time wasn't because it had no remaining strategies to continue trying to negotiate down the debt; severely limited as it was by the lack of bankruptcy protection and lack of sovereignty, it still could have lobbied the US government on humanitarian grounds. What Puerto Rico had run out of time for was the illusion that it had autonomy over its affairs, that its residents had full US citizenship, that it had anything resembling a self-directed economy.

There were still some theoretical legal arguments that could have potentially been exploited to turn the tide in Puerto Rico's favor. There was a pending appeal to the Supreme Court over the circuit court ruling that struck down the Ley de Quiebra Boricuas, or the Puerto Rico Bankruptcy Law, which was passed early in the García Padilla administration, as well as another case, *Puerto Rico v. Sánchez Valle*, which tested the legal principle of double jeopardy to show that if one could be tried for the same offense in Puerto Rico and the United States, then Puerto Rico had some form of pseudo-sovereignty. Finally, there was a theory proposed by ex-governor Acevedo Vilá that if Puerto Rico defaulted on its debt, the bondholder/creditors could and would hold the US government liable. Acevedo Vilá had gone to Washington with ex-governor Hernández Colón to meet with Weiss and lobby against the passage of PROMESA in the hopes of avoiding the governmental gridlock that would result from clashes between the board and the local government. He also asked about the United States' potential liability for Puerto Rico's debts. "Antonio Weiss admitted to me that if we go to default, they would be sued as well," he said.[39] Acevedo Vilá had been talking about this for at least two years, when he began referring to an obscure Supreme Court case about Guam called *Limtiaco v. Camacho.* The case involved a bond emission made by Guam, which is also a US unincorporated territory, that exceeded the legal limit. Guam attorney general Alicia Limtiaco refused to approve the emission and was sued by the governor, Felix Camacho, who won. Limtiaco lost on appeal, but the Supreme Court heard the case and found in favor of the attorney general. The court's decision included these lines: "The Governor mistakenly argues that we owe deference to the Guam Supreme Court's interpretation of the Organic Act. . . . The debt limitation provision protects both Guamanians and the US from the potential consequences of territorial insolvency. Thus, this case is not a matter of purely local concern."[40] These words seem to indicate that responsibility for the debt cannot be legally confined to its territorial origin. Yet none of this discourse was seriously pursued. It didn't feature in the main congressional debate on PROMESA nor in the activism that was slowly coalescing around the debt crisis issue.

In fact, mainstream Democrats—increasingly employing liberal darling and *Hamilton* playwright Lin-Manuel Miranda, who offered Republican members of Congress free tickets to his Broadway play in exchange for legislation on Puerto Rico— willingly, if somewhat reluctantly, embraced the PROMESA bill as the only solution possible at the moment.[41] Appearing on the popular HBO show hosted by John Oliver, Miranda suggested that the PROMESA bill, "if it were done right," would save Puerto Rico. "The hard part is convincing Congress that Puerto Rico matters so their heart is in the fight for relief / not a bailout but just relief / a belief that you can pass legislation to ease our grief," Miranda freestyled. He didn't specify what the terms of that relief would or should be.

July 1 approached, and it was clear that Puerto Rico was going to default on a $2 billion debt-service payment, a moment that would once again be heralded as a sign that Puerto Rico had run out of time. The days leading up to the nation's annual independence celebration were also the last few days that Congress would remain in session before a summer break. At least one Democrat, Washington senator Maria Cantwell, argued that the deadline was artificial and unjustified in its urgency. "There is so much discussion that somehow July 1 is a magic date," she argued as her colleagues were preparing to invoke cloture—or end any further debate and get to the business of approving the final version of PROMESA. "July 11 is the next scheduled legal hearing on this, and that is plenty of time for the Senate to weigh in on a few ways to improve this legislation and to make sure we are not suspending the constitution of Puerto Rico in the process. . . . Why is this important? Because there are hedge funds out there that took Argentina's debt and it took almost a decade to get a resolution."

Senators Richard Durbin and Harry Reid also alluded to the menace of the hedge and vulture funds, all to no avail. New Jersey senator Robert Menéndez said, "I came to this chamber in September and December of last year to raise the alarm bells about what was happening in Puerto Rico. The majority held the ball and ran out the shot clock, attempting to silence the voice of 3.5 million U.S. citizens living in Puerto Rico in this debate."[42] Menéndez's argument seemed compassionate enough, saying that, technically, any judgments reached through creditor

litigation would be unenforceable as long as Congress continued with its retroactive stay on litigation. In other words, there
was still time to debate or even fundamentally reconceive of
PROMESA because Congress could continue to grant stays on
debt collection actions in court. Yet he did not object in principle to the proposed oversight board, which would take away all
legislative powers from Puerto Rican elected officials and cost
hundreds of millions of dollars for Puerto Ricans.

None of this legal haggling would explain why, after so many
years of economic crisis in Puerto Rico, neither Congress nor
the Executive Branch did anything meaningful to confront it. In
fact, most Washington observers, including congressional Democrats, continually lamented that so little meaningful legislation
had passed in Congress at all because of Republican obstruction-
ism. How is it then that we got this extraordinary effort to pass
the bill quickly, suddenly signaling an unexpected triumph of
bipartisanship? And during a presidential election year, no less?

Whether it was a simple matter of radical Republican control
of the House or the optics of a bailout, the Executive Branch
and the Treasury Department had shown a lack of will to in-
sist on a different kind of solution that could avoid austerity and
would work with Puerto Rico on ways to develop a functioning
self-sustaining economy. Instead, they caved to protect the only
donors that matter—the financial community, from which both
Lew and Weiss had sprung. The ultimate message from the passage of PROMESA was that Wall Street called the shots. That
much was abundantly clear from the liability clause in the final
bill:

(2) LIABILITY CLAIM.—The term "Liability Claim" means,
as it relates to a Liability—

(A) right to payment, whether or not such right is reduced to judgment, liquidated, unliquidated, fixed, contingent, matured, unmatured, disputed, undisputed, legal,
equitable, secured, or unsecured.

In other words, PROMESA ensured the rights of creditors to payment regardless of whether the debt was deemed "legal" or "equitable." The ultimate protection against any finding of illegality in a debt audit was baked into the legislation. Would the hoped-for debt audit, then, be reduced to a way for Puerto Ricans—and, less likely, Wall Street—to learn from their previous mistakes or would claims of violation of Puerto Rico's constitution hold up?

And so on June 30, 2016, a new day dawned on Puerto Rico. In the coming year an unelected board—appointed by Republicans and Democrats in Congress, with a majority of Republicans and including three members of the Puerto Rican financial community that had helped create the debt crisis in the first place—would be the ultimate authority governing island residents' affairs. Given the unreasonable goals of balanced budgets and its imposition of budget cuts and wage and pension reductions as well as the inevitable out-migration that would occur in response, Puerto Rico was facing the possibility of a permanent debt crisis.

CHAPTER 5

PROMESA = *POBRεZA*

Mural on a public wall in Old San Juan. © Joseph Rodríguez

Credit is a means of privatization and debt a means of so-
cialization . . . debt is social and credit is asocial. Debt is
mutual. Credit runs only one way. But debt runs in every
direction, scatters, escapes, seeks refuge. The debtor seeks
refuge among other debtors, acquires debt from them, offers
debt to them. The place of refuge is the place to which you
can only owe more and more because there is no creditor,
no payment possible. This refuge, this place of bad debt, is
what we call the fugitive public. To creditors it is just a place
where something is wrong, though that something wrong—
the invaluable thing, the thing that has no value—is desired.
Creditors seek to demolish that place, that project, in order
to save the ones who live there from themselves and their
lives.
        —**Stefano Harvey and Fred Moten**, *The Undercommons*

When they invaded there was no debt. They created public finance to indebt what they designated as the people [of]
Puerto Rico. . . . The equation is simple. The colonizer makes
the colonized pay and the coloniality it imposes. And since
there aren't enough funds to pay the colonizer, then the debt
recurs, which cumulatively, also requires the colonized to pay.
        —**Luis Rey Quiñones Soto**, Preface, *PROMESA: Puerto Rico
        Oversight Management and Economic Stability Act*[1]

A debt is a promise.
        —**David Graeber**, *Debt: The First 5,000 Years*

When Barack Obama signed PROMESA into law on
June 30, 2016, it marked a transition in the US relationship with Puerto Rico, one that symbolized the
final shift of its priorities from Cold War empire building to the
urgent needs of global finance capital. Puerto Rico was no longer a significant strategic military outpost to guard against in-
cursions from the Soviet Union. Its captive economy had been
greatly reduced in significance by free-trade agreements like

NAFTA. Outside of still-sizable corporate profits and the use of the island's banks as tax havens, the primary source of revenue for US financial interests was no longer tax avoidance for pharmaceutical and other corporations but rather how Puerto Rico's bonds could be exploited through usurious interest rates and ultimately bought out by vulture funds. The core priorities underlying PROMESA were clearly stated early in the section Title 1—Establishment and Organization of Oversight Board:

> SEC 101. FINANCIAL OVERSIGHT AND MANAGE-
> MENT BOARD.
> PURPOSE—The purpose of the Oversight Board is to provide a method for a covered territory to achieve fiscal responsibility and access to the capital markets.

Thus, the essential purpose of PROMESA and the oversight board it creates was to allow Puerto Rico to right its sinking financial ship, get its "house in order" so as to be able to have "access" to the global casino of financial speculation. Its purpose was not to explore ideas about how to create the conditions for a sustainable economy, not to rethink its position in the globalist new order by engaging in regional trade in the Caribbean or with Latin America and Asia. It is to retrain Puerto Rico and Puerto Ricans, through the use of severe austerity and government shrinking, so as to allow re-entry to "the capital markets," which can be defined as markets where buyers and sellers engage in trading of financial securities like bonds, stocks, and whatever ingeniously devised financial instruments might exist when the PROMESA process concludes. This is far, far away from the moment in 1952 when Luis Muñoz Marín stood in front of the Puerto Rican people as the first Puerto Rican to have been elected governor of the territory, envisioning a moment when the island would develop enough to petition Congress for its independence.

The imposition of PROMESA and its mandated Fiscal Oversight and Management Board was nothing short of the absolute

derogation of any notion of democracy and autonomy in Puerto
Rico. The PROMESA law mandates an oversight board, a technocratic tool that, although conceived to address problems
in US municipalities like New York City and Detroit, turns
into an organ of discipline and punishment when applied in
Puerto Rico, particularly when its local government has no real
agency, unlike New York and Detroit. The use of the acronym
PROMESA can be read as insipidly naïve at best. At worst—
and most accurately—it is an expression of cruel sarcasm that
recalls the essential notion of a debt as a promise, now forsaken
and needing a blunt instrument to address the failure of Puerto
Rico's promise to repay.

Fiscal control boards first appeared in the United States
back in the nineteenth century, before the rise of twentieth-
century colonialism and imperialism, seemingly part of the
culture of industrialism and modernity. Yet they seem almost
designed to be the ultimate tool for a late-capitalist era, when
global financial concerns intervene to rectify "failures" of local
democracy.[2] These boards are designed to reduce the authority
of locally elected officials who are perceived to have generated
debt crises, and they aim to protect investors while supposedly
ensuring against future inappropriate indebtedness. The local
government is reduced to peripheral involvement in setting and
planning fiscal policy, and the board oversees debt restructur-
ings and settlements that greatly encourage privatizing public
resources, leaving the bill with the tax-paying victim.

Theoretically, the use of fiscal control boards offers a chance
to overhaul local politics that may have succumbed to corruption and inefficiency. They even claim to be strengthening
democracy. But all they accomplish, in reality, is transferring
power from the public trust to a new economic structure determined by corporate exigencies and ethics. In the case of Puerto
Rico, the FOMB represents a financial sector takeover of a local
government that is an anomaly in the United States, steeped in
Latin American tradition and the Spanish language, one that
had never existed outside of a colonial context.

State-appointed oversight boards for local jurisdictions began
in Missouri during the fiscal crises in the United States of the
1870s.[3] Although Missouri was no longer a territory and had long
been admitted to the Union, the board established a precedent
for laws addressing bad debt. Supreme Court decisions of the
era helped normalize control boards as an option by ruling that
the state legislature could define local revenue structures and
appoint individuals to manage local finances. The use of control
boards continued during the Great Depression, when states like
New Jersey, Michigan, North Carolina, Oregon, and Massachusetts all implemented some form of fiscal receivership, in which
budgets and appropriations were closely supervised.

The modern era of control boards began in 1975 in New York
City, which created something called the Municipal Assistance
Corporation (MAC) to work together with an Emergency Financial Control Board, made up of representatives of the major
corporations of the day. The move was prompted by the city's
pattern of borrowing that was intended to preserve a kind of
New Deal social contract with working New Yorkers. The kind
of liberal politics that still characterized New York and other
major cities was formed during the FDR era and continued well
into the 1960s, when it was meant to create a cultural renaissance for the white working class while only including residents
of color in a token fashion.

Class tracking students according to their "ability" was one
of several educational policies of this period that greatly affected my experience as well as that of my peers growing up in
New York City.[4] With a mandate presumably derived from test
scores, the system continually tracked me into more advanced
classes, where I served as a token representative of Puerto Rican
migrants, most of whom would be tracked into classes geared
toward vocational rather than academic career paths. This
down-tracking resulted from various factors: low test scores derived from racially or culturally biased tests could diminish a
student in the eyes of the teacher, but many instances—according to anecdotes I've heard as well as academic studies—merely

reflected a racial bias conditioned by negative portrayals in the media. From the late 1950s through the 1970s Puerto Ricans were continually branded as juvenile delinquents, gang members, drug traffickers, and substance abusers in the news media and Hollywood entertainments. I was given the opportunity to interact and learn with more privileged, ethnically European students, which reinforced my family's ideals about ultimately being accepted into the greater American social fabric and, in turn, upheld their faith that Puerto Rico's unincorporated territorial status would eventually be resolved in a similarly positive fashion.

New York City's fiscal control board was composed of seven members, just like the FOMB in Puerto Rico. Yet unlike Puerto Rico, the city was allowed to appoint the majority of its members. Its governor, reformist Democrat Hugh Carey, chose "private citizens," like the president of New York Telephone Company, the president of American Airlines, and the president of firearms manufacturer Colt Industries. Carey was an early neoliberal Democrat, leaving a legacy of corporate tax cuts as well as monuments to the city's new corporatist era: the Jacob Javits Center, Battery Park City, and the South Street Seaport.

Yet there were other, eerie ways in which New York's board presaged what would happen in Puerto Rico—its corporate slant actually prompted the *Village Voice* to call it a "junta," and local politicians strongly criticized it for not including representatives from labor unions or community organizations that focused on people of color. The narrative justifying the imposition of the New York City board was also chillingly reminiscent of what would happen in Puerto Rico. The fact that it infringed on democratic rights and processes paled in comparison to the fiscal need to balance the books. "The city is insolvent," said a MAC official to the *New York Times*. "To ordinary men and women, any outfit that has a huge deficit, that has used up its reserves and that can't borrow any money is insolvent. There has to be some sort of receivership by the state. It's not an assault on home rule. It's the facts of life." The official was reestablishing a narrative that endorsed placing a government's assets and rights into the hands of a responsible custodian, a fiscal control board.

Then, in 1978, Cleveland became the first large city to default on its bond payments since the Depression, prompting Ohio to not only create a fiscal control board but also to pass statewide legislation that would standardize the creation of fiscal control boards as a remedy for any similar crises in other municipalities. Washington, DC, had a board in place from 1995 to 2001, and Philadelphia has had one since 1995. By 2009 the number of fiscal control boards operating in the United States was forty-eight, up from thirty-six and thirty-four in the 1980s and 1990s, respectively.[5] Many of these boards oversee entire states that, like Puerto Rico, don't have access to Title 9 bankruptcy procedures.[6]

Even these more modern examples of fiscal control boards have their roots in the methods established with those of the nineteenth century. The idea was to provide an instrument to directly take over fiscal management of a state or municipality; provide a temporary stay on individual creditors' court actions, and devise a plan for debt restructuring.[7] Although there has been some lip service from Puerto Rico's FOMB about creating feasible plans and policies for sustainable economic development, it seems to prioritize these more old-fashioned aims. It's easy to understand why. As prototypical managerial instruments conceived of and implemented by technocrats with little feel for what real local economies are, fiscal control boards are not well suited to improving the economic health, quality of life, or civic empowerment of the communities whose finances they oversee. They have historically imposed varying degrees of austerity on local communities, hampered community members' participation in the democratic process, and set communities up for long-term challenges by creating conditions for economic growth that only serve outside investors.

In New York the establishment of the MAC and the Emergency Financial Control Board was a seminal event that seemed to encapsulate the turn American history was about to take.

The failure of the manufacturing sector was a major reason for eroding tax contribution—the loss of factory jobs deprived states and municipalities of not only tax income (real estate, capital gains, and payroll) but also consumer spending and tax-paying. This was a classic example of a multiplier effect that manifested itself in laying off workers and creating a new kind of working poor among people of color. The creation of an almost European-like civil society characterized by easy access to schooling, libraries, health-promoting community centers, and cultural events was too much for the system to bear—raising taxes was rapidly becoming out of the question, and the manufacturing-driven economy was no longer generating the tax income. Thus, capitalists were brought in to oversee the transition to a finance-driven debtor economy.

While the early days of the Emergency Financial Control Board foreshadowed the process in Puerto Rico in some ways, they were markedly different in others. The most important difference, of course, is that the New York board was at the beginning of the historical arc I've been describing, with more deference granted to local government because of that newness. And because New Yorkers not only had full citizenship but also lived in perhaps the most important city for business in the United States, New York was considered too big to fail—though that didn't mean it would be shielded from radical change. The "private members" of the board may or may not have had an ideological connection to mainstream liberalism, but for them the bottom line ruled, and they had the upper hand when it came to imposing budget cuts.

Within a few months after the NYC fiscal oversight board was formed, friendly overtures and mild disagreements between the board and elected officials had devolved into contentious debates over three-year economic plans. Cost-cutting technocratic proposals began to sound like genocide to community activists. Mayor Abraham Beame had reached office in part because he was willing to weaponize his constituents' racism—his campaign against Bronx Borough president Herman Badillo, perhaps the strongest Puerto Rican candidate for mayor of New York ever, was marred when Beame deployed Afro-Latinos playing loud salsa music on a flat-bed truck through middle-class white neighborhoods in Queens.[8]

In early 1976 Beame's choice for Housing and Development administrator, Roger Starr, proposed something called "planned shrinkage," which was intended to gut services from the city's poorest neighborhoods that were, not coincidentally, populated. by blacks and Latinos. Minority advocates' loud outrage eventually led to Starr's resignation, and Deputy Mayor John Zuccotti demurred politely, saying the plan wasn't "practical."[9] Over the long term, however, the idea stuck, becoming an operative part of MAC commissioner Felix Rohatyn's moves to make the city more hospitable to corporate investment. Planned shrinkage—or the deliberate withdrawal of services to impoverished neighborhoods—became the go-to method to prepare a neighborhood for its eventual gentrification. Herman Badillo devolved from a working-class champion into a bitter older neoliberal critic, switching to the Republican Party during the Giuliani era. Meanwhile gentrification displaced Latinx NYC residents from three different neighborhoods while Zuccotti had a rather famous park named after him near the Wall Street financial district.

THE FALSE PROMISE OF PROMESA

There is a strange irony behind the use of the word *PROMESA*. The name of this law that empowers a fiscal control board to oversee Puerto Rico's debt restructuring tries to fuse the axiom that a debt is a promise with the promise of a Puerto Rican future that is even less promising than its phase as a commonwealth. The way David Graeber describes it in his book *Debt: The First 5,000 Years*, debt was originally a way for societies to use their sense of morality to create a balance of payments in a local community. When metals began to be used for currency, money came into use to pay formalized debts, allowing it to "turn morality into a matter of impersonal arithmetic."

Italian economist and philosopher Maurizio Lazzarato sees debt as having evolved into a power relation, one that has moved the relationship between debtor and creditor formally into the political realm.[10] In his way of thinking, the power relation of social class, traditionally embodied by the conflict between the owners of production and workers, has morphed into a leveraged battle between investors and consumers. In the industrial era of political economy, power was primarily exerted through class conflict at the point of production through imposing discipline on workers. But power in a postindustrial society is increasingly wielded by owners of debt, intent on using contractual debt re-lations to surveil and virtually imprison debtors.

Although this paradigm might be most immediately obvious in the case of individual consumers struggling under the weight of credit card or student loan debt, with the rise of fiscal crises and fiscal-control boards, it is increasingly weighing on states and municipalities as well. As we have seen, the same kind of moral arguments made about the fiscal responsibilities of individ-uals are used to coerce compliance by imposing control boards. This, despite the obvious fact that the United States itself oper-ates under massive debt—currently upward of $22 trillion, with moral arguments against it rarely succeeding in Congress. Eso-teric questions about the United States' ability to "print" money to temporarily assuage shortfalls are also couched in moral lan-guage. Printing money outside of budgetary constraints would be as irresponsible as allowing a teenager to "print" money in or-der to go on a strip-mall shopping spree. Instead, the reluctance to simply create more currency is most likely a moral argument invoked to control the supply of currency and empower financial markets, as these profit in their role of policing the circulation of money while invoking the fear of runaway inflation.

In Puerto Rico the debtor-creditor relationship is being used to transform the premise of the United States' presence on the island. The PROMESA board is a tool to assert this power. It wields this power in even less democratic ways than fiscal control boards in the fifty states, rebooting the colonial controls and joining them with austerity techniques used globally. It has been set up to act as a laboratory for testing extreme methods, while its citizens are easily dismissed as people of color and non-English speakers. The more appropriate analogy for what Puerto Rico is experiencing is not so much the fiscal-control board imposed on Detroit just a few years ago but instead the Flint water crisis, where cost-cutting measures instituted when revamping access to the city's water supply wound up contaminating thousands of poor and working-class families of color.[11]

True to most of the speculation regarding the creation of the FOMB, colloquially called La Junta, the members who were chosen all represented either centrist or conservative elements and were involved with the financial sector in some capacity. The presence of bank executives and conservative economic think tanks reflected neoliberalism's progression since the New York fiscal board—presidents of large corporations had been replaced by figures from finance and economics. Three Democrats and four Republicans were named to the FOMB and, as a concession to appearances, five of the members were of Latinx background, with four of those being Puerto Rican. Fittingly—and echoing US colonial control over Puerto Rico—the governor had a representative on the board, though he had no vote, much like the resident commissioner the island sends to Congress each legislative session.

The fact that the clear majority of the board is Latinx and yet its members are bound to enforce a policy that doesn't sympathize with Puerto Rican citizenry demonstrates the power of finance capital's imperatives to transcend any idea about ethnic or racial solidarity. Though appointed by Democrats and Latinx, board chairman José B. Carrión III and board members Carlos García, Arthur González, José B. González, and Ana Matosantos were all deeply embedded in the financial sector.

García and Carrión in particular have so many links to banks that were involved in accumulating the debt that their presence on the board is staggeringly ironic. Two Hedge Clippers reports, "The Looting of Puerto Rico's Infrastructure Fund" and "Insured to Profit: Conflicts of Interests in the Career of José Carrión III," detail connections between them, Santander Bank, and the Government Development Bank (GDB). Both banks played a major role in amassing and profiting from Puerto Rico's debt, privatizing the island's telephone company, looting island infrastructure funds to facilitate GDB refinancing deals and making possible more bond emissions, and using pension funds for investing in capital appreciation bonds.

The first report systematically detailed how García diverted $1 billion intended for infrastructure improvement and maintenance to "a series of financial transactions that were intended to bolster the island's credit rating, but which became tied up in the issuance of billions in new debt." According to the report, Carrión and his wife benefited from government contracts that enriched various members of Carrión's brokerage firm, who also worked at the GDB as well as a private equity firm tied to the Health Insurance Administration, which Carrión's wife ran. Those Carrión associates were among a number of GDB employees who were shielded from prosecution about questionable actions by a provision in the PROMESA law.

By the spring of 2016 it became clear that the government had no power and was merely engaged in a back and forth with the FOMB that amounted to a kind of political theater staged for the benefit of whatever islanders still held on to some belief in their own political agency. The public was increasingly aware of the questionable roles Carrión and García played in amassing the debt, and there was widespread skepticism about the newly appointed executive director, Ukrainian American Natalie Jaresko, who had a salary of $625,000 a year. She had no experience in the Caribbean, and ethical questions have been raised about when she was CEO of the Western NIS Enterprise Fund (WNISEF), a $150 million US-taxpayer-financed investment fund, before becoming Ukraine's finance minister in 2014. WNISEF was a United States Agency for International

Development (USAID) organization intended to stimulate investment growth in the Ukraine and Moldova.

Before being named the Ukraine's finance minister, Jaresko managed over a ten-year period to collect $1.77 million in bonuses from WNISEF when her salary was supposed to be $150,000 a year. She apparently avoided publicly disclosing significant income by cofounding Horizon Capital Associates and the Emerging Europe Growth Fund, which were set up as privately owned investment funds whose earnings were considered "unrelated" to the WNISEF returns. In a subsequent annual report it was disclosed that one of these new organizations, Horizon Capital, made over $2 million in management fees associated with investment transactions. Jaresko's own husband, an original partner with her in WNISEF, noted her books cooking, accusing her in a lawsuit of improper loans to Horizon Capital. The Ukraine's economy failed to revive, despite Jaresko's management of a $17.5 billion grant from the IMF.[12]

In March and April of 2016, echoing the strikes of 2010 and 2011, students at the University of Puerto Rico engaged in renewed protests to shut down operations at most of its campuses, trying to tie together various strands of discontent that had been emerging as a result of the imposition of PROMESA. The students were responding to $512 million in budget cuts to the eleven branches of the university system over the course of ten years as well as the plan to privatize some of its buildings and grounds soon. Taking part in a history of activism within the University of Puerto Rico that went back to the early part of the decade, the students began demanding that the $72 billion debt be audited. The Ricardo Rosselló administration, which took power in 2017, was about to pass a bill to eliminate the debt audit commission that previous governor García Padilla had signed into law.

During the demonstration, a crowd of several hundred protesters swarmed the steps of the Capitolio building in Old San Juan. Mirroring events six years prior when protesting Luis Fortuño's job cuts, they were met with a barrage of pepper spray and night sticks from a belligerent riot squad. The return of violence to the capitol steps served as a reminder that the US Department of Justice had investigated the Puerto Rico Police Department in 2011 for excessive force, leading to a consent decree that placed the department under DOJ supervision. Puerto Rico ACLU president William Ramírez asserted that the use of pepper spray was in violation of the DOJ-enforced agreement with the PRPD. Further, he expressed concern that the police were emboldened by Trump attorney general Jeff Sessions's statement that such federal investigations of police abuses would be reevaluated, presumably in ways more favorable to the police.

I spoke with Bernat Tort, who teaches in the philosophy and women's and gender studies departments at UPR and was pepper sprayed in the face when he resisted the riot squad's attempts to push demonstrators away from the building. "We were prepared for the possibility that they might use [pepper spray], but no one was prepared for the stinging pain, all over the body," said Tort. "I lost my sight for forty minutes."[13] Tort, who belongs to a group called Self-Convened Professors in Resistance and Solidarity (PARES), felt strongly about supporting an audit of the debt. "The audit would reveal, one, how much of the debt is illegal, two, who is responsible for putting together the illegal bonds that were sold, and three, who was involved in the underwriting," he said.

While the student movement shared some similarities with the one that took place in 2010, there were important differences, largely involving the increased urgency of the island's fiscal crisis. "Back in 2010 students were fighting against a raise in tuition and an additional charge of $800 annually," said María de Lourdes Vaello, a first-year law student and activist. "The purpose of the university is to provide a high-quality education to the middle and lower classes, but now we're facing cuts that threaten the very existence of the institution. It's a much bigger moment."

Tort felt that the 2010 movement was important because it abandoned the hierarchical structure of the old left in favor of horizontalism, creating a new organizational base. "The difference is, despite the fact that the mobilization is happening over the cuts to the UPR budget, they're now linking to the general issue of the austerity measures imposed by the Fiscal Oversight and Management Board," he said. "It's the basis for what we hope to be a national movement against austerity measures in favor of the debt audit, in favor of a moratorium on payment on those portions of the debt that are illegal or illegitimate, and in favor of restructuring the debt so that the payments are linked to investments in economic development and the common good of the country."

The unrest at the universities, particularly on the storied main campus in Rio Piedras, a district of San Juan south of the colonial city, was happening at a key moment in PROMESA's process. On May 1 the freeze on debt litigation from creditors, one of the features of fiscal-oversight boards in general, would expire. Up to that moment there had been very little if any progress made on presettlement negotiations. It was widely expected that one of the two debt-settlement provisions of PROMESA, Title III, would be invoked. It provided for a continued stay on creditors, preventing any court cases to collect debt from going forward, and requiring that a debt-restructuring plan be formulated. This would be handled in a pseudo-bankruptcy court run by a US circuit court judge. Presumably it would allow the kind of bargaining that Detroit took advantage of in its reduction of debt just years before.

Yet the Title III provision brought into play again the strange silence—or sleight of hand—the players in this drama had been using to portray PROMESA as a fair process that would offer Puerto Rico the kind of debt relief and path forward it needed. The stay on creditors seemed positive, but the path forward was still envisioned as an ability or demonstration of creditworthiness so as to return access to the capital markets. Title III was conceived as a way to create a kind of bankruptcy proceeding that could play out under PROMESA's rules rather than conventional bankruptcy as well as a way to

keep all the murky and largely undisclosed behavior of Puerto
Rico's government, its development bank, its financial sector,
and its Wall Street enablers to escape scrutiny from those outside the loop.

In August 2016 I was invited to a conference put together by
the Ravitch Fiscal Reporting Program at the Craig Newmark
Graduate School of Journalism at the City University of New
York. During that conference then Governor García Padilla appeared via Skype to take questions from those attending, including journalists from the *New York Times*, the *Wall Street Journal*,
and *Bloomberg News*. When I asked García Padilla if he'd heard
of the preliminary audit report that was filed in the summer of
2016, after PROMESA was signed into law, he at first said he
hadn't understood my question. After it was repeated, he merely
invoked a platitude about all attempts at transparency being
welcome. At that point Richard Ravitch approached me, pulled
me aside, and correctly explained that Title III of PROMESA
contained explicit language about doing just that—auditing the
debt. All parties would be able to testify and wrangle over griev-
ances during the Title III court hearings. But this would be
a debt audit that would be entirely supervised by the FOMB,
which ultimately outsourced the job to Wall Street accounting
firm Kobre & Kim in 2018.

Months later Ravitch, who rose to fame as a negotiator
during the New York fiscal crisis, disclosed that he had been
retained by García Padilla as his representative on the FOMB
and would continue to play a role as the PROMESA process
played out on the island. He had famously been credited with
convincing New York City teachers' union head Albert Shanker,
over a desperate feast of matzo crackers, to prevent New York
City from going into bankruptcy by making up its shortfall with
teachers' pension funds.[14] In 2014 he had also volunteered to
play a major consultant role in Detroit's bankruptcy proceedings. Unsurprisingly—or not—he was convinced that Title III
was Puerto Rico's last, best chance and was uninterested in a
citizen-run or independent audit, just like most of the actors

who had been promoting the narrative that PROMESA was about saving Puerto Rico.

By the end of April 2017, with new governor Ricardo Rosselló in power, Puerto Rico's government dissolved its own independent citizens' audit debt commission, which had been signed into law by García Padilla in 2015, claiming that the $2 million expense of running it was too costly. In its place the island's Senate passed a resolution requiring the US comptroller general to audit the debt, which it correctly claimed is provided for by PROMESA. Opposition party PDP senator Eduardo Bhatia countered by insisting that "Section 411 of PROMESA does not say that, it does not say that an audit will be done; it says that a report will be made on how the debt is increasing and decreasing, and that it will have some elements. That's not a debt audit; it's a debt report."[15]

The tension climaxed on May Day in San Juan, when several streams of demonstrators—worker and student groups, faculty members, a feminist contingent, street artists, and an increasingly politicized middle class—coming from different points around the city converged at the Milla de Oro (Golden Mile) in the Hato Rey business district. The crowd, numbering tens of thousands, came to hear a mix of speeches and musical acts on a stage set up in front of the World Plaza Building, which once housed the failed Westernbank and in April had acquired a new tenant: the FOMB.

The protest—which was centered around proposed budget cuts and tuition increases for the university system but became a lightning rod for objections to austerity and the power of the FOMB—was massive and peaceful. There was an almost festive atmosphere. Still, there was a great deal of angst and concern over the future of the island and its public institutions. The demonstrators had no idea that by week's end the governor and the FOMB would invoke Title III of PROMESA. This began a legal process that would lead to a form of bankruptcy, one many believed would be weighted toward the creditors' interests, intensifying the air of uncertainty over the island's future.

The Milla de Oro represents the triumph of modernity that US colonialism intended to bring to Puerto Rico in the 1950s and 1960s. A palm-tree-lined boulevard called Luis Muñoz Rivera Avenue, festooned with glass-box buildings housing banks and corporate offices, signaled a level of prosperity that didn't exist in the rest of the Caribbean. Now that the FOMB was headquartered there, it became even more of a symbol of an external force symptomatic of the lack of democracy on the island and emblematic of Puerto Rico's second-class status.

The crowd gathered around the stage on Muñoz Rivera Avenue was unaware that just around the corner on Bolivar Street a small, rogue contingent of masked demonstrators was throwing stones at the main headquarters of Banco Popular, the island's largest bank, shattering some of its largest windows. Police—regular forces and the riot squad—reacted aggressively, moving into the area and marching en masse toward the main stage down the block. They launched tear-gas canisters and pushed into the crowd as stage announcer Millie Gil, a local media personality, was desperately calling for calm. "Don't be provoked. . . . We don't want the headlines of tomorrow's newspapers to say that we lost control of a peaceful demonstration!" she pleaded.[16]

But the police, even after a negotiated standoff with impartial observers from Amnesty International, the Puerto Rico chapter of the ACLU, and the Colegio de Abogados (the Puerto Rico Bar Association), engaged in continual confrontations with protesters, pushing, striking, and gassing peaceful demonstrators and masked provocateurs alike. This was not unlike the pattern observed during the protests of 2010–2011, when the police force brought in heavily outfitted riot squad personnel who escalated conflict after provoking mild pushback from the more militant demonstrators.[17]

Images of vandals, tear gas, and students running under late-day thunderstorms dominated the evening news. It was a tailor-made media op for the conservative, law-and-order statehood party (NPP) government. Governor Ricardo Rosselló held a press conference denouncing the vandalism, but he lumped the vandals together with the marchers. His tone of moral opprobrium was underscored the next morning in a staged media tableau that showed him helping workers sweep up shattered glass in front of the Banco Popular tower.

The mayor of San Juan, Carmen Yulín Cruz, as well as Representative Manuel Natal Albelo, who was one of the first elected officials to champion the idea of an independent debt audit, quickly denounced the governor equating peaceful protesters with vandals. The ACLU's William Ramírez held a lengthy press conference in which he, still recovering from the effects of the tear gas he endured while acting as a negotiator and observer, displayed the tear-gas canisters and even rubber bullets that the police had used. His statement directly contradicted one made earlier by Police Superintendent Michelle Hernández, who denied their use. Ramírez also criticized excessive use of force and violations of protocol, including the lack of warnings and plainclothes officers not wearing badges.

Eyebrows had also been raised when Banco Popular filed a lawsuit on the afternoon of the protests and disturbances. The lawsuit named forty-two plaintiffs, including community organizations, labor unions, and "unknown demonstrators." Ariadna Godreau-Aubert, a human-rights lawyer at a legal action committee devoted to drawing attention to frivolous suits brought to intimidate people who take part in demonstrations, found the suit to be highly irregular and part of a disturbing pattern. "This suit came out just an hour after the events, and even the president of the Banco Popular said that the lawsuit was made in a preventive way, that they had it ready in case something happened. You can't have a demand ready in case something happens—lawsuits exist to remedy real damages and include people that caused real damages, not something prepared or speculative," she said. Godreau-Aubert pointed out that a previous suit against demonstrators engaging in another protest in late April was dismissed because of lack of evidence.

The following week Governor Rosselló signed into law revisions in the penal code that increased criminal penalties against demonstrators who wear masks, seemingly aimed at students and young protesters; made it a crime to obstruct construction sites (up to three years in prison), aimed at union protests; and imposed a fine of up to $30,000 for interfering with tourist activities, spurred perhaps by the closure of an access road to the airport on May Day, and for obstructing access to or functions in health or government offices or learning institutions.

This last element was particularly relevant because, just days after the governor and the PROMESA board invoked the Title III clause and its modified bankruptcy provision, Education Secretary Julia Keleher announced that 179 public schools around the island would be closed. Although the continued population exodus from the island has decreased the number of enrolled students, the closures still heavily affected poor and working-class areas and placed on many families an increased burden of extra commuting time to more distant schools.

Many political observers derided Governor Rosselló's decision to request the invocation of Title III, recalling his previous insistence that the island could pay its debt in a restructuring process that would not require bankruptcy proceedings. PDP senator Bhatia filed an injunction to force the release of a copy of the proposed budget the governor had sent to José Carrión, the head of the FOMB, arguing that the island's citizens were entitled to full transparency.[18]

The Title III proceedings began on May 3, presided over by New York District Court Judge Laura Taylor Swain. Taylor Swain is an African American appointed by Bill Clinton in 2000 and a bankruptcy judge ostensibly not particularly aligned with Wall Street bankers. The primary order of business would be to focus on the fates of the COFINA and general obligation bonds. Although the matters would be considered "jointly," creditors from the two sides began warring against each other, each claiming priority. The two groups of creditors generally represented two types of investors. GO bond investors had fewer late arriving vultures and felt strongly that their investments should be paid in full because of the Puerto Rico Constitution's requirements, whereas COFINA investors featured more vultures who knew that the sales tax that backed their investments was not going away anytime soon and could count on direct extraction from whatever population remained over decades.

There were many troublesome aspects about the debt-restructuring negotiations. First, pensioners remained a potent force as they attempted to claim a higher priority on a debt that, also part of the restructuring process, added $49 billion to the already contested $70-plus billion bond debt; the government might be forced to sell off a substantial amount of its properties to lessen the blow of the "haircuts," or downward negotiation of payouts to creditors. Next, collective-bargaining agreements with unions representing government workers might be suspended to renegotiate contracts. Finally, the "absolute priority" rule in PROMESA for the general-obligation debt of $12.7 billion might mean it must be paid in full.

But a huge problem was also developing, a political one. Governor Rosselló, the executive branch, and the legislature would be stripped of much of its power because the FOMB would need to approve all of its budget appropriations. Consequently, the government would be limited to the role of manufacturing good public relations for its stances for and against the FOMB and the judge's rulings. The imposition of the FOMB forced Puerto Rico's government to practically cede control of the majority of the issues that had to do with developing public policy. Rosselló's government would still create a budget and fiscal plan, but it would not be enacted unless approved by the FOMB and could not be changed after its certification. In effect, Puerto Rico's democratic process, in which the people elect legislatures to make decisions about its policies and finances, was in trouble.

That August the FOMB and the government were openly engaged in a kind of theater of the absurd. Their periodic meetings—technically open to the public but held before a restricted audience required to register beforehand—were being held in both San Juan and the financial district in New York. Some also took place at the luxurious Hotel El Conquistador in Fajardo, a remote fishing town on the island's northeast corner, far from the urban milieu of protest in the capital city of San Juan.

On one such occasion, with few public spectators besides members of the press, bond-holding reps, and policy wonks, the meeting was held in a sterile conference room resembling that of any US hotel chain. Over the course of about two hours La Junta went through the motions of hearing fiscal-plan testimony, making resolutions, voting, asking each other questions, and almost robotically responding with prepared texts. Then, seemingly out of nowhere, a sharp exchange between the government of Puerto Rico's nonvoting representative and members of the FOMB revealed the growing tension. La Junta announced a plan that would impose unpaid furloughs on government employees two days a month, claiming that the resulting savings of $218 million were "necessary to ensure that the proper budget savings are achieved." Although the proposal was a step down from the original plan of four days per month, Christian Sobrino—who, as the representative of Governor Ricardo Rosselló, had no vote—strongly took issue with the move. "On the issue of furloughs the government understands that a line has to be drawn. There will be no furloughs. You can take that to the bank," he announced without irony. The confrontation seemed to signal that, while Rosselló's government would for the most part cooperate with La Junta on the goals and cost-saving strategies of the fiscal plan, the government would wield what little political capital and autonomy it had on a few key issues.

The only problem was that back in March Rosselló's NPP (pro-statehood) government unreservedly celebrated La Junta's certification of the fiscal plan—including the *four* days of furloughs per month—as a triumph that left behind the "times of incoherence and improvisation" that previous governments had promulgated. Junta board member Carlos García bristled in his response to Sobrino, insisting that "the government representative said nothing in March; nobody said there was any opposition. The government has known about this."

Meanwhile the media and several elected officials of the pro-commonwealth and pro-independence parties reacted with skepticism toward the government's sudden decision to embrace confrontation. Crusading PDP (pro-commonwealth) representative Manuel Natal Albelo called it an attempt to "save face with public servants," an argument to cast La Junta as "the bad guy. But the reality is that they are both the mother and father of this." Even Sobrino joked about his outburst when, as the press assembled for a Q&A following the Junta meeting, he remarked, "If this were a drama we would be nominated for an Oscar."

In that same meeting the FOMB finally announced it would create a committee to "investigate" the debt. A petition in Title III bankruptcy court for a forensic debt investigation had motivated the action. That petition, which was lodged by a group of creditors holding unsecured debt, seemed to have unnerved both the government and the FOMB.

The following week the FOMB filed suit against Rosselló, claiming that in March neither he nor his then representative in FOMB, Elías Sánchez, raised an objection to the furloughs, when the fiscal plan was approved, nor in June, when the budget was approved. The suit claimed that "Congress provided [the FOMB] sole and complete discretion regarding the fiscal plan certification decisions."

The FOMB was making it clear that it had always been a *control* board hiding behind the euphemism "oversight and management." Ironically, the "oversight" language had first appeared in former governor García Padilla's term, when he suggested an oversight board as part of the law he proposed to allow Puerto Rico to write its own bankruptcy terms. It was picked up on, as described in the last chapter, in the Treasury Department–driven push to create the PROMESA mechanism for debt restructuring.

The process of PROMESA was deliberate, creating the board's opportunity to become the central authority in Puerto Rico in stealth-like fashion. Embedded in its directive to rein in expenses by cutting budgets and labor force and promote privatization of publicly owned resources and properties were other, more subtle mechanisms. In both the monthly FOMB meetings and the Title III court of Taylor Swain, under the mandate of debt restructuring, there were decisions made that may result in long-term suffering for Puerto Ricans. One is the suppression of a forensic debt audit that could at least cause massive political protest as well as a moral authority to pressure the reduction of the debt—keeping in mind that PROMESA's language seems to imply that all debts can be collected, even if they were made illegally. The other is probably the main reason for PROMESA's swift implementation: a series of court rulings that would foster debt deals that would be considerably more favorable to creditors than if Puerto Rico had real bankruptcy protection.

Two 2018 decisions in Taylor Swain's court illustrated the kinds of debt settlement deals that create a terrible burden on the people of Puerto Rico: the deal to settle PREPA's debt, which not only set unfavorable terms but primed the Electrical Authority for privatization, and the COFINA deal, in which creditors were granted 55 cents on the dollar in the form of bond swaps. But Taylor Swain's ruling months earlier on a lawsuit brought by disgruntled creditors over the unconstitutionality of the FOMB itself, claiming it was invalid because the way its members were appointed violated the Constitution's Appointments Clause, was an even more chilling indication of Puerto Rico's powerlessness as an unincorporated territory. In rejecting the claim, Taylor Swain opined that "Congress has plenary power under the Territories Clause to establish governmental institutions for territories that are not only distinct from federal government entities but include features that would not comport with the requirements of the Constitution if they pertained to the governance of the United States."

In other words, because Puerto Rico is a territory rather than a state, the FOMB can basically do anything it wants without needing to worry about constitutionality. The unerring logic of "belonging to, but not a part of"—essentially an abstraction based on race and racism—was for a moment given legal cover by a moderate-liberal African American judge from Brooklyn. A court of appeals overturned Taylor Swain's ruling in February 2019, allowing the FOMB to continue to operate while giving the Trump administration ninety days to either reappoint the members or appoint new ones. In May 2019 he opted to reappoint the existing board.

In August of 2018 the FOMB released a 615-page report by independent investigators Kobre & Kim that cost $3 million. The report was extremely thorough, documenting many of the abuses that have been recounted here and in much of the reporting by independent groups like the Hedge Clippers and the Action Center on Race and the Economy. It found that ending Section 936 exacerbated the pattern of borrowing and that the GDB was irresponsible and vulnerable to interest-rate swaps, incurred massive underwriting fees, and was not transparent, which further inhibited detection of Puerto Rico's descent into an economic death spiral. Yet when Kobre & Kim interviewed key witnesses, it was not done under oath, and the questions were not as probing as they should have been.

Regarding one set of swaps, known as the GO Basis Swaps of 2006, under the administration of Aníbal Acevedo Vilá, the report reads,

We interviewed the lead banker on Goldman's Puerto Rico team in 2005, who was identified by GDB management and in contemporaneous documents, as having proposed the legislation or advocated for the Swaps. When we asked this senior Goldman investment banker if he was involved in drafting or commenting on the 2005 legislation, he told us he did not recall. We also asked him if someone on his team would have been designated to comment on or draft the legislation. He told us he did not recall. When we asked the senior Goldman investment banker about the GO Basis Swaps specifically, he told us he did not recall the specifics of any Swap transaction, including where an Issuer received upfront money as part of a Swap, and did not recall any pitches Goldman made in connection with a Swap.

In another commentary on the preference for higher-risk investments, with neither UBS (a Swiss multinational investment bank) nor Santander Banks communicating the terms of those risks to local investors, the report revealed,

> The witness noted that bank clients routinely sidestepped tailored investment strategies in order to weigh their portfolios heavily with fully tax-exempt investments, namely Puerto Rico–Related Bonds and Local CEFs. Santander Securities' witnesses did not recall the same wide disparity between the popularity of Santander Securities' Local CEFs and Santander Securities' offerings in open-end funds.

Apparently, few feet were held to the fire. The FOMB report, while impressively detailed and packed with relevant details, was content to describe much of what happened without explaining why it happened and whether that should be taken into account when deciding the fate of the staggering, overwhelming debt, which was four times as much as Detroit had incurred. This is not to mention the much more favorable deals Detroit got, where legal violations involved in incurring the debt were understood to warrant significantly reducing the principal in many cases. By acting as Puerto Rico's representative in debt restructuring, the FOMB produced a report that fell short in protecting the interests of a municipality filled with US citizens.

"The report does a great job in many ways—I agree with the practical recommendations and there were a couple of interesting nuggets," said Alvin Velazquez, a longtime lawyer for SEIU who has testified before Congress on PROMESA. "They go after the drug users, but not the drug dealers; they put all the blame on the politicians." If anything, the Kobre & Kim report demonstrates that both the Commonwealth and pro-Statehood parties failed the Puerto Rican people almost equally by not facing the reality of restructuring the debt sooner, instead continuing to borrow to stave off the inevitable.

Late in November 2008 the Puerto Rico Center for Investigative Journalism (CIJPR) revealed that the FOMB was an even more direct imposition of Congress than previously imagined. Having sued for the FOMB's emails through a Freedom of Investigation Act request, the CIJPR published several that clearly demonstrated that members of the board, including its chairman, were receiving direct instruction from members of Congress regarding the terms of austerity they required. These actions belie the language of PROMESA, which states that the FOMB "shall not be considered to be a department, agency, establishment or instrumentality of the Federal Government."

The emails included an exchange between Andrew Vercera, who works for Rob Bishop in his capacity as chairman of the House Natural resource committee, and FOMB chair Carrión. In one email to Carrión, Vercera tells him that "we wanted to reiterate the power the Board has in regards to the Fiscal Plans to push back on the Governor's recent actions." To which Carrión responded, "We understand this is essential to our mandate and will hunker down."[19] The emails show a strong suggestion by Bishop's subordinate that the FOMB make sure to exert its power over a fiscal plan that might be unacceptable to Governor Rosselló or other Puerto Rican elected officials. Although the original mandate of PROMESA is that the FOMB should not be an agent of the Federal Government and a representative of Puerto Rico's interests in debt restructuring, one might think it to be autonomous. But this autonomy appears even more limited than that promised by the commonwealth status itself.

All of this, of course, doesn't even shed light on the role that Governor Rosselló plays. While he purports to act as a defender of the Puerto Rico government and its people, he also remains complicit with the politics of austerity and creating as much opportunity for opportunistic "disaster capitalists" as possible. Although he suffers from an inevitable decline in popularity because of how clearly his government has dramatically limited power, he and the NPP are essentially in the process of normalizing an authoritarian government that uses its base to ensure that popular movements run into plenty of interference. Because of the way the imposition of PROMESA has eviscerated the idea of the commonwealth and made attempts to petition for statehood even more inert than before, the argument over Puerto Rico's political status has been rendered moot.

Puerto Rico's long-running status debate was premised on the existence of the commonwealth as a semi-autonomous state that straddled the boundaries between its association with the United States and sovereignty. Pro-statehood and pro-independence forces argued against it as a form of colonialism, and they have been proven correct. However, granting statehood is not likely, given that support was low before, as Congress was hesitant to take on new expenditures to support entitlement programs and any push for independence is weighed down by the fact that the island territory is far from economic self-sufficiency. The new normal created by PROMESA in a post-hurricane world has opened up new possibilities for Puerto Rico's politics far beyond its long-running status debate.

CHAPTER 6

STATUS UPDATE?

Puerto Rico senator Eduardo Bhatia (PDP) at a 2017 legislative hearing in San Juan.
© Joseph Rodríguez

"Puerto Rico was not being groomed . . . for independence or statehood. Puerto Rico was to be held in perpetuity, or as long as needed, firmly under the control of Congress."
—José Trías Monge,
Puerto Rico: The Trials of the Oldest Colony in the World

"The political status of Puerto Rico is one of free association with the American Union. It is a new way of abolishing a colonial status under the constitutional system of the United States. I do not say that the details of our relationship cannot be improved, both from the point of view of the American Union and that of Puerto Rico, but the principle that such relationship, however it may change, is one of free agreement, makes the step we have taken the definite one in self-government."
—**Luis Muñoz Marín,** from a speech delivered
at the University of Kansas City, April 23, 1955

"This year Puerto Rico celebrates its hundredth anniversary as a territory of the United States. Let's let them freely express their status preference and if they choose, let's welcome them as the fifty-first state. It's only fitting that a Republican Congress should give the people of Puerto Rico what so many Republican presidents sought to achieve: a way to determine for themselves the government they should have."
—**Ralph Reed,** Century Strategies, from "Remarks before the
Puerto Rico Chamber of Commerce," February 5, 1998

On July 25, 1952, Luis Muñoz Marín, the first elected governor of Puerto Rico, gave the speech that inaugurated the new commonwealth, or Estado Libre Asociado (Free Associated State) status for the island territory. Until the ascension of Muñoz Marín, all of Puerto Rico's governors had been appointed by the US government, and the island's status as an unincorporated territory was just that: colony, territory, non-state, ultimately ruled by external forces. The new ELA status was an idea that germinated through a connection between Muñoz Marín, President Franklin Roosevelt, and his appointed liberal governor, Rexford Tugwell. It was finally carried out by the Truman administration, motivated by the UN's pressure on the world's major powers to decolonize after World War II.

On that day Muñoz Marín made a long and rambling speech that compared unfavorably in terms of dynamism and charisma with his archrival, the nationalist leader Albizu Campos, whose driving oratory style had motivated a popular movement that threatened US rule over the island. The central theme of Muñoz Marín's speech was the lone-star flag that anticolonialists had used since the 1890s and had been prohibited in 1948 by a Puerto Rican law that resembled something from the repressive McCarthy era designed to harass suspected communists. At the end of his speech Muñoz Marín raised the flag in public for the first time since its prohibition, declaring, "This flag is for all Puerto Ricans, without exception. For those who have used it with the terrorism of the past and those who display it as a symbol of peace in the present."

Muñoz Marín's speech and raising of the flag as a symbol of the commonwealth were both attempting to put an end to a period of nationalist violence that had destabilized Puerto Rico and marking the beginning of a political era that would ultimately be defined by three political parties primarily driven by their support of one of three status options—commonwealth, statehood, and independence. These categories are a kind of reinvention or replication of earlier categories that went as far back as the nineteenth century, during Spanish colonialism. Back then they were called autonomy, assimilation, and separatism. The separatist movement made its big splash with the Grito de Lares rebellion in 1868. However, after the Spanish revolution and subsequent abolition of slavery in 1873, Puerto Rican politics under Spain were dominated by a bipolar opposition between a Liberal Reformist Party, which preferred reform that would favor autonomist "Creole" (Puerto Rican–born) interests, and the Liberal Conservative Party, "assimilationists" who favored the interests of those born in or who held strong ties to Spain.

The Liberal Conservative Party eventually became obsolete because it was grounded in the Creole/Peninsular dichotomy that dominated Latin American discourse and political parties. It faded in the face of shifting power dynamics of transitioning from Spanish to US colonialism. That transition was marked by the poignant episode in which the Liberal Reformist Party, renamed the Liberal Autonomist Unionist Party—led by Luis Muñoz Marín's father, newspaper publisher Luis Muñoz Rivera—briefly succeeded in reaching an agreement with Spain for autonomous rule and Muñoz Rivera became Puerto Rico's first autonomous prime minister. The new government was supposed to take power in May 1898 but was delayed by the onset of the US war with Spain. The nascent legislature managed to convene on July 17, but eight days later, on July 25, US forces landed in Puerto Rico's southern port of Guánica. Puerto Rico's politics was turned upside down as the US government appointed the eleven-member executive council and military governor, effectively taking away any semblance of self-rule for which Puerto Ricans had fought for thirty years.

Yet slowly a new political landscape, entirely a reaction to the US colonial apparatus, began to take shape. Muñoz Rivera resurrected his Autonomist Party as the Federal Party for five years between 1899 and 1904. During that time they controlled most of the municipalities in local elections. Meanwhile, in 1899, José Celso Barbosa, an Afro–Puerto Rican physician who had once belonged to the Autonomist Party, created the Republican Party, which favored statehood. The US government appointed Barbosa and some fellow Republicans to the Executive Council, setting up the political opposition lines between autonomism and assimilation, or annexation as some would call it.

In 1904, after years of frustration with the lack of real political power, Muñoz Rivera formed a new coalition, the Unionist Party. It incorporated pro-statehood, pro-autonomist, and pro-independence factions, united by Puerto Ricans' desire to make their own political decisions. They called for the creation of an Estado Libre Asociado, or Free Associated State.[1] That was three years after *Downes vs. Bidwell Insular* was decided, famously stating that Puerto Rico belonged to but was not a part of the United States. Again, the undercurrent of racial difference exemplified by the racist testimony in Congress after the acquisition of Puerto Rico and reinforced by the discriminatory Insular cases decided by the Supreme Court served to undermine Puerto Rican self-determination. While not rejecting the citizenship granted them through the Jones Act in 1917, they wanted to free themselves from strict colonial rule.

Dissatisfied Unionist Party members formed the Nationalist Party in 1922, with future leader Pedro Albizu Campos joining as vice president two years later. By 1932, after a temporary alliance between pro-statehood Republicans and Liberal Unionists, the Unionist Party separated into the Liberal and Republican Parties, with the Liberal Party abandoning autonomism for independence. A short-lived alliance between Republicans and socialists threatened the Liberals, demonstrating the strength of the emerging constituencies of Puerto Rican workers, who had been taught to organize in part by the arrival of Samuel Gompers and the American Federation of Labor earlier in the century. The onset of the Great Depression served to focus Puerto Rican politics on the fate of the working class and not so much on status change. Albizu Campos supported a series of labor strikes that fused his Nationalist Party with working movements and created a new militant strength in the party.

In 1938 Luis Muñoz Marín founded the Popular Democratic Party. The PDP, which reneged on its call for independence in favor of a kind of populism, had been working since the late 1930s to co-opt the radical separatism of Pedro Albizu Campos's Nationalist Party and the land- and labor-reform policies of the socialist-labor coalition called the Central General de Trabajadores (General Confederation of Workers). It found a natural ally in surviving New Deal elements of the FDR years. President

Harry S. Truman, who had recently declared that the old ways of "imperialism" had no place in America's postwar vision, even gave the PDP his blessing. But in retrospect Truman's moral pronouncement was a euphemistic device developed by US policy makers to grant a limited sovereignty to camouflage Puerto Rico's still-existing unincorporated territory status. By creating the commonwealth status, also known as the Estado Libre Asociado (ELA), the US government postponed Puerto Rico's quest for nationhood indefinitely.

Puerto Rican politics were restructured after the ELA was established. This was accomplished through the fiction that, with a new constitution and a political status that seemed to afford limited sovereignty, Puerto Rico's ultimate quest for statehood or independence held a new position of strength. It firmly entrenched its political discourse in a debate over the three status options that defined its three major political parties. Earlier attempts to bring about independence had been significantly disrupted by the unrelenting repression of nationalist and anticolonial discourse made possible first and foremost by the Gag Law, or La Ley de Mordaza. This law was approved by Governor Jesús Piñero, the first appointed Puerto Rico governor, and Muñoz Marín, despite protests against prohibiting speech or actions that advocated for the end of US control of the island. It was arguably part of a US attempt to control speech about independence when it was trying to bring about a new form of Puerto Rican political status in the new era of decolonization.

An almost exact copy of the Smith Act of 1940 (formerly the Alien Registration Act), which made it a criminal offense to advocate for the violent overthrow of the government, the Gag Law suppressed tens of thousands of votes for the Independence Party in the 1948, 1952, and 1956 gubernatorial elections; muffled dissent at the University of Puerto Rico, a pro-independence hotbed; and provoked Nationalist Party members to commit violent acts protesting it. These acts produced an even more efficient backlash from the government, which was still ruled by a US-appointed governor.[2]

During the first fifty years of US control over the island there were various early parties, such as the Socialist Party, the Unionist Party, the Federal Party, and, of course, the Liberal and Republican Parties—the forerunners of today's commonwealth pro-independence and pro-statehood parties. This multitude of political forces created an unstable landscape of pluralism and interparty coalitions. However, the post-ELA era would feature a near replication of the US two-party system, represented by the pro-statehood NPP and the pro-commonwealth PDP, with the Puerto Rican Independence Party adding a muted third option, albeit one that, in an informal way, was aspirational for many Puerto Ricans who, despite their pragmatic status preference, favor independence in their hearts.

There is a tension between what is apparently a two-party system and the reality that many want independence but don't see it as a realistic political goal because of colonialism, global economic realities, and US-led repression, creating a dense layer of surrealism to Puerto Rican politics. In addition, the island's politics are in an almost permanently atrophied state because political discourse prioritizes the status question over local social, political, and economic concerns. Perhaps most importantly, the fictitious "commonwealth" and its delay of a real solution to Puerto Rico's status has made the island vulnerable to corruption, helping to perpetuate its untenable economic development and ultimate descent into debt crisis.

Today most Puerto Ricans—both on the island and the diaspora—wrestle with the ineluctable contradiction between putting the status debate and even the formal aspects of decolonization on hold and the reality that because of its history as a colonial possession, Puerto Ricans, both within and outside the island's territory, have a kind of hyper-obsession with national identity. The Spirit Republic of Puerto Rico, created by a coalition of Nuyorican artists and activists like Pedro Pietri, Adál Maldonado, and Eddie Figueroa, issued a Spirit Republic of Puerto Rico Passport. It was a kind of satirical art performance in the 1990s in Uptown art spaces in which officials would issue anyone a passport from an "imaginary nation," perhaps inspired by island independence activist Juan Mari Bras, who in 1994 traveled to Venezuela to renounce his US citizenship in the hopes that asserting his local residence in Puerto Rico would resonate. In the late-twentieth-century media environment, where logos and branding had become paramount, all three political parties began to use the lone-star Puerto Rican flag, all attempting to claim national identities within the context of independence, commonwealth, and statehood.

The racial and cultural differences distinguishing Puerto Ricans from stateside Americans motivate Puerto Ricans' sense of national identity. Puerto Ricans do not "see themselves" as mainstream Americans—this can mean lack of identification with either blackness or whiteness, although a racism persists on the island. Many don't speak English as their preferred language, and they often seem untethered from the central aspects of American music, dance, and culinary culture. Yet pro-commonwealth forces have often presented this distinct national identity as a way to "have it all," to "be ourselves and US citizens at the same time." Statehooders, meanwhile, imagine full US citizenship and direct participation in state and federal government, despite maintaining a unique national identity that does not adhere to the established tenets of quotidian American life.

The installment of Muñoz Marín's PDP government in 1949 began a period of dominance by the pro-commonwealth party. This was particularly true because the pro-independence or nationalist movements and parties had been repressed, and the new commonwealth status had temporarily rendered statehood forces irrelevant. The blunting of nationalism was carried out not only by the Gag Law but also the onset of FBI surveillance, begun by Director J. Edgar Hoover, who mandated the creation of dossiers on independence activists and sympathizers. When the *carpetas*, or FBI files, were finally made public in 1987, they revealed that the FBI had tracked upward of seventy-five thousand people.[3]

Many of those under surveillance were members of the Puerto Rico Independence Party (PIP), formed in 1946 by

Gilberto Concepción de Gracia, Fernando Milán Suárez, and Antonio J. González as the electoral wing of the Nationalist movement. Concepción de Gracia was a one-time lawyer for Pedro Albizu Campos and great-uncle of René Pérez Joglar and Ileana Pérez Joglar of the alternative rap group Calle 13 as well as *Hamilton* playwright and protagonist Lin-Manuel Miranda. The PIP has pursued a rigorous pro-independence agenda regardless of the fate of the Nationalist Party's leader, who was imprisoned for most of his life, and they garnered 19 percent in the 1952 election that made Luis Muñoz Marín governor. Their politics can best be described as democratic socialist, and at times they make strange bedfellows with the NPP, with whom they agree that Puerto Rico's current status can best be described as "colony."

The PIP appeals to a broader group of voters than their vote totals—less than 10 percent and usually around 5 percent—usually indicate. There is a bloc of Puerto Rican voters sometimes referred to as *melones*, or melons, because they are "green" on the outside and "red" on the inside, meaning they openly support Independence Party policies (their main color is green) but vote for the PDP (whose color is red). They apparently have the aspirations of independence close to their hearts but vote pragmatically for pro-commonwealth PDP candidates, much as a Bernie Sanders voter may have voted for Hillary Clinton in 2016.

The PIP's main figurehead over the years has been Rubén Berríos, a perpetual candidate for governor and constant critic of US policy and presence on the island. He was most prominent during the resistance to the US naval base on the island of Vieques, even as major figures of the PDP and NPP voiced their support for its closure. Although the PIP enjoyed a period of popularity in the years after the commonwealth was formed, the pro-statehood forces regrouped. By the mid-1960s they had formed the New Progressive Party and, in 1967, forced the first plebiscite—or nonbinding—vote on changing or retaining Puerto Rico's political status.

There have been four plebiscites on Puerto Rico's status—
in 1967, 1993, 1998, and 2012. All have been complicated by
vague and sometimes inaccurate descriptions on the ballot of
what "commonwealth" meant. At times the commonwealth
choice reflected the desires of the PDP to present an option
for enhancing the status to allow for greater autonomy in self-
governance, adhering to federal tax laws, engaging in trade with
other countries, and receiving entitlement program benefits.
Further complicating the matter was the fact that the autonomy
baked into the commonwealth status was largely illusory and
detracted from a coherent idea of what exactly the status is. In
the first two plebiscites, held in 1967 and 1993, commonwealth
won, with statehood gaining more traction in 1993. But the last
two plebiscites were strongly disputed votes favoring statehood
and largely boycotted by the PDP because the plebiscites were
designed during a period of NPP control of the executive and
legislative branches. The high participation in most Puerto Rican elections reflected voters' passion, as they turn out to vote
at a much higher rate than their US counterparts. However, the
plebiscites were largely symbolic in nature because they were
nonbinding and Congress never took the voting results seriously.

Although in some ways the adversarial nature of the PDP
and the NPP parallel the opposition between US Democrats
and Republicans, there is a lot of overlap and divided loyalties that reflect the US–Puerto Rico colonial relationship. In a
sense the PDP and the PIP represent a politics that stands for
a notion of self-determination while continually falling short
of it. But the NPP essentially acts as a Trojan horse for US bipartisan politics within the island territory's politics through its
ties to both Republicans and Democrats. It has long sustained
itself through lobbying on K Street while ostensibly offering its
voters the illusory promise of statehood. Although the NPP will
most likely never achieve its stated goal, it has succeeded in
creating conflicts of interest with that goal by participating in
the cutting edge of neoliberal politics, where government has
allowed a hostile takeover from global corporations and finance

capital, and political influence is bought and sold like commodity shares on the floor of the New York Stock Exchange.

The evolution of current politics in Puerto Rico is intimately tied with two intertwined phenomena: the conscious yet somewhat covert policy carried out by the NPP to engage both the US Republican and Democratic parties and the acceleration of attempts to influence Washington focusing on K Street lobbying, which has an outsized influence on congressional wheeling and dealing. The former was belied by the NPP's often clear association with conservative Republican rhetoric: the law-and-order regimes of Carlos Romero Barceló and Pedro Rosselló from the 1970s to the 1990s; Luis Fortuño's and Ricardo Rosselló's invocation of Catholicism and family values; and the embrace of downsizing government, cutting taxes, and privatization. Yet the NPP could extract various concessions from Democrats, particularly concerning issues like releasing political prisoners and increasing federal entitlement programs. Because of this, they cultivated strong ties with the Democratic Party as well, with some of its major figures actively enrolling in the Democratic Party itself, like Rosselló father and son, and Pedro Pierluisi, former resident commissioner.

The origins of the NPP's shift toward influencing both parties in Washington apparently began during the Romero Barceló administration in 1979. This happened at the same time that the commonwealth government and the ELA in general were reeling from the period of recession that ended the heyday of Operation Bootstrap and Puerto Rico being held up as the "Showcase of the Caribbean." When the governor and the Commonwealth of Puerto Rico were facing lawsuits from the families of two murdered independentistas in the Cerro Maravilla case, which the government had covered up despite clear evidence that there was entrapment and intrusive involvement by the FBI in the killings, Governor Romero Barceló met with President Jimmy Carter's attorney general, Benjamin Civiletti. Immediately after the meeting Romero Barceló announced his support for Carter in the Democratic primary, and two months later Civiletti announced he was ending the DOJ investigation of the Cerro Maravilla incident without charges.[4]

Romero Barceló found two other reasons to work with Democrats. The first was the result of his successful Statehood for the Poor platform, encapsulated in an eponymous book published in 1973 in which, in the hopes of expanding his base beyond Puerto Rico's upper- and upper-middle-class elites, he argued that statehood would mean full entitlement in social welfare transfer payments.[5] Democrats were still the strongest supporters of FDR's welfare state policies, while Republicans were beginning to scapegoat those programs to politicize white middle-class discontent. The second was his recognition of the importance of asserting more influence over appointing federal judges, which was controlled by whomever was in power in Washington. The remarkable thing about Romero Barceló's strategy is how he went from overseeing an early example of an authoritarian right-wing NPP administration, which remained the public face of the party while he was in charge, to becoming a fusion politician working both sides of the aisle, mostly out of view from the average Puerto Rican.

During the Pedro Rosselló administration, which coincided with the Clinton era in Washington, the NPP became more overtly involved with the Democratic Party. The Clintonian DNC's neoliberal shift made this easier. Further, as mentioned earlier, Rosselló and Clinton bonded over the "crime-fighting" experiment of setting up police occupations in the island's housing projects, a strategy that went hand in hand with the increasing mass incarceration that Clinton presided over.

In the late 1990s the Rosselló administration also became heavily invested in passing the Young Bill, sponsored by the ethically challenged Republican representative from Alaska, Don Young.[6] The bill, called the United States–Puerto Rico Political Status Act, would provide for a US government–approved plebiscite that would allow for either a change of status to statehood or independence within ten years or a stay on the commonwealth status for the same period.

The bill just managed to pass the House in March of 1998, but it quickly died in the Senate, opposed by conservative Republicans. The farcical theater of the Young Bill clearly indicated how Republican-supported lobbying and fundraising would inevitably crash and burn when it came up against the reality that most Republican senators had no stomach for Puerto Rican statehood. It was all just a show that allowed a lot of money to change hands, with no Republican politicians losing any credibility or suffering true political loss, as none of them had Puerto Rican residents as their constituents.

It can be said that the only way Puerto Rico can really operate politically in the United States is through lobbying. Because it has only a nonvoting representative in Congress, the resident commissioner, it can only act through that representative in the form of lobbying. Although such lobbying is not formalized as part of the private-sector lobbying structure, in practice it's a reality of life in DC. In 1998, with Carlos Romero Barceló holding the position of resident commissioner, the NPP-dominated Puerto Rico government spent about $4 million on lobbying in Washington for Puerto Rican status interests. At the time that amount was more than the combined sum that the municipal governments of Denver, Los Angeles, Miami-Dade County, and Chicago spent on lobbying.[7] The PDP, for its part, spends heavily on federal campaign contributions as well, particularly for Puerto Rican–identified representatives Nydia Velásquez and Luis Gutiérrez, both of whom garnered tens of thousands of donations when the Young Bill hit the House Floor.

The statehood movement's connection with the seamy netherworld of right-wing conservatives, most of whom have played infamous roles that have led to the current Trump authoritarian regime, is perhaps far more troubling than its dealings with Democrats. It's rather remarkable how the NPP continues to this day to work with everyone from centrist and even liberal Democrats to hard-right Republicans while maintaining party loyalty. How do they do it? The answer is the same as for the question of why they do it: lobbying money.

One of the most infamous lobbying connection stories begins with the College Republicans of the early 1980s—students finding ways to empower themselves on campuses while surrounded by the burgeoning left liberalism and subsequent apathy of the youngest Baby Boomers coming of age. In 1981 Ralph Reed, Jack Abramoff, and Grover Norquist bonded over their ideas of activism and political theater. Like much of this New Right, they read Saul Alinsky and aimed to refashion New Left tactics and remake them into a fresh message of social and fiscal conservatism. The three figures not only deeply influenced the Republican Right over the next twenty-plus years; they also were heavily involved in either making lobbying deals or engaging political consultancies that combined dirty business with leveraging political causes, paving the way for the horrific synthesis of white supremacism with oligarchic corruption that Donald Trump epitomizes.

After moving on to get a PhD in history from Emory University, Reed ultimately crossed paths with evangelical Christian Pat Robertson and, with $64,000 donated by the National Republican Senatorial Committee, formed the Christian Coalition. The cynical use of fundamentalist Christianity to create a large swath of the right Republican base was one of the origins of the revived white supremacist use of victimization to amass political power. By 1994 Republicans were calling for "draining the swamp" in Washington. Three years later Reed began to transition to political consultant, forming Century Strategies, which combined a host of media relations, voter outreach, business development, and organizing services. One of his first major clients was the infamous Enron Corporation, which had already entered a tailspin when it hired him but still paid him $30,000 a month until it went bankrupt.

Reed's next venture was Puerto Rico. Following up on Ronald Reagan's idea that Hispanics were all Republicans but just didn't know it yet, Reed spun a narrative that framed Puerto Ricans as victims of colonialism and, as a family-oriented and Christian people, deserving of an immediate path to determining their own status. This kind of rhetoric fit nicely with the NPP's conservative tendencies, including not only law-and-order but also "family values" rhetoric. It resonated with the conservative Catholicism of the NPP's base in the sprawling San Juan suburbs. As he was lobbying in Puerto Rico, Newt Gingrich and Tom DeLay—who would later be convicted of money laundering, conspiracy, and campaign finance violations[8]—threw their support behind the Young Bill. Among the lobbying firms hurling money at Congress were Jack Abramoff's pro-statehood Future of Puerto Rico, Inc. and Grover Norquist's Americans for Tax Reform. Abramoff had been famously involved in scandals involving cheating Native American groups who wanted lobbying force to get casinos built on their territory as well as activities in the Marianas Islands that involved fraud, labor exploitation, and even covering up sex slavery.

In the 1980s the firm Black, Manafort, Stone, and Kelly was involved in lobbying for Puerto Rico. It had been hired by the Puerto Rico Federal Affairs Administration, essentially the island's main connection to lobbyists. Paul Manafort and Roger Stone were both subjects in the Mueller investigation of potential ties between Russian operatives and the Trump administration, and both have a long history of questionable financial and public relations actions and tactics. Charles Black has been lobbying for PRFAA since the 1980s, and long been associated with Jack Abramoff, and has also been a lead lobbyist for the PDP.

The connection between College Republicans and the Puerto Rico Statehood Students Association, formed in 1979 by Luis Fortuño and one-time Resident Commissioner Kenneth McClintock, is not clear. However, it does share a link with the Young Republican Federation of Puerto Rico, the organization that first nurtured current Resident Commissioner Jenniffer González, who is an active supporter of conservative policies, as her uncritical support of Trump indicates. PRSSA is also a nexus for the crossover between centrist statehooders, like Pierluisi and McClintock, and hardliners, embodying the strange continuum within it. The NPP seems to encapsulate both tendencies

of the seemingly insurmountable partisan divide of the United
States without any of its fraught complications because it
cannot be a part of US politics. It's not a contradiction that
McClintock backed Vietnamese American US Representative
Stephanie Murphy (Democrat) in her primary race,[9] while the
Rosselló administration sent out press releases congratulating
Jeff Sessions when he was appointed attorney general. Rosselló
can support Andrew Gillum for governor of Florida while Jenniffer González supports Rick Scott. That's what happens when
it's openly acknowledged that lobbying and paying for political
access is the only route to being influential in Washington.

In the aftermath of the Young Bill's failure, the Rosselló administration pushed on, insisting on a plebiscite that November
anyway. The 1998 vote was famous because the option "None of
the Above" won 50.3 percent of the vote. It was favored by supporters of what was called Enhanced Commonwealth, which
would provide for some of the extended powers listed earlier.
However, the US State Department position since the time of
the plebiscite has been that such enhancement is unconstitutional. Furthermore, the idea that the United States could sign
on to a new status designation that Puerto Rico independently
conceived of is well beyond the US conception of territorial
law. These realities—as well as the rhetorical resonance of the
phrase "none of the above"—suggested to Puerto Ricans that
the status argument itself was becoming futile, particularly because of the threats to national integrity of countries all over
the world as global capital was reorganized—national sovereignty itself was seemingly a rapidly vanishing illusion. The rise
of authoritarian nationalism in France, like Marine Le Pen's
National Rally Party, and the Brexit phenomenon in England as
well as other European examples demonstrate pushback against
the globalizing force of the European Union.

This became evident to certain sectors of the Puerto Rican
left around the turn of the millennium. The 1998 referendum
was a spectacular failure for the independence option, which
received only 2.5 percent of the vote, well below what PIP can-

didates receive in general elections. The erosion of support indicated a lack of passion not necessarily for independence but for the PIP establishment itself, which had become increasingly perceived as a party for elitist liberals who did not necessarily have a worldview in step with an increasingly intersectional and antinationalist globalized left. Puerto Ricans who lean toward independence, particularly in the intelligentsia and among university students, have sought political expression through labor struggles as well as other socialist projects. There is also the factor of the "melon" voters, who vote for commonwealth out of pragmatism yet ultimately prefer independence.

A group of seven academics captured much of the impetus behind the new progressive movement. Having studied at the University of Puerto Rico as undergrads, in 1998 Juan Duchesne, Chloé Georas, Ramón Grosfoguel, Agustín Lao-Montes, Frances Negrón Muntaner, Pedro Ángel Rivera, and Aurea Maria Sotomayor proposed the idea of "radical statehood" in an attempt to wrest the goal of becoming the fifty-first state from conservative reactionaries and make it into something of a progressive political strategy. They had all made significant contributions to interdisciplinary Latinx studies, Puerto Rican studies, the decolonial school, and queer studies, both in the United States and Puerto Rico. Together they authored "Statehood from a Radical-Democratic Perspective (An Invitation to Dialogue for All Inhabitants of the Puerto Rican Archipelago)," which at first garnered considerable support among progressive activists and thinkers. However, nationalist Puerto Ricans generally rejected it for its suggestion that they abandon the quest for independence to engage in a Quixotic pragmatism that could allow colonial subjects to change their oppressor from within.

The manifesto was on the cutting edge of a line of thinking that seeks to unify islanders and the diaspora through a notion of identity that isn't a stark binary choice between total assimilation to the United States and a kind of rigid nationalism—found in hard-socialist states like Cuba, Venezuela, and Nicaragua—that still seems to affect socialist and progressive movements in Latin America. Radical statehood was an attempt to recapture what had been lost from the movements of the 1960s that tried to fuse disparate agendas like class struggle, feminism, and gender liberation.[10]

Although I understood the nationalist rejection as passionate and righteous, at the same time I felt that the radical statehood idea was visionary in the way it assessed Puerto Rico's postcolonial and neocolonial reality. In addition, it suggested a blueprint for the role of US Latinos as supporters and collaborators of Latin American workers and marginalized people that still resonates today. The radical statehood doctrine, which suggests that Puerto Rico would be better off as a progressive democratic fifty-first state than an independent country, reflected a desire for the island to play a role in helping to "forge a multiracial, multicultural, democratic, pacifist and internationalist Nuestra América," echoing Cuban icon José Martí. The authors also said they didn't want to "Americanize" by assimilating culturally.

On the contrary, because Puerto Ricans have long participated in "institutions, practices and discourses of the metropolis," as US citizens living on both the island and the mainland, their call for statehood is intended as an act of radical democracy. "We need to make alliances with the more liberal sectors in the U.S.," it asserts early on in the text, alluding to those Puerto Ricans who have been able to increase their engagement with the "political, professional, trade union, ecological, sexual, feminist, public health, educational, artistic, and social practices" of the mainland left.

The manifesto also points out how blind nationalism can gloss over the ways elite sectors of Latin American nations collaborate with the hemispheric neoliberal agenda at the expense of subordinated local social classes, many of whom are forced to emigrate to the United States. Indeed, in the United States—in cities like New York, Chicago, and Los Angeles—many Latinx can potentially come to understand the power of unifying as Latinos, comparing notes about our idiosyncrasies and common ground and learning to struggle together.

The manifesto suggests that the best choice for Puerto Ricans is to "fight from inside the U.S. body politic, to extend to all groups the rights that white citizens of the metropolis enjoy—to increase the minimum wage, to improve environmental legislation, and to restructure the welfare state along more human dimensions." It is a call to break away from stagnant ideas about cultural nationalism in Puerto Rico that view independence as a panacea (without coherent strategies for postindependence economic development), and to instead ally with US progressive movements in the hopes of addressing the persistent racism and homophobia that existed either overtly or covertly in Puerto Rican nationalism.

The challenges facing radical statehood today are twofold. One, the most obvious, is that any kind of statehood is virtually politically impossible given the state of Puerto Rico after Hurricane María and its massive debt. Further, even without those realities, Congress has never seemed enthusiastic about the idea, and they have the final say. Secondly, Congress's implementation of PROMESA has made statehood an idea unappealing to most Puerto Ricans who consider themselves progressives or on the left. Still, as US Democrats took control of the House in 2019, some observers have floated the idea that progressives might call for statehood for both Puerto Rico and the District of Columbia if a Democrat takes the White House. In the end there is a strong need for US Latinx to engage in a political agenda that seeks to merge the interests of nonelite classes living here and in Latin America. Yet in Puerto Rico, it's hard to imagine progressives embracing statehood at this point.

Although this idealism was soundly rejected both by academics and activists as well as citizens at the ballot box, it set the stage for new political perspectives to emerge in Puerto Rico in the new millennium. The fragile notion that Puerto Rican politics would forever be a contest between commonwealth, statehood, and independence was rapidly falling apart even before the debt crisis set in. In the mid-2000s, under Governor Fortuño, the NPP started to move more in the direction of authoritarianism, focusing on social conservatism, anti-unionism, shrinking government aid programs and responsibilities, and heavy-handed use of police authority. Meanwhile the PDP scrambled to float new ideas about an enhanced commonwealth that appealed to voters but had little chance of happening, and progressive-left forces splintered, with many abandoning the PIP to form political alliances that focused more on everyday struggles for workers, marginalized people, and the environment.

LOBBYING, THE NPP, THE DEMOCRATIC PARTY, AND A DOJ INVESTIGATION: A CASE STUDY

The unhealthy symmetry between lobbying, the NPP, and the Democratic Party came into sharp relief during the early 2010s, when Obama's Justice Department, headed by Eric Holder, investigated overzealous and discriminatory police procedures enacted by the Puerto Rico Police Department. The investigation came after successful pressure by the ACLU chapters in both New York and San Juan. Unwarranted police violence was used on multiple occasions, including when students and workers demonstrated after Governor Fortuño announced that he was going to cut twenty thousand government jobs and increase tuition at the University of Puerto Rico. There was also evidence of over a decade of systematic police abuse directed against residents of poor neighborhoods like La Perla in San Juan and Loiza, the island's most Afro–Puerto Rican municipality, and Dominican immigrants, both legal residents and undocumented.

Immediately following an incident at the capitol building in San Juan involving police use of tear gas and billy clubs, which had resulted in several injuries, the Colegio de Abogados, or Puerto Rican Bar Association, held hearings. Many of the injured and aggrieved testified before a stunned audience, and within a month the Colegio de Abogados issued a 132-page document detailing the various violations the department committed, testimonies of the victims, and its recommendations.

Predictably, this report did not generate the desired response; instead, NPP senator Roberto Arango announced legal action to revoke the bar because of its defense of students who, he said, had committed "illegal actions."

Since its inception in 1840—but particularly since membership became compulsory in 1932—the Colegio de Abogados had inspired attacks because of its function as a forum for advancing civic debates, and it had weathered them all. But even though its membership contained partisans from all three of Puerto Rico's major political parties, the attack from right-wing supporters of Governor Fortuño only intensified. In 2010 the law firm of Indiano & Williams won a class-action suit against the Colegio de Abogados, claiming that its practice of requiring members to purchase compulsory life insurance to practice law violated the First Amendment. The ruling awarded over $4 million in damages. But because most of the members of this class-action suit were never informed that they were in the class and in order to lower the amount of damages, Colegio de Abogados president Osvaldo Toledo began urging its members to opt out of the class in the lawsuit. In response, Judge José A. Fusté, who had been appointed by President Reagan in the 1980s, charged Toledo with violating a gag rule imposed on the case and ordered him to be imprisoned for five days after Toledo refused to pay a $10,000 fine. Fusté, who also happened to be the judge who sentenced Al Sharpton to ninety days in prison for protesting Vieques, is an old friend of Carlos Romero Barceló. The Vieques protests at least temporarily united local activists with those in the diaspora, making it an international struggle. Sharpton, along with figures like Harry Belafonte, salsa singer Rubén Blades, and other social justice activists, all made appearances at protests in New York, at times allowing themselves to be arrested as an act of civil disobedience.

In the summer of 2011 I went to visit Toledo in his office as part of my investigation of the circumstances that led up to the police misconduct in Puerto Rico. I was curious about rumors that mysterious lobbying on behalf of the NPP was delaying or even attempting to quash the DOJ report. Toledo, however, wanted to talk about the continuing harassment campaign against the Colegio de Abogados and shared the same suspicions about the delay. "The government wants to strangle us," he said. "They say the Colegio is filled with Communists, that we are a bunch of terrorists. On our thirty-two-member board of directors I have seven statehooders. Some of them came to the jail to support me."

One of the lawyers who participated in the Indiano & Williams suit was Harvard Law School graduate Andrés W. López, who is an ardent statehood supporter.[11] López is a prominent pro-statehood activist who is a DNC member, and in September 2009 President Barack Obama appointed him to the Committee to Study the Potential Creation of a National Museum of the American Latino. It's striking that he shares this NPP affiliation with Luis Fortuño, whose reign as governor resulted in slashing government jobs and increasing authoritarian use of police repression against demonstrators.

According to Open Secrets, a database run by a nonprofit research organization focused on tracking lobbying and campaign contributions, López was one of Puerto Rico's principal donation bundlers for the Obama campaign, having raised at least $500,000 on his behalf. López had been prominent in Obama's outreach to the Latinx community, including coordinating the president's appearance at a Super Bowl party at the Miami home of Emilio Estefan, López's fellow member of the National Latino Museum study committee. López was also a key figure in helping to organize Obama's fundraising visit to Puerto Rico in June of 2011.

One of López's key connections to Obama was Jeffrey Berman, who was hailed during the 2008 presidential campaign as the main force behind the Obama camp's ability to secure uncommitted delegates, delivering the surprise victories in early primaries that allowed him to overwhelm the Clinton campaign in the long run.[12] After Obama entered office, Berman left government for a job in the private sector at Bryan Cave Strategies,

the public-policy division of Bryan Cave, a major K-street lobbying firm.

Public filings showed that Berman accepted over a million
dollars in contracts from Puerto Rican agencies like the Puerto
Rico Federal Affairs administration and PREPA. They lobbied
for things like the passage of the Puerto Rico Democracy Act,
a plebiscite project to decide the political status of the island
that was, of course, biased toward the statehood party's goals.
Representative Luis Gutiérrez told me that he was intimately
tied to Pedro Pierluisi, who had castigated him as "insulting"
and "disrespectful" when he took the House floor in one of his
many forceful speeches denouncing the civil rights violations
tolerated by the Fortuño administration. While Gutiérrez had
a famous falling out with Obama over Obama's lack of urgency
on pushing for immigration reform, he was equally frustrated
that Obama's major campaign bundlers in Puerto Rico, like
Andrés López, were deeply tied to the NPP, which continually
affected other parties' abilities to influence Obama on Puerto
Rico affairs. Many local observers called Berman a bridge between Fortuño's government and federal agencies in Washington, facilitating Puerto Rico's inclusion in both federal stimulus
programs and the Obama healthcare reform plan. His connection to Obama's inner circle can be measured by a few influential associations. His boss at Bryan Cave Strategies is Broderick
Johnson, a Hollywood agent and producer nominated for an
Academy Award for *The Blind Side*, starring Sandra Bullock.
Johnson was also an adviser on Obama's 2004 Illinois Senate
campaign and his 2008 presidential campaign and is close to
Attorney General Eric Holder.

Toledo, who had been at the incident at the capitol building
as an observer and was personally sprayed with tear gas, was
frustrated by how the Fortuño administration had cast aside the
many Colegio de Abogados attempts to produce reports about
the police problem. He believed in the process of the DOJ investigation and wanted to believe that Obama himself was not
aware of the suspicious nature of the delay in issuing the report.

"The problem is the lobbying was paralyzing this thing," Toledo said wearily. "Earlier in the year, in January, one of the DOJ investigators came here and asked me for a meeting," he shared as he picked a business card out of his wallet and placed it on his desk. It belonged to a member of the Special Litigations Division. "This is the guy. He admitted it to me. He told me that the report was almost done, that he had met the governor the same day. Two weeks later we found out about Bryan Cave and Jeffrey Berman."

That September, months after the report was supposedly done, Assistant Attorney General Tom Perez finally issued the DOJ Report, which put the PRPD under a consent decree—meaning direct supervision by the DOJ. This would last until issues raised by the report—including "staggering levels of crime and corruption" among police officers as well as systematic abuses of poor Afro–Puerto Ricans, and Dominican immigrants—were addressed effectively. It's still a mystery why it took so long.

WHEN IN DOUBT, PUSH FOR ANOTHER PLEBISCITE

The following year the Fortuño administration doubled down on the NPP's central political strategy: pushing for a plebiscite using the party's relentless rhetoric. The plebiscite of 2012 further polarized the left and right by squeezing out most liberal statehooders, demonstrating the commonwealth's collapse into irrelevance and independence's near impossibility. Much to the delight of the NPP message controllers, the numbers were striking: 61.2 percent of 1.8 million voters said they favored statehood. But of course it wasn't quite that simple. The ballot options came out of a tortured political process that involved consultation with the president's Puerto Rico Task Force and, in the end, was never authorized by Congress.

Unlike previous plebiscites, the voting procedure involved a two-step process. The first question on the ballot asked, "Are you satisfied with the current territorial status?" On that question, 54 percent voted no, which didn't necessarily mean the voter was against commonwealth per se but that they were simply unsatisfied with the current version of commonwealth. The second question was: "Which status do you prefer?" It then offered the options of statehood, a "Sovereign Free Associated State" (an undetermined nonterritorial hybrid of commonwealth and independence), and independence.

The vote went to statehood (61 percent), with "Sovereign Free Associated State" winning 33 percent of the vote and independence garnering 6 percent. But although this appeared to be a clear victory, during the campaign leading up to the vote the PDP had urged their followers to simply enter a blank vote in protest of the way the NPP constructed the plebiscite to favor statehood. If one counts the blank votes, statehood won only 45 percent of the vote—not a majority—and it gained fewer than the combined total of "sovereign free association" and blank votes. The Sovereign Free Associated State and blank ballots together amounted to 51 percent of the votes, virtually the same result as the plebiscites held in 1967 and 1993. This is almost a mirror image of the 1998 plebiscite, which was won by "None of the Above" (rejecting statehood, commonwealth, independence, and free associated state) by margin of 50.3 percent over statehood's 46.5 percent. To complicate matters even further, the 2012 plebiscite occurred the same year pro-commonwealth PDP candidate Alejandro García Padilla defeated Luis Fortuño, the incumbent pro-statehood governor, leaving the statehood party without its primary advocate.

Pierluisi, at the time the island's incumbent resident commissioner, would continue on the inside track to lobby for statehood with Barack Obama, because unlike Fortuño, he was a DNC member with ties to the president. For his part García Padilla announced that he would hold a Constitutional Convention in Puerto Rico in 2014 to seek a new plebiscite that would be approved by Congress. Even after Hurricane María, his successor, Governor Rosselló, continued to pursue statehood projects. Rosselló announced at once point that he would be implementing the "Tennessee Plan," which was designed to promote gradual entry as a state, without acknowledging that this method was originally designed to increase the number of slave states.

In the aftermath of the PROMESA FOMB and Hurricane María, Puerto Rican politics has become even more fragmented and mired in disarray. The NPP continues to advocate for statehood in a climate where it is increasingly unlikely to be granted. In June 2017, after a dubious back and forth with the Jeff Sessions–headed DOJ—which refused to sanction the plebiscite, much less agree that it would be binding—the NPP pushed through a plebiscite vote in which statehood won 97 percent. The lopsided victory reflected the fact that almost all other voters boycotted the election. With so little support from Washington as well as at least half of the Puerto Rico electorate, the NPP seems to be bent on pushing through plebiscites as one of the only forms of political action left for them. Despite the fact that the votes are nonbinding, not certified, and virtually ignored by Congress, the pro-statehood party continues to advocate for new plebiscites and new proposals to bring to congressional committees, whose priorities are elsewhere. Yet on the island each of these plans and plebiscites are front-page news for months, giving the NPP an appearance of political viability.

The farcical outcomes of the most recent plebiscites unfortunately draw attention to the almost untenable position of the Commonwealth Party. After the García Padilla government lost its legal appeal of the ruling against his Puerto Rico Public Corporation Debt Enforcement and Recovery Act and the *Puerto Rico v. Sánchez Valle* "double jeopardy" ruling, there is no longer any sense that there was anything special about Puerto Rico's "autonomous" relationship with the United States. The long road that could be traced through the Autonomous Charter with Spain in 1897, presided over by Prime Minister Muñoz Rivera, and leading to the 1952 Commonwealth of Puerto Rico constitution, ushered in by his son Muñoz Marín, had ended in the cold realization that Puerto Rico was still an unincorporated territory with no recourse against its ultimate legal owners, Congress.

So what is to be done, then, about the PDP? It continues to function as a party antagonistic to the right-wing tendencies of the NPP, although not necessarily to its neoliberal tendencies. Representative Manuel Natal Albelo and San Juan mayor Carmen Yulín Cruz represented the PDP's left wing (until Natal Albelo left the party in 2018), continually denouncing mainstream politics' abandonment of working-class issues and, of course, the brutal indifference demonstrated by President Trump after the hurricane. Many on the island and in the diaspora welcomed Cruz's announcement in March 2019 that she would be running for governor, but it remains to be seen if she can pull the party itself out of its political miasma. The party's existential position—holding on to the nonexistent autonomy promised by the ELA—looks increasingly indefensible. It is unclear how much of a difference it can make as Ricardo Rosselló's pro-statehood government is continually exposed as powerless and ineffectual in the wake of the PROMESA FOMB.

The PDP turned eighty years old in 2018, and, as if the Luis Muñoz Marín speech never happened, the long-held illusion of an autonomous commonwealth has been revealed for what it really is. In the summer of 2018 former governor Aníbal Acevedo Vilá wrote a somewhat incendiary column in *El Nuevo Día* calling for the PDP to change drastically. "We have to come up with a new economic relationship with the United States and that should evolve into a new political relationship," he told me in an interview a few weeks later.[13] "The values of being in the 'center' and having an association with the US are still valid, but [Puerto Rico's political future] has to be outside of the Territorial Clause, and it has to be something completely different. It has to be something that will give Puerto Rico the economic tools for development but will keep the bond, which is basically citizenship." With this, he again sidestepped the issue of the fundamental imbalance caused by US control over

Puerto Rico's economy, which only considers favorable conditions for outside investors. He also identified a crucial issue for Puerto Ricans on the island: uninterrupted access to US citizenship, something that's difficult to negotiate while holding onto the radical politics of separatism. What's more, Acevedo Vilá praised the left-liberalism of Bernie Sanders and Elizabeth Warren for their strong focus on class-based solutions, mentioning that he had been the first major mainstream elected official on the island to announce his support for Sanders. He saw Sanders's benevolence as a source of access to "tools" necessary for "economic development" while keeping citizenship, which in a sense is not far from the radical statehood position.

Then, after bristling about the indignities of rediscovering Puerto Rican inequality, just as everyone on the island has since the hurricane, Acevedo Vilá restated the classic PDP position: Puerto Rico is a unique culture and society that still desires important ties to the United States. "After María everybody was saying, oh, you can't do this to them—they are Americans," Acevedo Vilá lamented. "I say this with all due respect: I'm not an American. I'm a US citizen, but I'm a Puerto Rican, and that's a big distinction that has to be made. So that has to be the point of any kind of discussion about what to do with Puerto Rico."

I was reminded of the many times my father told me almost the same thing with the same exact words, and I still don't know if they're the words of someone unable to see the reality of colonialism or someone with a pragmatic view about living life while playing the cards he's dealt. Still, soon after my interview with Acevedo Vilá a major scandal broke out involving emails revealed from early 2017 that seemed to show the DNC intervening in the election of a Puerto Rican Democratic party head at the expense of the Bernie Sanders's Our Revolution faction led by Senator Eduardo Bhatia. The DNC faction was made up of NPP elected officials affiliated with Resident Commissioner Jenniffer González, famous for her constant photo opportunities with President Trump and her continued refusal to criticize the administration's neglect of Puerto Rico.

In November of 2018 Governor Rosselló was still trying to drum up the possibility of yet another plebiscite, tweeting a letter from the House of Representatives calling for a plebiscite, accompanied by a simple question: "Statehood: Yes or No?" Once again there was no guarantee that the vote would be binding, and the signees of the letter were the usual suspects: Representative Rob Bishop, who was not only involved in drafting PROMESA but also attached to some disaster capitalist initiatives on the island; Don Young, the author of the 1998 plebiscite initiative; and Jenniffer González. Unsurprisingly, Bishop's largest bloc of donations in early 2017 came from Puerto Rico, notably families associated with the NPP.[14]

If the status debate between the PDP and the NPP is rapidly fading into Puerto Rico's past, it would seem that the island can't enter the poststatus future fast enough. Although ultimately deciding Puerto Rico's status—hopefully through independence—is important to me and to Puerto Rico, there is so much work to be done just to survive intact as a people that it's best to shift the focus away from status for now. Candidates who didn't belong to any of the three traditional parties won over 10 percent of the votes in the last gubernatorial election. Puerto Rican politics now include factions of identity-based politics and the new democratic socialism that seems to be on the rise in the United States. Members of the Independence Party, like María de Lourdes Santiago and Juan Dalmau, have pioneered much of this move to the left. They have been unwavering in rejecting US colonial practices and social injustice against women and Afro–Puerto Ricans.

The change in the Independence Party is noticeable, although it has been difficult for the party to break away from its image as an elitist party for intellectuals and out of touch with the ranks of the poor and working class. It's been forty years since PIP president Rubén Berríos defiantly called for a socialist Puerto Rican Republic after having attended the inauguration of ill-fated Chilean president Salvador Allende, who was killed in a CIA-backed coup in 1973. These days the strongest memory I have of Berríos is that he became symbolic of a party that did little to appeal to voters outside of a small elite. Still, the question remains: Does the fact that the PIP continually fails to win much more than 5 percent of the Puerto Rican vote stem from its elitism or from decades of repression?

As someone who has stared into the weary eyes of the late, pro-independence radical Filiberto Ojeda Ríos, languishing in the Metropolitan Correctional Center in lower Manhattan, complaining of being fed fatty food despite a circulatory condition, I have to ask myself: Don't all Puerto Ricans want to be independent in their hearts? It certainly seems that way during the Puerto Rican Day Parade every summer when, despite the barrage of corporate logos on the floats that carry dancers, singers, politicians, and union workers, everyone remembers how to sing the plena "Qué Bonita Bandera" (What a Beautiful Flag). That anthem invokes a cultural nationalist identity with more surviving power than Muñoz Marín's 1952 flag-raising speech.

For so many of us there is a burning desire that that day, the one of independence, will inevitably come. It's simply a question of on whose terms it will be. But with the terrible swift sword that Hurricane María wielded on September 20, 2017, that dream was violently and indefinitely dashed.

CHAPTER 7

HURRICANE MARÍA DESTROYS THE COMMONWEALTH FANTASY

A woman walking through a debris-ridden San Juan street. © Joseph Rodríguez

I n August of 2017 I was in Puerto Rico reporting on the "showdown" between La Junta and the Rosselló government when the governor claimed he'd commit civil disobedience and risk being jailed if the FOMB insisted on its plan to furlough government workers for four days a month. As usual I was staying at my family's home in the Luquillo Mountains, not far from the El Yunque National Rain Forest. One afternoon, when I was not shuttling to Fajardo to cover the FOMB meetings or in San Juan to do interviews, I went to a small strip mall in Rio Grande to do some grocery shopping and pick up meds for my elderly mother. As I returned to the car with my groceries, I noticed looks of concern on other drivers' faces as they looked out from the parking lot to the main road, Route 3.

Then I noticed that there had been a massive power outage, something that would occur locally in our barrio near the rain forest but had now engulfed the entire municipality of Rio Grande. There were no traffic lights working, and swarms of cars were inching through intersections, hoping that the cars zooming down Route 3 would see them and let them pass. Within a matter of minutes I was one of them, peering in both directions and gingerly pushing the nose of my car forward, trying to guess if another car entering from the opposite direction would turn left, wondering if I'd be able to get through quickly enough to avoid an accident and work my way back east toward my mother's home. I could feel a blanket of uncertainty falling all around me with the setting sun, wondering if this kind of event—a sudden plunge into darkness without knowing when power would return—would reoccur with increasing frequency.

While driving up and down the mountain on a winding road surrounded by dense foliage from the edges of the tropical rain forest, I'd noticed that the overgrowth was spilling into the roadway, swallowing up the poles that carried the electricity. The maintenance provided by crews of workers cutting away at the foliage seemed even less frequent than usual. Earlier in the month PDP representative Ramón Luis Cruz Burgos had claimed that during the first twenty days of July 2017, 65 percent of Puerto Rico's municipalities reported blackouts. In 2016, when the problems began escalating, UTIER, a labor union that represents thirty-six hundred of the ninety-five hundred PREPA employees, had accused PREPA of purposely not performing proper maintenance of electrical lines because of workforce cutbacks. UTIER president Ángel Figueroa Jaramillo had been making the media rounds, claiming that the lack of maintenance was intentionally designed to create a climate of public acceptance of the failing agency's ultimate privatization. Just a week before my run-in with the blackout, the Puerto Rico Senate launched an investigation into the increasing incidence of blackouts on the island.

I'd also been growing more uncomfortable about my mother's arrhythmia, which required unpredictable visits to the emergency room at the local hospital in Fajardo. It was the same one where my father had a surgery on his intestinal tract several years earlier, where necessary anesthesia exacerbated his existing Parkinson's disease and incapacitated him for the final two years of his life. He was unable to move or speak, relegated to a bed in our home while being fed through gastrotomy tubes and breathing with a respirator. My mother is unusually strong and capable for her advanced age, but every time I left her in the house on the mountain to go back to New York, I felt uneasy about her vulnerability.

When hurricane season hits its peak in late August and early September it can be an anxious time for Puerto Ricans in the diaspora. In years past we depended on rumors or phone calls from relatives about storms that may or may not be approaching, but in the age of the internet, it's easy to check the National Hurricane Center website run by the National Oceanic and Atmospheric Center or, better yet, follow local newspaper and television websites in Puerto Rico that feature clips of meteorologists like Deborah Martorell, who is a minor celebrity because of her work on WAPA TV. This year the threat of Hurricane Irma drew my attention, and I nervously watched the progress of the storm through charts made up to track its size and reach.

When Irma passed, it left about a million Puerto Rican residents without electrical power, and three people had been killed. At the time it was the most powerful Atlantic hurricane on record, and although it left scattered damage on the island due to winds and flooding, it gained much more attention because of its spectacular destruction of smaller islands like Barbuda, St. Bart, and St. Martin. Irma's path culminated with another strong hit on Cuba, whose yearly battering from one storm or another goes largely unnoticed in the US media. It then gave a considerable pounding to the Miami-Dade County and Tampa areas of Florida. It took about a week or more for power to be restored to my mother's house as well as to many of my friends on the island, demonstrating again the rickety nature of the power grid, but all in all it felt like we had dodged a bullet. Multiple hits by storms on Puerto Rico were rare, and if this was the worst that the peak of the season could offer, it seemed safe to hope for the best.

But of course, the trouble was far from over. On September 20 Hurricane María made landfall on the southeastern coast of the island, devastating towns like Humacao and Naguabo. It then continued on in a northwestern path through the Cordillera Central, or central mountain chain of the island, finally exiting through the northwest corner near the town of Isabela. It hit with the power of a Category 4 storm, with winds and gusts well over a hundred miles an hour, and was a direct hit on most of the island.

The irony for media crews on the island, who staggered out of their homes with cell phone cameras, to television and radio stations that were being pummeled and flooded, was that no one in Puerto Rico could see the reports they transmitted. Instead, they were broadcast on outlets like WAPA America, a network that rebroadcasts programs from local station WAPA TV to cities in the United States, Univision, and other Spanish-language media outlets. For decades the media had ignored Puerto Rico, in what some have designated as an intentional blackout. Now, suddenly, it was the biggest story on the national media.

In the following days island residents were shell-shocked by a new landscape of myriad twigs where Ceiba trees once grew, zinc roofs shattered into shards, and a rising tide of noxious, contaminated water flowing through what were once quaint Caribbean towns. One of the major motifs of this panorama left in the wake of the devastation was the poorly maintained infra- structure, which the storm exposed. Electrical cables attached to unstable posts all around the island had fallen to the ground, creating an obstacle course of exposed wires.

The Trump administration, performing crisis mode, chose to display military deployment for the cameras, first with US Army North deputy commander Richard C. Kim, then with Lieu- tenant General Jeffrey Buchanan. Offstage there were under- the-radar DOD private contract firms like Strategic Response Partners spotted prowling the streets of San Juan. But despite some favorable reports in the press of remote mountain-area rescues and deployments to deliver diesel gas for electric gen- erators and restore cell towers, the fragile fabric of this island society was fraying quickly.

The reality-show ethos of Trump continued to distract: he invited Resident Commissioner González on Air Force One for a photo op to discuss his plans, and soon afterward, at the in- famous press conference with Melania, Rosselló, and a muted Carmen Yulín Cruz, Trump bullied the governor into admitting that there were only four casualties of the hurricane when in fact the bodies were already piling up at morgues and, for those less fortunate, in people's backyards. Then he entered the evan- gelical Cavalry Church, located in the basement of a strip mall in NPP-loyal Guaynabo, and famously tossed rolls of paper tow- els at a roomful of about two hundred people who had been bused in from shelters in nearby towns.

The untold, lied-about death count would become one of the two more powerful motivators for the new politics that would coalesce around post-María Puerto Rico. The other was the media phenomenon created by Mayor Cruz, who appeared on Anderson Cooper's show on CNN and berated the sluggish response from the administration as hundreds, if not thousands were slowly dying or suffering from lack of access to health care or medications. She seemed, understandably, emotionally raw at times, shedding tears and expressing despair, and viewers echoed her obvious indignation. The scandal around the government's inability to come to grips with the crisis became a major storyline in the media and central to the stinging rebuke islanders were beginning to deliver to the Trump administration's condescending, thoughtless, if not hateful colonial attitude toward Puerto Rico and its people, which had been laid bare.

Hurricane María has been compared to Katrina because of the extent of the damage and suffering as well as its potential to illustrate that Trump, as Kanye West famously suggested about George W. Bush, doesn't care about people of color. But New Orleans emerged from the storm with some areas decimated, others intact. María had spread its destruction across an entire island 110 miles long by 40 miles wide and made it a deforested, barren wasteland. More than 80 percent of the island's power lines were flattened, and its entire population—save those with generators, which operate on gasoline and other fossil fuels in short supply in the aftermath—was without electrical power. It was not so much a disaster area as it was a disaster nation, a nation of bleak, hot, humid, thirsty radio silence, fighting to bring basic necessities and relief aid to its citizens despite an inability to communicate with each other through normal digital channels.

For several days after the hurricane I was unable to contact my mother and her nearby relatives and friends in her rural community. Because there was little information about the damage outside of San Juan and a handful of other featured areas, I had no idea what had happened to our home or whether my mother and aunt, who had ridden the storm out with her, had enough access to food and water. I tried to rationalize that, because of the slope the house was on and the improbability of flooding in her community, a catastrophe was unlikely. But nightmares about her possible condition still haunted me.

Finally, after over a week of worry, my sister received a call from my mother's neighbor reassuring us that she was okay, was eating well, and had no immediate health problems. The house was made of concrete, as so many houses in Puerto Rico were, so it was sturdy enough to stand up to the storm. The concrete architecture reminded me of the fortune that the family of pro-statehood supporter and former governor of Puerto Rico Luis Ferré made, allowing them not only to influence government but also to own the island's largest daily newspaper, *El Nuevo Día*. The family founded Puerto Rican Cement, which was at the center of infrastructure development as the island transitioned from agriculture to industry thanks to Operation Bootstrap. But on the roof of my mother's house was an object that to me symbolized the island's future: a modest solar energy unit that my parents purchased in the 1990s to generate heat for the hot water in our house, and Hurricane María hadn't even dented it.

My sister and I spent several days booking flights to San Juan that the airlines continually canceled because of widespread reports of overcrowding and electric power failures. It was later reported that the airport suffered $86 million in damages. We were finally able to get a flight in early October. The flight was the grimmest I'd ever taken to Puerto Rico—or anywhere, for that matter. A no-frills Jet Blue flight on one of its older planes, it was filled with worried families and military personnel. When we landed, there was none of the typical applause that occurs when Puerto Ricans land on their native soil. I'd been poring over media images of the destruction, but I was still shaken by what I confronted as we drove the twenty-five miles or so from the airport to my mother's home in the rain forest.

When we set off on the drive, we could immediately see the effects of the damage—buildings with roofs blown off, cracked façades, rubble along streets and highways. All along the Baldorioty Highway were cars pulled over with their flashers on, which I soon learned were people talking on their cell phones in one of the small areas where a signal could be found.

Everywhere I looked were dystopic vistas of piled debris—pieces of zinc roofs, cracked porcelain fixtures, discarded mattresses, and an uninterrupted cavalcade of once-verdant tropical trees stripped, snapped, and splintered.

Along the Espiritu Santo River near Mameyes, the town at the foot of the mountains that are home to the El Yunque Rain Forest, I saw people washing their clothes by hand, returning to a nineteenth-century reality that didn't depend on electrical appliances. Up the road a brigade of workers struggled to restore fallen lines. The road snaking up the mountain was almost empty, and as we approached our family home I saw how the small barrio had most of its tree cover destroyed. It looked as if a California redwood fire had swept through the area, and this cluster of homes that housed poor, middle-, and working-class residents was visible in ways I'd never imagined. The huge old Ceiba tree that once guarded the entrance to my grandfather's old twenty-two-acre property was eviscerated, and the site of so many childhood memories had been swept away, replaced with sagging trees and strewn electrical poles.

When we reached my mother's home, we found her stoic, yet a little shell-shocked. In her living room, immaculate as usual, she sat across from a municipal government–issued packet of crackers, applesauce, and bottled water, looking up watery-eyed and saying, "I was wondering whether you even wanted to talk to me anymore." It was then I realized what it must have been like to be incommunicado for so long. With cell service and internet out, island residents like my mother were caught up in a pervasive wave of disconnection and chaos, one that exposed the inadequate response of the federal government as well as Rosselló's reeling government bureaucracy.

The Rosselló government had been quick to exploit the relatively light impact that Hurricane Irma had, trying to claim a public relations victory despite the fact that electrical power had been out for a week to ten days. But the utter destruction and chaos that María had brought overwhelmed them. They ineffectively leaned on public relations strategies, which, coupled with the shortcomings of Trump's FEMA, were a recipe for disaster for Puerto Rico. Local people wound up taking matters into their own hands, clearing the streets with whatever tools and vehicles they could muster. In the case of my mother's barrio it was our neighbor Melvin who helped to organize a brigade of local residents to use machetes to clear the road that connected with 191, the artery that leads to the entrance of the rain forest park. After hours of work in hot, humid conditions, they trekked up 191 to a well that was operated by barrio residents, cutting through an intense tangle of flayed foliage. Within days of the hurricane, water was restored, just as it had been in the days following Irma.

The longstanding rift between metro San Juan and its far-flung municipalities became more pronounced after María, as urban areas like Condado and Guaynabo saw their power return—albeit slowly—while the countryside remained blanketed in darkness and, often, desperation. Puerto Rico is famous for its gated communities, but in many cities and towns the social divide is marked by a kind of "intimate segregation," where better-off residents live in close quarters with their poorer neighbors, who are clustered in housing just a block or two away. This is evident in San Juan, where the posh Ocean Park community abuts neighborhoods like Barrio Machuchal, which has a large elderly and poor Afro–Puerto Rican population.

One of the borders between Machuchal and Ocean Park is Calle Loíza, which was currently undergoing a renaissance not unlike that of Bushwick, Brooklyn, with cafés and art galleries driving a vibrant youth-culture scene. Mariana Reyes Angleró, the leader of La Calle Loíza, Inc., a nonprofit that tries to keep a reverence for local residents and Afro-Caribbean culture in the midst of the area's revitalization, was a bit rattled when we sat down to talk. I met her at a Chinese restaurant across the street from the apartment she shares with her husband, folkloric plena musician Héctor Matos. She had been using the organizational capability of La Calle Loíza to help send out volunteers to take inventory on what residents need, often trying to connect with relief efforts of Diaspo-Ricans on the mainland.

"We're trying to get a mattress for one of our ninety-year-old neighbors," she said, visibly strained from both Irma and María. "We organized a brigade of construction workers in the neighborhood to clear the streets—anything we can do." She and her husband were also in the process of raising funds for the bar-restaurant they owned and operated, which was ironically called La Junta. They ultimately had to abandon it because their landlord was unwilling to make repairs after María. The restaurant was named after a group of former UPR students who coalesced in New York in the 1990s—university professors, artists, and workers—who remain in contact as they participate in a circular migration between New York and Puerto Rico. It had been an important site for preserving the legacy of bomba and plena music, which represented the Afro-Caribbean working class in a way similar to salsa and hip-hop in New York.

"We are people with some means, though by no means wealthy," sighed Mariana. "But I think about the average people who live here. The people we employ are mostly at the poverty level and now have no job and no source of income, and maybe the roof flew off their house. What are they going to do?" Reyes was worried about how—after the gasoline shortage and diesel-distribution problems get solved and ATMs and hospitals struggle to get back to full operation—people would react to a new normal of shuttered businesses that will not recover; neighbors lost to illness, death, and migration; and the prospect of sporadic electricity and spotty cellular service.

Almost everyone I spoke with was considering leaving Puerto Rico, even if their hearts were not in it. Many were saying they would stay only because they had an elderly relative they couldn't abandon who stubbornly wished to remain. The postal worker in charge of the annex in the small town of Palmer, where my mother receives her mail, looked at me sadly and said, "I wish I could leave, but I can't. What's coming I can't imagine and am afraid may be very difficult. Of course you should take your mother back with you. You're doing the right thing."

The stories of shock and devastation were legion: the director of the communications department at the University of Puerto Rico lamenting the damaged classrooms and the destruction of most of the school's archives; an administrator at another local university frantically trying to apply for FEMA aid not only for herself—her apartment had been flooded with several inches of water—but also for her father and sister, whose houses had lost their roofs. Then there was the couple who lived in Cayo Martín Peña, a poor area that had been desperately trying to clean up the lagoon whose polluted waters were threatening neighbors and who found a crocodile in their house after the hurricane, and another woman in a working-class area adjacent to the high-end tourist area El Condado who had spent $4,000 to repair her roof only to see it torn off like the "lid of a tin can" during the storm.

Many people I spoke with reacted with derision or indifference toward Trump's and Vice President Pence's interventions. The president's imbecilic behavior has not surprised many, but the spirited response from San Juan mayor Carmen Yulín Cruz earned her new respect from many locals who had not been fans before. Pence's visit, which came two weeks later, had the unpleasant effect of throwing metro-area traffic into complete chaos, prompting the closure of the Baldorioty Expressway, which is something like Manhattan's FDR Drive. I had been conducting interviews all afternoon in the metro area, and when I finished I realized that all surrounding avenues were closed. I was forced to drive back toward Old San Juan, which was still without electricity (as opposed to Condado, where billionaire hedge funder John Paulson bought three of the area's most luxurious hotels in 2014 and 2015: the Vanderbilt, La Concha, and the San Juan Towers). Driving south toward Río Piedras in the hopes of avoiding traffic, I encountered flash floods that made Avenida Muñoz Rivera a one-lane lake. Pushing on to the old Route 3 on the way back east to the rain forest, a feeling of dread overtook me as I realized that night had fallen and thousands of cars were surging along highways with stoplights that didn't work.

Amazingly, the anxious civility that had permeated the island kept us all safe, and I maneuvered the painstaking miles through a torrent of headlights, drivers hanging on to fading cell signals, flooded roadways, and yawning potholes. The landscape had become an unrecognizable blur of twisted highway signs, with familiar landmarks distorted and useless. Entire communities that had previously been invisible, cocooned in foliage, now emerged, ghostlike. There was no light anywhere, just a full moon that seemed to swallow all of Route 66 as it cut through the beginning of the mountainous interior.

NEGLECT, MORE DEBT, MORBID DEATH

In those early days after the storm PDP leaders, backed by allies in Congress like US Representative Nydia Velásquez, lobbied for a federal humanitarian grant between $15 billion and $30 billion. In late October the House passed a $36.5 billion disaster-relief bill that would cover the storms that hit Houston, South Florida, Puerto Rico, and the Virgin Islands as well as the wildfires that had plagued the West Coast. The relief designated for Puerto Rico would come in the form of roughly $5 billion in loans, as opposed to the $7.4 billion in community development grants made to Texas and Florida in September.[1] It was a cruel joke for a territory already drowning in debt.

There was much debate about permanently ending the Jones Act, which restricted shipments to Puerto Rico, permitting only ships that were built and maintained by the United States. This effectively banned aid from non-US ships in the aftermath of the storm, but ending the Jones Act completely was never seriously considered after its ten-day suspension that September. Rafael Bernabe, the Worker's Party candidate for governor, advocated for the use of a force majeure legal argument to have the debt sharply reduced or eliminated. He argued that not only did the hurricane fundamentally change Puerto Rico's circumstances, but the debt's existence could also make it difficult to assure the "life, well-being and security of its citizens" under these new conditions.[2]

Early discussions about electrical infrastructure rebuilding revolved around the interactions between Pedro Rosselló and US inventor Elon Musk, who wanted to implement a system of micro-grids to replace the centralized, south-to-north delivery of electrical power from one source in the southern town of Guayanilla. Although the power grid idea never really took hold, Musk sent hundreds of Powerall battery packs to capture energy generated by solar panels, a solution some local hospitals implemented. The Musk intervention symbolized the use of entrepreneurial solutions to Puerto Rico's major problems involving a high-profile figure. This distracted attention from those who had been developing solar energy on the island long before the hurricane. Soon the discourse would turn to Rosselló's announcement in January of 2018 to privatize PREPA, the electrical energy authority.

Perhaps the most disturbing of the many horrors that beset Puerto Rico in the wake of Hurricane María was the local and federal governments' inability or willful refusal to acknowledge the number of people who died as a result of the storm. Omaya Sosa, a reporter from Puerto Rico's Center for Investigative Journalism, first uncovered the scope of the casualties. Like some Puerto Ricans on the island and most in the United States, she had seen the nightmarish press opportunities for Trump and his wife, Melania, when they visited: the paper towel tossing of course, but also the strange gathering around a table in an aircraft hangar in which Trump bragged about the US response to the storm.

During this press conference Trump scolded Rosselló and the island's residents as if they were children, as if he were talking to his daughter Ivanka after she spent too much money at Henri Bendel's as a teenager. "I hate to tell you that you've thrown our budget a little bit out of whack, because we've spent

a lot of money on PR and that's fine. We've saved a lot of lives."
Then, in his typical condescending tone, he invoked a kind of
passing sympathy that was designed to lead in to another success story he could spin about the US Trump Organization. "If
you look at the—every death is horror. But if you look at a real
catastrophe like Katrina and you look at the hundreds and hundreds and hundreds of people that died, and you look at what
happened here with really a storm that was just totally over-
powering, nobody's ever seen anything like this." At this point
he turned to Rosselló and asked, as if they had rehearsed the
response: "And what is your death count as of this moment,
seventeen?" To which Rosselló replied, like an obedient vassal,
"sixteen, certified."

"Sixteen certified!" bellowed Trump. "Sixteen people versus,
in the thousands. You can be very proud of all of your people
and our people working together."

This press conference did not yield what many had speculated—negative exchanges between Trump and Mayor Cruz,
who was present. But in this one brief exchange with Rosselló
Trump had revealed the cynical, dismissive nature of the US
colonial treatment of Puerto Rico, the one that Obama only
hinted at when he passively handed off the debt crisis to Congress. It will probably not be revealed for years—and perhaps
never—whether Rosselló had agreed to go through with the
farce of corroborating this ridiculously low death estimate at
the direction of Trump or just to save his own rapidly deteriorating reputation. But it wasn't a stretch for most Puerto Ricans
to have that perception.

Everyone knew that estimate was appallingly low, because
everyone knew about the failing hospitals, the impossibility
of transporting the many sick and elderly people to hospitals,
the lack of electricity, and the reporting challenges of local
morgues. I knew precisely because of the anxiety I'd felt years
before when the electricity failed in the rain forest, knowing
that if my father was off the respirator for too long, he might die
despite my mother's best efforts. And I knew that it would take

time before his body could be moved, and that if a power outage lasted for a long while, his death would not be recorded for weeks or it would be written off as succumbing to the precariousness of his disease-ridden body. After directly experiencing what had happened to Puerto Rico's infrastructure as a result of this storm, I knew these kinds of stories would be happening thousands of times over.

Sosa, who was doggedly visiting hospitals and morgues to look for unreported deaths, knew much better than me. She started pounding the pavement days after the hurricane, visiting people in towns across the island and scouring local hospitals and morgues. She found that the original count of sixteen, parroted by Rosselló in the Trump press conference, was obviously inadequate given the clear lack of access that thousands of elderly and ill Puerto Ricans had to oxygen-providing units, dialysis treatments, and other forms of medication and treatment. She found a woman in Lajas who waited in vain for battery-operated electrical generators that were never delivered to her town in time to save her father, an aging man whose children had unsuccessfully fought a major hospital, the Pavía in Santurce, against releasing him because there was no electricity in his home to power his respirator. She found that the morgues at hospitals were filled to capacity and that the Institute for Forensic Sciences was also filled with cadavers, 25 percent of whom were presumed to be victims of the hurricane and its aftermath.

Besides the fact that many of these hospitals were unable to function normally because they lacked power, staff, and sufficient supplies, they also struggled with the suspension or complete lack of communication and coordination. It was almost impossible to get a cellular signal. Most cell phone towers, like the poles that convey the island's electricity, had been knocked to the ground and were inoperable, plunging the entire island into a kind of panicked shock over disrupted communication. It cut off family members from each other for weeks, and people's inability to know about their loved ones' fortunes caused a trauma syndrome like the one I'd seen stirring in my mother when I arrived at her house. It was a common sight to see Puerto Ricans pulled over on highway roads or clustered together near the offices of cable-internet or cellular signal providers, latching on to that signal for a few moments on the phone with a relative who had done the same halfway across the island.

To Sosa the communications breakdown was central to understanding the problem of undercounting deaths caused by María. More than that, it was implicated in the way the Puerto Rico government used public relations to sustain itself as it presided over the disintegration of island life. Sosa's reporting and instincts were confirmed as the months passed, first by a *New York Times* investigation, then when two studies, by Harvard and George Washington universities, showed that the death count had been vastly understated. In the interim the Puerto Rico Center for Investigative Journalism, CNN, and the *Washington Post* filed Freedom of Information Act requests and took other legal actions to force the disclosure of government actions and records that furthered the findings.[3]

The methods used in analyzing the hurricane death toll ranged from esoteric to more straightforward, but their basis was to compare the average number of deaths per month in the months following the hurricane to the average compiled over the two previous years, 2016 and 2015. On September 29, the day that Héctor M. Pesquera, the secretary of Public Safety, doubted that the death toll would "double or triple" the way it would in the aftermath of an earthquake, the *Times* investigation found that 127 people died, which is 57 more than had died in 2016.[4] Pesquera, who had previously been named Puerto Rico police commissioner in the aftermath of the DOJ's investigation in 2012, had served in the FBI for twenty-seven years and had been based in Broward County, Florida, as the head of the Southern Command of DHS in 2005, the year of Filiberto Ojeda Ríos's assassination.

The investigation estimated that three weeks after the storm the death toll stood at 739, which would have made it the sixth-deadliest hurricane in the United States since 1851.

It found that the greatest proportion of deaths occurred in towns and municipalities along the direct route of the storm and that the number of deaths due to sepsis—a bacterial infection transmitted through drinking water, much of which had been contaminated after the storm—had the greatest increase of all causes of death. The Harvard T. H. Chan School of Public Health/Beth Israel Deaconness Medical Center report, published in the *New England Journal of Medicine* in July 2018, estimated that the death toll was at least 4,645, a number that stuck in the public imagination both in Puerto Rico and among the diaspora, becoming a familiar device used on placards in demonstrations, artworks, and internet memes. The dead had suffered injuries from flying debris, were swept away by floods, were prematurely discharged by overworked and overflowing hospitals, and died in ambulances unable to reach hospitals because of traffic snarled by signal lights that were not working.

In late August of 2018 the George Washington University Milken School of Public Health released a report that estimated 2,975 deaths. Because this study was commissioned by the Rosselló government, its estimate became the finally accepted number, changing its total from the 64 it had risen to a few months after Rosselló asserted a death toll of sixteen. Two weeks later Trump tweeted that "Democrats in order to make me look as bad as possible" had somehow inflated the death toll, despite the fact that the study had been commissioned by the same pro-statehood party that had refused to call him to task for months over the litany of failures of the US federal government to provide adequate relief to Puerto Rico.

An investigative report in *Politico* in March of 2018 showed that everything about the Trump administration's approach to Puerto Rico exhibited a consistent bias toward providing aid to victims of Hurricanes Harvey and Irma, which had struck Texas and Florida, respectively. The fact that FEMA director Mike Byrne remained in Houston during the crucial early period of the María aftermath was just part of a broader pattern in which US efforts were consistently shown to have fallen short in Puerto Rico. While seventy-three US Northern Command helicopters were deployed over Houston within six days, it took three weeks for the same to happen in Puerto Rico.[5] The study found that FEMA sent three times as many meals to Houston, 40 percent more liters of water, and four times as many blue tarps that would be used as temporary roofing.[6] The hurricane damaged 50 percent more homes in Puerto Rico than Houston (335,000 to 204,000), whereas the number of people sheltered in Texas more than doubled the number in Puerto Rico (37,000 to 15,000). But Puerto Rico's island-wide loss of power that lasted for months created a sustained need for such provisions. Three times as many FEMA and military personnel were sent to Houston, and it took forty-three days for the administration to approve permanent disaster work in Puerto Rico, as compared to seven days in Houston.

The Rosselló's government's inability to pressure the Trump administration was also notable. The governor himself did not criticize US efforts until Trump's insulting tweets in September 2018, a full year after the hurricane, and Resident Commissioner Jenniffer González was even more subservient, disagreeing with Trump only when he announced on September 24, 2018, that he was an "absolute no" as far as favoring statehood for Puerto Rico, in part because of his antipathy toward San Juan mayor Carmen Yulín Cruz. González's critique amounted to a refusal to accept that statehood would inevitably be denied because of Cruz's defiance to Trump, something that he continually pointed out when he argued that Puerto Rico should not receive more relief funds.

The Rosselló administration's obfuscation of facts and lack of transparency—which wasn't much better under the PDP government of Alejandro García Padilla nor Rosselló's NPP predecessor Luis Fortuño—had long plagued Puerto Rico. Although it's highly notable that this tactic was key in amassing the $72 billion debt, the Puerto Rico government has evaded and muddied public perceptions as part of its governing strategy. A case in point occurred in 2010, after Puerto Rico passed a law requiring all Puerto Ricans to fill out a form to have their birth certificates reissued because of what they called a rapid increase in identity theft. The reason for this, according to documents issued by the Fortuño administration, was that it affected US national security. More to the point, in a press release issued on January 22, Secretary of State Kenneth McClintock asserted that the reason for the law was that there was an identity fraud crisis in the United States set off by hundreds of copies of Puerto Rican birth certificates. Because of the quaint custom that Puerto Rican institutions have of requesting copies of birth certificates for everything from driver's licenses to Little League teams, he claimed that there were "thousands" of copies floating around, waiting to be used by identity scammers, drug traffickers, and terrorists. McClintock went on to say that 40 percent of all identity theft cases in the United States used Puerto Rican birth certificates.

This was, of course, hard to believe, but there was little uproar in the Puerto Rico news media. When challenged, McClintock claimed that the US Department of State's Bureau of Diplomatic Security reported that Puerto Rican birth certificates have been used in about 40 percent of *passport* fraud it had recently investigated. He was now admitting that he had narrowed down the sample to passport applications, not all US identity fraud cases, as originally claimed. Yet in many articles in *El Nuevo Día* and *Primera Hora*, Puerto Rico's two largest dailies, it continued to be reported that fraudulent Puerto Rican birth certificates were causing an "identity fraud crisis" in the United States, with the only evidence cited being the original assertion that 40 percent of *all* of the cases of identity theft in the United States are tied to Puerto Rican birth certificates.

Although it is true that there have been many cases of fraud involving Puerto Rican birth certificates, this hardly constituted a threat large enough to invalidate the identity proof of an entire island of four million US citizens. The minimal cost of $5 per new birth certificate was seen as a desperate move to raise money for an economy racked by high unemployment and recession. The process also created hardship for many seniors who lacked copies of their original birth certificates or other proof of identification. I had to fly down to Puerto Rico one week specifically to testify that I was my mother's son. Because she had lived in the United States most of her life and took my father's surname, she had almost no proof of who she was in the eyes of the Puerto Rico government.

HEALTHCARE CRISIS DEEPENS

Puerto Rico's healthcare system was already in crisis before María, and the storm only made things worse. Over three thousand doctors had left the island between 2010 and 2015, largely because of deeply embedded problems in the healthcare infrastructure, including that most of the population relied on Medicaid, and the privatization of the rest of the insurance system rendered it grossly inefficient. Besides that, practicing medical professionals had to deal with overcrowded conditions and an overwhelming number of patients while only earning about half the pay of their mainland US counterparts.

A disproportionate part of Puerto Rico's population is over sixty, and more than 60 percent of its residents receive federal entitlements like Medicare or Medicaid. However, because of the island's colonial status, they do not receive the full entitlement as they would in a US state, and the aid for such federal programs is capped. As a consequence, the Puerto Rico government has had to borrow for many years to make up for the shortfall of funding, which is responsible for $25 billion of the $73 billion debt in 2015.[7] Funding for these programs is always precarious and needs to be renewed by Congress in its budget yearly—with no guarantees it will come through.

Meanwhile thousands of elderly and sick patients, suffering from some of the highest asthma and diabetes rates in the United States, sit for hours in waiting rooms for routine doctors' appointments, often creating a testy atmosphere between themselves and the staff. A fall for an elderly person that causes a broken wrist can result in long waits for the few remaining orthopedic physicians as well as extended waiting times of several weeks for surgeries. The privatization of the healthcare system did nothing to solve these problems. Instead, it set up an infrastructure that was not only incompatible with the island's previous emphasis on public health clinics but also created the same kinds of barriers to care that plague US health insurance systems, which make primary care physicians gatekeepers to keep all health care in-network. Senior citizens were also steered to Medicare Advantage plans that required additional monthly payments and are slow to reimburse patients.

The earlier model of Puerto Rican health care came from programs developed by the US Centers for Disease Control, funded by FDR New Deal programs, and featuring diagnostic and medical treatment centers in all seventy-eight of Puerto Rico's municipalities.[8] It was a regionalized model designed to be emulated by the developing world through organizations such as the World Health Association.[9] In the 1970s the privatized part of the system began to grow, ironically because of the advent of Medicaid and Medicare, which began in the United States in 1965. Because funds for these programs were capped in Puerto Rico—another manifestation of the territory residents' second-class citizenship, who did not have full entitlement—Medicare in particular encouraged the growth of a private medical sector for those who could afford it. Through a new set of changes in the healthcare system known as "La Reforma" in the 1990s under NPP governor Pedro Rosselló, Puerto Rico aligned itself with the neoliberal healthcare reform implemented by President Bill Clinton. It decentralized the regional system and separated funding streams from administrative agencies, taking many physicians from the public to the private sector. The smaller clinics were largely dismantled, and public hospitals were privatized, with physicians arguing that "the payment and organizational structures embedded in the current privatized managed care system reduce the capacity to coordinate care . . . and shift the focus of care from prevention to treatment."[10]

Because of Puerto Rico's subordinate position to the United States, which in this case involves its healthcare system, US-style solutions are often imposed without much internal debate. Further, that debate can be controlled by elected officials who don't want to do anything to disturb the island's path in America's orbit. Although it's true that the previous system benefited from New Deal–inspired methodologies, Puerto Rico now has a US-like privatized healthcare system, which is forbidding enough for mainland Americans, operating in a place where there's a much higher percentage of the population using government-backed insurance (coupled with privatized Medicare Plus plans), with fewer economic resources and a lack of access to preventative medicine. According to Puerto Rico's Center for Investigative Journalists, almost two thousand Puerto Ricans left the island specifically because the healthcare system could not meet their needs.

All of this snowballed after María, when it became common for doctors to perform surgeries illuminated by smartphone flashlights. Doctors and hospitals on various parts of the island found it difficult, if not impossible to communicate with each other, so more doctors left for the mainland. In one particularly poignant situation, the only significant healthcare facility on the island of Vieques to provide dialysis, among other services, remained closed well into 2018. The abdication of care is even more disturbing when you recall that Vieques had been used as a bombing range for decades, and people who live there are eight times more likely to die of cardiovascular disease and seven times more likely to die of diabetes than those on the main island of Puerto Rico.[11]

Massive problems remained more than a year after the hurricane, from the instability of the electrical system to keep supplies like insulin refrigerated to the cuts in visiting nurse programs, from the chronic worsening of diseases like diabetes and hypertension to the lack of access to treatment for those

in rural areas. A slew of new health complications has pro-
liferated, not the least of which was a disastrous diminution
of mental health. Although the anxiety and dislocation most
island residents experienced had receded a bit, the most vulnerable have experienced increases in panic attacks, PTSD,
and depression. The difficulty of merely maintaining one's
existence with the threat of continuing blackouts, crumbling
roads and infrastructure, and an agricultural crisis that has
hampered access to healthy food has engendered the kind of
low-grade paranoia often associated with war zones. Suicide
attempts increased dramatically, up 30 percent in the months
following María, as well as those admitting to contemplating
it. Most painfully, many of those were children under eighteen:
six teenager suicides were recorded between September and
December 2017.[12]

OUT-MIGRATION AND SMALL RETURNS:
THE CIRCULAR PATH OF PUERTO RICANS

The colonial relationship between the United States and Puerto
Rico entails the continued migration to and from the unincorporated territory. Even before Puerto Ricans were extended US
citizenship in 1917, they were migrating northward because of
convulsions in the local economy. They found varying periods of
employment and then, often, returned to the island. Earlier in
this book I've recounted how the Great Migration of the 1940s to
1960s helped create the basis for a Puerto Rican presence in the
United States, influencing American politics, economy, and culture almost as much as islanders were influenced by the United
States. As a result of the economic downturn after the Section
936 tax breaks were phased out, out-migration from Puerto Rico
began to average anywhere from forty to eighty thousand people
a year. Hurricane María, unsurprisingly, intensified the exodus.
First it was those who needed immediate medical attention, followed by those who'd long had doubts about the island's fate.

Moving to the mainland has now become an open question for most Puerto Ricans.

Yet this is not simply a story of Puerto Ricans abandoning their beloved "Isla del Encanto" to find a new life in the United States—or sometimes even returning. It's a story of attempts to create a life change—perhaps with the intention of leaving temporarily or perhaps failing in that attempt altogether—in the face of the at-times overwhelmingly desperate situation on the island. One study done by tech firm Teralytics, which harvested information from smartphone data, shows that about four hundred thousand people, or 12 percent of the island's population, left between September 2017 and February 2018, but apparently only half of those remained in the United States in 2018, while the other half returned to the island. The highest concentration of migrants—about fifty-seven thousand—went to Orange and Osceola Counties in the Orlando area, with about fifty thousand others spread among counties near Miami and Tampa. For comparison, the Bronx, Central Massachusetts, and Philadelphia received about eighteen thousand altogether.

Other methods of assessing the migration ranged from measuring net airline passengers leaving Puerto Rico for the United States, applications for FEMA disaster relief for María filed from the United States, and new Puerto Rican enrollment in Florida schools and address changes on file at USPS from Puerto Rico to locations in the United States. FIU professor Jorge Duany, an expert observer of Puerto Rican demographics, called it "the biggest migration from Puerto Rico since records have been taken," while the Center for Puerto Rican Studies in New York estimated that between 2017 and 2019 Puerto Rico may lose up to 470,335 residents, or 14 percent of its population.[13] It may be true that such a dramatic shift will occur, but it remains to be seen whether factors driving the exodus remain constant or, at least, predictable at this time.

Certainly the economic outlook does not favor retaining the current levels of population. Even the much-noted influx of disaster capitalists and billionaires, lured to the island with tax breaks by the last three governors, will not do much to interrupt the general trend of population loss. But so many problems have been besetting early migrants—many of whom were only able to stay for a period of months because they were being temporarily housed in hotels under one of the FEMA programs—that it's not clear how many Puerto Ricans will stay.

There's no doubt, however, that the Orlando area in Central Florida has become one of the new centers of Puerto Rican diaspora life, spawning new terminology to transcend late-twentieth-century notions of "Nuyorican" that previously dominated thinking about Puerto Rican life stateside. Dubbed "Flori-Ricans," "Diaspo-Ricans," or "Other-Ricans," Orlando-area migrants have established themselves in a terrain similar to their tropical island, carving out the kind of lower-middle- to middle-class lifestyle that was the building block for Puerto Ricans fortunate enough to remain on the island after Operation Bootstrap in the 1950s and 1960s. The area has become a unique meeting point between New York/New Jersey–area Puerto Ricans who decided to move south for retirement or employment reasons and island Puerto Ricans looking to escape the effects of the territory's ten-year recession and, now, the aftermath of a catastrophic hurricane.

As far back as the 1930s and 1940s both Orlando and Tampa were used as escape valves for what US bureaucrats deemed Puerto Rico's "population problem." But the combination of the existence of military bases near Orlando that lured Puerto Rican service members and, in 1971, the opening of Disney World attracted family-oriented tourists from the island as well as job seekers and retirees frightened by the crime waves of the 1990s. Although a significant number of Puerto Ricans came to Orlando with a high educational level, most migrants are not part of a "brain drain"; they do not overrepresent the most educated and professional sectors of the population. Many Puerto Rican migrants are low-skilled workers who take service jobs at Orlando's tourist attractions, notably Disney World, which has heavily recruited workers from the island. In the late 1990s Disney

offered between $900 and $1,500 bonuses and free airfare to
those willing to relocate from the island to Orlando. The largest
percentage of worker occupation during the peak of the 1990s
migration were operators, fabricators, and laborers (23.3 percent), followed by service work (20.7 percent), administrative
support (18.9 percent), and sales (13.7 percent). Among those
over twenty-five years of age, 33.5 percent had some college
education or an associate's degree, but only 10.9 percent had
completed their bachelor's degree. This figure compares unfavorably to the 15.5 percent of people over twenty-five with a
bachelor's degree in the United States as a whole and 14.3 percent for Florida.

The influx to Orlando after Hurricane María was mainly
composed of relatively unskilled workers, with many of the
professionally trained residents choosing instead to relocate to
major cities in the Northeast. Several prestigious private universities, from Brown to NYU, offered free tuition for UPR
students whose fall semester had been shattered by the storm.
Puerto Ricans who landed in Orlando have largely replicated
island life, with an impressive array of restaurants, clubs, and
grocery stores that serve Puerto Rican–style food and play its
Afro-Caribbean music. Because of the overlapping nature of
Puerto Ricans' political loyalties, with PDP and NPP voters not
necessarily easily divided into Democratic and Republican categories, there is no consensus about what kind of effect Puerto
Ricans will have on Florida elections. However, the continuing
verbal abuse and physical neglect coming from the Trump administration will likely depress his support from Puerto Ricans,
except among the most hardcore NPP rightists.

THE PRODIGAL MOM

My mother, whose name happens to be María, was one of
those who came north after the hurricane, largely because of
her health needs and the uncertainty of when electricity would

return to the island. When I went down to retrieve her, my sister and I spent several days using flashlights and candles, traveled down the mountain when we needed to call people, and shopped in supermarkets that had limited selection and quantities. We used the unplugged refrigerator to store things like cheese and vegetables that would last for a few days before spoiling.

Victor and Migdalia, a couple who had lived across the road from my mother, left for Orlando to stay with their son, who had left two years earlier and successfully been employed by a security firm while his wife found work at a bank. She'd just given birth to her son, and they were thinking of flying in her side of the family to be closer to them as well. With Victor and Migdalia gone, my mother was much more willing to leave for New York—she now had few people nearby who could take her to a hospital at a moment's notice when necessary.

My mother had long resisted attempts to convince her that she should come back to the States so we could take better care of her. She preferred the home my parents built for their retirement on property that had been part of what was once a twenty-acre farm maintained by her parents. She had been born there, and many in the small community who remained were partially related to her. Her father—my grandfather—had come to work in the barrio at a YMCA camp that attracted some travelers from the United States, and he built a small home where he raised farm animals, milked cows, and sold eggs from his hens and small crops like plantains, mangos, and even coffee in the town at the base of the mountain. He acquired those twenty acres of land, according to my relatives, because he'd lent $20 to a neighbor, who died before he could pay him back. In his will the neighbor left him the bulk of the twenty acres, which stretched down to the Río Mameyes, the border between Rio Grande and Luquillo. I still have distant relatives who live on the other side of that river and physically cross it to get to the road that leads down the mountain to the coast. My mother refers to them as the ones who live *en el otro lado*—on the other side.

When the day finally came for us to leave, we did so with great sadness. We locked up the house without knowing when we would ever return, our rental car slowly descending the mountain she'd walked down to go to school when she was growing up during the Great Depression in the 1930s. Her new home would be with my sister in Orange County, New York, in a town that was a kind of exurb home to civil service workers and people looking for a good deal just close enough to the city to be affordable. Readjusting to the Northeast would come fairly easy for her—after all, she was a veteran of city life, having shuttled us around the Bronx and Manhattan on public transportation and had even taken a job at a Midtown jewelry business when we'd moved into our high school and college years.

The first thing she seemed to notice was the vast abundance of suburban supermarkets, with the explosion of "healthy" food choices, endless availability of fresh fish and exotic cheeses, as well as the exurbs' relative paucity of customers. My sister went through hours of struggle getting a new health insurance plan for my mother, whose Puerto Rico plan was not valid in New York. But once she did, my mother marveled at not having to wait hours to see a doctor and how the one she saw could speak Spanish, and she commented that he was very handsome and polite.

I was surprised to learn my mother was even more bilingual than we'd thought. With the steady high-speed internet at my sister's replacing the intermittent service she'd received on the island, she became more voracious than ever consuming national news on her tablet and increasingly held conversations in English with us and the people in my sister's neighborhood. A new pair of eyeglasses allowed her to read without the bouts of strained, tearing eyes she'd suffered in Puerto Rico.

When the Christmas holiday came, we all celebrated together for the first time in many years—with snow on the ground. My mother experienced the snow, bare trees, and below-zero temperatures for the first time in decades, and she embraced them ambivalently—happy to relive the ambience of holiday seasons

past but not thrilled about how the cold forced her to stay inside most of the time. It was around then that she began to ask
people back home whether they'd gotten their electricity back.

In a few months, much of the San Juan metro area had gotten power back, and life had returned to something of a sense
of normalcy in tourist areas. Up in mountainous areas like the
El Yunque the power was still out. Some residents were able to
afford limited electricity through gasoline-powered generators,
but many, if they had been able to repair damage to their roofs
and property, were still living the 6 a.m. to 6 p.m. existence of
their ancestors from the early twentieth century—keeping per-
ishables in ice chests, illuminating their evenings with candles
and flashlights, and turning in early to be able to awaken at
dawn.

As winter turned slowly into spring, my mother began to
miss the rhythms of her rural barrio, where neighbors stopped
by now and then to check on her and give her a ride so she
could go shopping and pick up her medication. This is a community that still engages in subsistence agriculture even as they
hold jobs in the tourist sector or as nurses, emergency medical technicians, house cleaners, or security guards. Most keep
plantain and mango trees or grow tubers like pana and yuca in
their backyards.

One day in April my mother's neighbor called to tell her
power had been restored in the barrio. Although my sister and
I wanted so much for her to stay, we knew she needed to be
where she felt alive. Her sister Mercedes, who had come with
us on the flight a year before, had already returned. Victor and
Migdalia were coming back to one of the houses across the road
from my mom's. We knew it was the right thing for her to go
back.

I visited my mother in August 2018 and found her healthier
and more vibrant than ever. The gentle mountain breezes don't
allow the summer heat to get too overwhelming. Much of the
foliage torn apart by María has grown back, and the main problem she seems to have is that the cable company has not been

able to restore her high-speed internet service. I taught her how to use her phone as a hotspot, and by the time I left, she had caught up to all her shows and knew the latest in the Mueller investigation.

I've always believed that there was a spiritual energy in the El Yunque that protected its people from all kinds of natural and political hurricanes. Sometimes, in the middle of an intense rainstorm, I walk outside to try to feel it. All at once the wind and the rain, the storm and the earth all seem to come together inside me. In those moments I understand the power of the land where I come from and why, despite everything, my mother needed to come home.

CHAPTER 8

THE TRUMP FACTOR

Vultures, Lobbyists, and Disaster Capitalism

Collapsed electric light pole in Santurce. © Joseph Rodríguez

"I think Puerto Rico was an incredible unsung success. In a certain way the best job we did was in Puerto Rico, but nobody would understand that."

—US president Donald J. Trump

"We're here to help Puerto Rico. We're here in service, and we serve through gifting. We're here to take our skills—our superpowers—and figure out how to help Puerto Rico, the Earth, and the people."

— Bitcoin investor Brock Pierce

"Even before the storms we had opportunities, but now we have a blank canvas where we can start thinking anew, where we can take bold steps into investment and innovation and rebuild Puerto Rico much more effectively."

— Puerto Rico governor Ricardo Rosselló

M ost Puerto Rican and diaspora thinkers and activists were strongly disappointed with the PROMESA process, its imposition of the Fiscal Oversight and Management Board to supersede local government, and its clear mandate to carry out debt restructuring to favor the US financial sector. The mainstream Democratic Party was by no means exempt from this disappointment, as its members in Congress for the most part had acquiesced to the PROMESA deal as the only resort to address the spiraling debt crisis. They accepted the neoliberal premise that a "bailout" from the Federal Reserve was unacceptable and acknowledged that the best thing that could be done for Puerto Rico was to put it on a somewhat painful path to regain "access to capital markets." Yet as exasperating as the Democrats' (with the exception of Bernie Sanders and, to some extent, Representative Luis Gutiérrez) accommodationist stance turned out to be, the election of Donald Trump turned Puerto Rico's situation from bad to much worse than could have been previously imagined.

As I've chronicled through much of this book, Puerto Rico has long been a kind of fantasy island for all manner of US economic and political ventures as well as ways of reformulating its power through the control of nonterritorial subjects as well as offshore economies. It has been a scientific laboratory for dangerous chemicals and unproven birth control methods, a dumping ground for unwanted or overstocked products and a place where American industry leaders could test their ability to work with a large population of employees who didn't speak English. It's been a place where the idea of North American free trade could be proven to benefit large corporations, and non-white men with limited English skills could be drafted into the armed forces. Lastly, it's been a place where the United States could experiment with tax policies that allowed for the accumulation of capital under conditions that were virtually offshore yet still within US territory and under the laws of the US banking system.

Now, with the end of Keynesian demand-side economic policy, the decline of labor unions, and the turn toward universal neoliberal privatization and worker disempowerment, Puerto Rico was poised to enter a new phase of extreme exploitation. With the twin devastation of the imposition of PROMESA to restructure the island's debt in favor of hedge and vulture fund investors and the widespread devastation caused by Hurricane María, Puerto Rico became a ripe target for what Naomi Klein calls "disaster capitalism."[1]

The disaster of Hurricane María created the perfect conditions for neoliberal capitalism, which needs a contraction of population and resources in order for a new capital project to expand quickly *ex nihilo*—from "nothing." The "blank canvas" Governor Ricardo Rosselló alluded to at an investor's showcase in New York in February 2018 sets disaster capitalists' mouths watering. Even better, from their perspective, was the reality that—unlike New Orleans, a recent setting for disaster capital explosion after Hurricane Katrina—Puerto Rico lacked the full protection of US laws and had already created laws to nurture a community of super-rich speculators. There was also the scope of the destruction to consider. It wasn't just neighborhoods like the Lower Ninth Ward that were severely affected; it was the entire island. The *Shock Doctrine*—a phrase coined by author Naomi Klein to describe how neoliberal powers take advantage of national economic and political crises to push through new policies that disaster-fatigued citizens find difficult to mount a resistance against—was looming to become Puerto Rico's way of life, its new normal.

Just weeks after Hurricane María, on October 2, the government of Puerto Rico awarded a $300 million contract to reconstruct fallen power lines on the island to a company based in Secretary of Energy Ryan Zinke's hometown of Whitefish, Montana. The company, called Whitefish Energy, had two employees, including its CEO Andy Techmanski. Apparently Ricardo Ramos, the CEO of PREPA, had already been in contact with Whitefish during the recovery period for Hurricane Irma. Ramos said he felt the company had "special skills" because of its experience with rebuilding electrical infrastructure in the mountainous areas of Montana.[2] Despite the fact that Whitefish did not have numerous linemen on its staff and had no experience working in disaster conditions nor a tropical climate, Ramos quickly signed a deal with Whitefish, ostensibly because they did not ask for any money upfront.

Ramos had the option of asking for mutual aid help through the American Public Power Association, but he was quoted telling CNN's HLN network that he didn't think they would respond quickly enough because their resources were already stretched thin in Texas and Florida dealing with Hurricanes Harvey and Irma. Almost immediately questions were raised about Zinke's involvement with the deal, but in late October he issued a statement denying any ties. Yet a few weeks later it was revealed that Techmanski had hired Zinke's son as an intern and that the firm's biggest investor was a Dallas-based firm that had given huge campaign contributions to Rick Perry, John

McCain, and Marco Rubio.³ Ramos also rebuffed these concerns, saying, "The doubts that have been raised about Whitefish . . . are completely unfounded"—implying that competitors who were disgruntled from having lost their bid were spreading the criticism.⁴

The contract was rather rich by even normal standards. The hourly rate for a site supervisor was $330 and a journeyman lineman would receive $227.88 per hour, but even worse, the rates for subcontractors, which were the majority of Whitefish's workforce, were $462 per hour and $319.04 per hour. Nightly accommodation fees of $332 per worker, with an $80 a day meal money rate, also attached. These rates compared with reports that Whitefish's subcontractors from the Jacksonville Electric Authority were making $90 an hour (twice as much as subcontractors normally made), which would mean Whitefish would be pocketing over $200 per hour per worker through the terms of the contract.

The Whitefish contract was followed in mid-October by a $200 million contract with Cobra Acquisitions LLC, a subsidiary of Oklahoma City–based oil company Mammoth Energy Services, Inc. The contract contained the same language as the Whitefish contract, stating that neither PREPA, the commonwealth governor, FEMA, nor the US comptroller general would have "the right to audit or review the cost and profit elements of the labor rates" in the contract.⁵ The Whitefish controversy ended with the cancellation of its contract at the end of October 2017, with Rosselló calling for a federal investigation of the contract award process, ultimately forcing Ramos out of his job by mid-November.⁶

FIRST ON THE NEOLIBERAL LIST:
THE PRIVATIZATION OF PREPA

The Puerto Rico Electric Power Authority was under fire from all sides in the aftermath of Hurricane María. Already targeted for privatization before the storm because of its $9 billion debt and ample evidence of the electrical grid's deterioration, PREPA was now elevated to a number-one priority in the disaster capitalist playbook. Although this plan had been considered during the original stages of the PROMESA board and would be just the latest in a series of privatizations that go back to the Pedro Rosselló administration in the 1990s, dissolving PREPA would kick off the island's new era. Since then Puerto Rico has privatized its phone company, its international airport, the toll collection for its major highways, various municipal medical clinics, and parts of its aqueduct and sewers authority. None of these moves have improved service to consumers, and almost all have resulted, as was the case when Chicago and Detroit privatized their parking meters, in higher costs.

The FOMB itself had been explicitly on the privatize-PREPA bandwagon months before Hurricane María. In an unapologetic opinion piece for the *Wall Street Journal* toward the end of June, board members Andrew Biggs, Arthur González, Ana Matosantos, and David Skeel endorsed the privatization move, saying they came to the decision after rejecting PREPA's restructuring proposal filed in March of that year. The FOMB used a simple, neoliberal logic to justify privatization: "Puerto Rico's electricity costs are two to three times as high as mainland levels. The board concluded that lowering the price of electricity and spurring economic growth depended on reforming PREPA's operations, not merely restructuring its credit. Affordable electricity could boost growth by up to half a percentage point annually, raising family incomes on the island, stemming out-migration and increasing funds available to repay creditors."[7]

This reasoning leaves out a crucial reason for the higher rates: electricity generation in Puerto Rico is almost entirely dependent on imported oil. It also failed to take into account that there is no guarantee that privatization would lead to more affordable electricity or that because a variety of factors—including access to education, stable employment, and health care—cause out-migration, lowering electricity costs, if achieved at all, would not necessarily "stem" it. This logic is often used to disguise the guiding principle of neoliberalism, which is neatly embodied in public-private partnership (PPPs) projects: selling off public corporations is most efficient at making the public pay for the costs of something like providing consumer electricity while also making it easier for private companies to obtain profits from production and distribution. This model can most clearly be seen in the oft-considered strategy of privatizing the generation and sourcing of electrical energy, while PPPs would handle transmission-line infrastructure rebuilding and repairs.[8]

A Puerto Rico Center for Investigative Journalism report revealed that as early as October 18, 2017—less than a month after Hurricane María—Arizona senator Jeff Flake and Utah senator Mike Lee had been pushing for privatizing PREPA. This was uncovered through emails written by their representatives to FOMB member Andrew Biggs. The report claimed that Flake and Lee "delayed granting supplementary disaster-relief funds to Puerto Rico" until amendments to reform the island's "energy sector," including privatizing PREPA, were included in the legislation. Biggs apparently acted as a conduit so that messages could be sent to FOMB budget director Ana Matosantos, providing a backdoor channel of interest—out of the public view—to promote the interests of ExxonMobil, Duke Energy, and Chevron. These corporations were among the oil and electric utility companies that had donated almost $800,000 to Flake in previous campaigns. Lee's donations, which included funds from Chevron, Haliburton, and Koch Industries, totaled almost $550,000.[9]

The following January Governor Rosselló announced that PREPA would be privatized. Calling the system outdated and inefficient, the governor criticized PREPA as monopolistic; noted that electricity generation was obsolete and depended almost completely on importing gasoline and that its south-north delivery system was inefficient, in which gas is manufactured from coal ash in southern towns like Peñuelas and electricity is then transmitted to a plant just west of San Juan; and cited how, in the last five years, 30 percent of PREPA workers had been laid off—all without mentioning the government's role in perpetuating the system's ills. This privatization would be accomplished in three stages: first, the legal framework would be defined, then buyout offers considered, and finally, the winning bid would be awarded. He promised a "transformation" of the system that would be "community centered," innovative, technologically advanced, and—this is key—"financially viable."

There are several ways to interpret what the still-in-negotiation privatization of PREPA will mean. Will Rosselló be able to fulfill his fantasy of some kind of variation of Elon Musk's proposed micro-grid reorganization, whose benefits seem significant but whose control could fall into the hands of external corporate interests? How would the settlement of its $9 billion debt—the restructuring of which was completed in November 2018—affect bidding? Finally, how exactly would different parts of PREPA, including electricity generation, be sold off? Even as four bidders were announced in January of 2019—Exelon Corp; PSEG Services Corp; a consortium of ATCO Ltd., IEM Inc., and Quanta Services; and Jeff Flake campaign contributor Duke Energy—there were clearly inescapable problems to privatization. Whether you take the bottom-line humanist angle of UTIER president Ángel Figueroa Jaramillo, who declared passionately that "PREPA is a public good that belongs to the people and not to the politicians of the day. . . . Energy is a human right and not a commodity," or the economist position that the public-private partnership mechanism that dominates this process will make decisions about the need for restoring and extending services on a purely for-profit basis, it's clear that this is just another way to subject Puerto Ricans to crucial policy decisions that are made far beyond their control and completely lacking their input. When the executive director for the island's Public-Private Partnership's Authority, Omar Moreno, while addressing investors in a San Juan hotel, equates "the people" with "the people of the private sector" as the just authority over what projects would be picked to modernize Puerto Rico's infrastructure, it's a clear indication of the Orwellian doublespeak involved in this process.[10]

There is an irony to the arguments over PREPA's privatization that involves who ultimately controls what happens in its restructuring processes on both the debt-restructuring and infrastructure rehabilitation and reconstruction side. The interests for privatization say that PREPA has been held hostage by its "politicization," meaning that it has been corrupted by favoritism in handing out contracts to cronies of whatever political party is in control. Yet privatization and its public-private partnerships are designed to create favoritism based on relationships outside the island and in the mainland United States. The Puerto Rican people are essentially being asked to accept a shift in favoritism/corruption from its own elites to "mainstream" elites who are arguably even less likely to intervene in their favor. It's essentially a neoliberal process of favoring globalization over local capital and/or governance, using the same sort of mainland US scams—like "retail choice," which largely has the effect of imposing higher rates on the consumer—something that has produced markedly unfavorable results to electricity consumers in the New York area for years.[11]

One of PREPA's earlier forays into privatization involved investing in private companies that generated electrical power from coal ash. The main problem with this strategy is that the residue of the coal ash left in the water supply generates a tremendous danger to the environment, particularly the fragile ecosystems of a southern Puerto Rico coast, which is dotted with the ruins of the failed petrochemical plants of the 1970s. In early August of 2017, in the southwestern town of Peñuelas, there was an uptick in police violence against a stubborn group of one hundred or so protesters fighting the deposit of toxic coal ash in local landfills. The ash had been transported by the energy company AES, which operates a Guayama, Puerto Rico–based electric-power plant, to the Dominican Republic in 2016. This severely contaminated a small town, caused widespread disease among adults and children of another small town where the ashes were dumped, and was subsequently rerouted to a landfill in Peñuelas, a community that had in the past been subjected to contamination from the petrochemical plants.[12] The government said at the time that coal produced about 15 percent of the total amount of electrical energy generated by PREPA. PREPA warned in mid-July that if its use of coal was disrupted, the cost of electricity would rise by 2.5 cents per kilowatt-hour, or 15 percent, and that this would also increase the number of blackouts.[13]

On July 4, 2017, the Puerto Rico government passed a law stating that a toxic element of coal ash, called fly ash, could not be deposited anywhere on the island. This prompted AES to turn to using a new product called Agremax, which mixed fly ash with other forms of ash and water. On August 6 a court in nearby Ponce dismissed a suit that claimed dumping it would cause health and environmental damage, such as chronic respiratory and coronary disease and contamination of rivers and reservoirs. The ruling said that, according to Puerto Rico's Environmental Quality Board, the dumping was in compliance with law and did not pose an environmental threat. The Puerto Rico Center for Investigative Journalism has reported that the coal ash was shipped in freighters to the Dominican Republic, where it wreaked havoc with that island's ecosystems, and there was a brief panic in Puerto Rico after Hurricane María concerning Agremax's inability to contain the ash during the storm. Studies remain to be done about any effects that may have had on local streams and rivers.

The presence of the toxic dumps in their communities naturally led students and environmental activists to begin engaging in organized activism. Gerardo Medina Rivera, an adjunct professor at the University of Puerto Rico–Ponce and a Peñuelas resident, argued that despite the court ruling, Agremax contains highly toxic elements and that the government should explore safer ways of producing energy. Medina Rivera had been part of a protest encampment that the community had sustained for two years. The encampment was similar to the one that protested the imposition of PROMESA, and like the university-based resistance movements of 2010, 2011, and 2017, in the wake of the imposition of the FOMB, it combined youth with labor and environmental activists and was organized in a horizontal rather than hierarchical structure.

Tactical police and a riot squad regularly visited the encampment, deploying tear gas and similarly violent confrontational methods. Puerto Rico is vulnerable to the kinds of harsh police oppression of environmental activism that has been increasing in Latin America, most notably in countries like Mexico and Colombia. Questioning the primacy of global oil and energy interests is a role a resistance movement can play that can create a volatile situation in terms of public protest. In Puerto Rico's case, direct ties to lobbyists for those interests, represented by Congress members like Rob Bishop and Jeff Flake, provide an incentive for the state to protect those interests over those of their own citizens. One of the more notable examples of the perils of environmental activism was the movement led by eco-activist community organization Casa Pueblo, which led the fight against Luis Fortuño's ill-fated Gasoducto project in 2011.

Building Gasoducto would have been a double victory for Fortuño because he wanted it to be a positive part of his campaign for election and, secondly, because it could have established a precedent for using government force against activists. One of many laws his administration pushed through as soon as he took power made obstructing any new construction project in any way a felony.

Arturo Massol, the associate director of Casa Pueblo, the community group that he formed with his father, Alexis, in 1980 to protest a government initiative to mine for silver, copper, and gold in the mountainside of Adjuntas, had been fighting this battle for many years. Arturo was clear about the direct threat of displacement being used against local residents who were "being menaced by a private firm that is trying to force them out of their property with threats and intimidation." He and civil rights activists like William Ramírez, head of the Puerto Rico chapter of the ACLU, were concerned with the possibility that Fortuño could press felony charges against demonstrators. But in a rare victory, however, demonstrators kept up such a sustained and sympathetic presence that Fortuño eventually had to abandon the plan, something that had a small hand in his electoral defeat in 2012.

Casa Pueblo established itself over decades as a community center that promoted arts, culture, and the environment. It is perhaps most famous for educating Puerto Ricans about building and installing solar panels in their homes and businesses to usher in a green-energy paradigm change "from below." Their main site, a breathtakingly beautiful house nestled in the foothills of mountainous Adjuntas, is a prime example of what they call *auto-gestión solidaria*, or "self-generated action in solidarity." They make their own coffee, operate a radio station, and have opened the first entirely solar-powered movie screening room on the island.

A model of engaging, community-oriented, aesthetic, nonviolent passive resistance, Massol and Casa Pueblo hardly project the image of "violent" anarchists. Yet mysteriously, on the evening of July 26, 2018, the same day that the FOMB reached a restructuring deal for PREPA's debt, Massol was arrested after leaving a pizzeria in Adjuntas with his daughter. The circumstances of the arrest raised questions about the police's motivations, as he was initially stopped under suspicion that his registration was not up to date, a violation that would have only resulted in a summons, and was eventually arrested for driving while intoxicated.

In Massol's recounting of the events, he claimed that because he clearly knew he was not intoxicated, he agreed to take a breathalyzer test, which the officer claimed verbally gave a result of .081—just over the legal limit—but refused to show Massol the reading on the device. At that point the officer escalated the investigation by accusing Massol of not cooperating, which Massol claimed he had done by taking the test. The officer then arrested him.[14]

He was taken to the local precinct, where he remained hand-cuffed without being allowed to consult a lawyer, later posting a photo that showed the marks the handcuffs made on his wrists. He said he was confronted with the .081 result, which could no longer be confirmed on the device, as it was long after the test was given. He admitted that the registration on his vintage 1952 Jeep was not current, but the owner of the pizzeria he had been in told *El Nuevo Día* that Massol had not consumed any alcoholic beverages while he was there.

"They have accused Casa Pueblo and my family of everything, tried every means to intimidate us, to undermine our fighting spirit and reputation," Massol said. "Although I never speak about the repression that we are living through, it's time for me to face this intimidation agenda. These kinds of actions do nothing but feed our conviction to continue building self-sufficiency and defending our national resources. Our doors are open to everyone who wants to listen and join, building for our country." In December 2018 Massol was cleared of all charges.

In November of 2018 PREPA announced that it would convert parts of its San Juan power plant from oil to natural gas, and the contract to refit its San Juan plant was awarded in March 2019. Governor Rosselló lauded the switch as a commitment to "clean energy," despite the fact that the debate about whether natural gas is "clean" is dubious about that.[15] It could be called "clean" because it gives out half as much carbon dioxide as coal when burned, but it produces methane, which is a potent greenhouse gas. The deal has been criticized because it was awarded to a relatively new contractor with little track record, recalling the Whitefish dynamic. The company, New Fortress Energy, has no track record of doing business in Puerto Rico and its director, Wesley Edens, is a "longtime supporter of the U.S. Ski and Snowboard Foundation" and a major donor to the Democratic Party. He is also the co-owner of the Milwaukee Bucks NBA team with Puerto Rico debt owner and Hillary Clinton fundraiser Marc Lasry.

PUERTOTOPIANS, BLOCKCHAIN, AND
BILLIONAIRE MIGRANTS

Developed by the mysterious Satoshi Nakamato in the wake of the 2008 recession/crisis, Bitcoin open-source p2p currency was designed to be a kind of libertarian tech solution to the untrustworthiness of the world banking system. To this day it is not known whether Nakamato is a pseudonym for a person or a group, but whomever he/she/they are, nothing has been heard from Nakamato since just after the currency's invention. Its proponents optimistically describe it as a cashless way for people to control economic transactions without a banker/middleman, eliminate interest, and dispense with metal-based currency systems as well as what is called "fiat currency," or the money that governments create based on the global faith in their gold and currency reserves, balance sheets, and potential to create capital and wealth. Bitcoin is constructed through a process that involves complex mathematical calculations and record keeping, and it is preserved through the methodology of blockchain, which provides an always-existing and accessible written record of transactions, with a set of rules and verification procedures.

David Graeber has posited that debt, as a social regulation mechanism, preceded money as currency and that the birth of philosophy in China and the Indian subcontinent was directly connected to the need to account for a sense of value crystallized not in "god" but in an object. From that perspective we can imagine Bitcoin as the new form of exchange value that might someday create a way to get out from under the paralyzing weight of worldwide debt. Our current global debt problem, not just restricted to Puerto Rico, is a primary driver behind the explosion of wealth inequality. It is clearly plagued by an abuse of transaction fees and exploitative interest rates charged by out-of-control financial institutions that supposedly would be on the path toward extinction if cryptocurrencies like Bitcoin took hold and served people in the decentralized open-source form that they promise.

Enter the Puertotopian narrative, primarily driven by Brock Pierce, a fusion of LA celebrity culture, gamer geek essence, Burning Man–hipster aesthetics, and post–Silicon Valley tech visionary gospel. Pierce had been coming to Puerto Rico since 2013 to spread the gospel of Bitcoin. Estimated by Bitcoin devotees to have a net worth of $1 billion, he is the chairman of the Bitcoin Foundation, an early blockchain venture-capital enterprise, and he preaches a vision of cryptocurrency as the next big evolution that will change everyone's life. A former child actor who had parts in family fare like *The Mighty Ducks* and *Little Big League*, Pierce left Hollywood while still a teenager to become a professional video game player in Hong Kong.

Pierce then entered a sordid association with a technology entrepreneur named Marc Collins-Rector who ran a company named Digital Entertainment Network. Collins-Rector invited Pierce into the fold. The company fell apart when Collins-Rector and his partner, Chad Shackley, were charged with child molestation, but Pierce absorbed enough of their vision from his experience—which taught him that static television and movie entertainment was about to be usurped by the interactive experiences promised by internet streaming—that he moved to Marbella, Spain, and founded a company called Internet Gaming Entertainment (IGE). He built this new company on the strength of his game-playing ability—his favored character was a dark-elf wizard called Arthrex—and soon realized there was money in selling virtual weapons, armor, and currencies he acquired in his gaming.[16]

Pierce began with platinum coins from a game called *Ever-Quest*, which began to develop into a market worth millions before establishing the gold accumulated by his Azeroth character in *World of Warcraft*—a game that once had eleven million subscribers—as the most heavily traded virtual currency. His virtual currency business had become so attractive that IGE was luring millions in investment capital from Goldman Sachs, and the company wound up hiring one of their bankers, Steve Bannon. Pierce described the infamous entrepreneur/right-wing media baron who, ten years later would make it all the way to Trump's White House as his "right-hand man."[17] Bannon felt that Pierce was at the center of a "fourth industrial revolution" that would take his vision of a "populist revolution" closer to its goal. Although there is no clear sign that Pierce is aligned with white supremacist movements, his connections to Bannon-style mysticism, combined with allusions to populist evasions of the global order, have imbued a kind of smoke-and-mirrors oratory—or, less charitably, subdued twenty-first-century huckster-ism—that pervades his public appearances.

Soon after Hurricane María Pierce decided the time was right to make the island his base, moving himself and his oper-ations there in late 2017. In his first major presentation during a conference he called Restart, held in San Juan in March 2018, he made clear his understanding of his role in language simi-lar to Bannon's. His narrative ties together the birth of crypto-currency with the aftermath of the tech bubble and the 2008 financial markets crash. He also scoffs at doubters by compar-ing skepticism about blockchain with the skepticism about the internet itself. The early adopters of the internet, he suggested, were fringe adopters, just like his fringe-y hipster self.

Although his ridiculous outfits, including a large hat with playing cards affixed to it, can make him seem like an eminently dismissible figure, Pierce knows how to use sophisticated lan-guage that combines techspeak and Bannon-like teleology, in which personal gain is fused with an outsized form of spiritual self-importance that pretends to be on the cutting edge of his-tory. "Bitcoin is digital value, a token with fixed supply," he said, with two large screens on either side showing a large "ME" with the "M" inverting in a motion graphic so that the screen even-tually shows "WE." "Blockchain can have programmable rules written into it like a contract—it is a decentralized and incor-ruptible public ledger. It's a public source of truth." Pierce's anarcho-libertarianism promises "decentralized autonomous communities" that create "an alignment of interests," some-thing that the developing world needs most.[18]

It's clear that Pierce is very good at connecting dots. He parlayed his fifteen minutes of fame in Hollywood into a video-game career, then used his playing skills to develop and exploit an emerging market of virtual currency. This put him into contact with venture capital backed by one of the world's most powerful banks, the one that is a central player in underwriting and charging exorbitant fees for Puerto Rico bond sales and loan adjustments. He likens Puerto Rico's blank slate to the conditions that allowed a market involving the use of prepaid cell-phone minutes to develop in Kenya, and he asks the all-important question: "Does Puerto Rico have tech unicorns?" alluding to Puerto Rico's potential for developing a gifted tech-savvy entrepreneurial class. By May 20 Puerto Rico's Department of Economic Development and Trade launched a Blockchain Advisory Council, headed by department secretary Manuel Laboy Rivera, to develop a friendly regulatory and legal framework for the nascent industry.

Since then blockchain technology has been cited as a way for new energy entrepreneurs to directly sell products to community cooperatives and, in this way, revolutionize the way energy is created and distributed in Puerto Rico. Yet all of this seems to ignore that very few significant developments have been made since the blockchain buzz began and that the central benefit seems to be a vague notion that attracting significant numbers of super-rich entrepreneurs and venture capital will somehow lead to innovation that will trickle down to benefit the post-María landscape of Puerto Rico. Pierce and his comrades know that their true purpose is to be at the center of a venture-capital bonanza that will invest in their companies and that profits will be protected by the Act 20 and 22 tax benefits that Luis Fortuño passed ten years earlier.

Pierce has already faced some noisy pushback in his public appearances. Nonetheless, he continues to carry on his bro-network in a rented Airbnb in Old San Juan, riding the wave until it crashes. So far he hasn't experienced pushback from the emerging revelation that the environmental consequences of blockchain farming could accelerate climate change through the tremendous amount of greenhouse gas emissions that the computers needed to mine Bitcoin would create.[19] Ironically, blockchain miners prefer areas of the world with relatively low electricity costs to get the best return on their investment, and the privatization of PREPA is unlikely to make prices in Puerto Rico more favorable for them.

The privatization of PREPA aside, the Puerto Rico government's strategy to attract the ultra-rich borders on the absurd: most come for the tax dodge, and although many invest in beach properties that could produce some jobs, there is no mechanism to ensure that a significant portion of their investment goes to Puerto Rican economic development. Over 1,500 well-heeled transients have established residency in Puerto Rico since 2012—when Acts 20 and 22 began, setting a low corporate tax rate of 4 percent—and make personal income from capital gains, interest, and dividends tax-free. To benefit, an individual must spend at least 183 days a year on the island, but just spending one minute on the island counts for one day—conceivably one could land on a private plane, buy a coffee, and go on to another Caribbean island destination.[20]

Various small businesses have sprung up to service the ultra-rich who buy up valuable properties along El Condado and the relatively remote beach town of Dorado, once a favorite of the Rockefeller family. Hedge-fund billionaire John Paulson, a major donor to New York University and once considered as a possible financial adviser to the Trump White House, has become a prime mover and shaker in El Condado. He hosts most of the major investment-attracting events, including the one where Puerto Rico was declared a potential Singapore of the Caribbean. The setting for the successful Hollywood comedy *Crazy Rich Asians*, Singapore is one of the most expensive cities in the world and is home to 188,000 millionaires, with 1,500 characterized as "ultra-rich"; has a low income-tax rate; and is also experiencing rapid growth in wealth inequality.

THE NEOLIBERAL "RIGHT SIZING" OF
PUERTO RICO'S EDUCATION SYSTEM

In July of 2018 Puerto Rico Secretary of Education Julia Keleher was interviewed by *CBS News* reporter David Begnaud and made a comment that set the internet on fire. Unfortunately the comment that was widely circulated was a misquote that appeared in an excerpt of the interview on Begnaud's Facebook page: "Hurricane María was the best thing to happen to Puerto Rico." The outrage and condemnation were swift, largely because Keleher, though her Spanish accent was passable, had grown up in an Italian American neighborhood in South Philadelphia and was generally perceived as an outsider in Puerto Rico. But what she really said—that the hurricane may have been a positive for the public-school system—was indicative of her purpose on the island and perhaps just as damnable. "Under normal circumstances here, it would have been very difficult for me to try to extend the school day," she said. "The other option I had was in the summer—that never would have flown—people were adamant about not having school in June. It was almost as if it was by law. And now all of a sudden it's an option."

Keleher meant that because the hurricane had closed schools for so long, she had a much better opportunity to implement something she had wanted to do for some time: institute various charter-school-like reforms, such as extending the school day, something she previously felt was impossible to do given the history and tradition of the school system. She was indirectly referring to rules set by the system of unionized teachers, who despite being vastly underpaid, had access to paid health insurance and a pension system, two expenses that education systems across the United States and Puerto Rico wanted to eliminate gradually by expanding the implementation of charter schools. In this way Keleher is acting as a kind of Trojan horse as she attempts to foist privatization plans on Puerto Rico in the wake of a crisis.

Keleher's remarks were eerily similar to those made by former Obama secretary of education Arne Duncan, who, in an interview with journalist Roland Martin in 2010, said that Hurricane Katrina was "the best thing that happened to the education system in New Orleans."[21] Similarly to Keleher, he explained that the city's education system was a disaster and that the community needed to be woken up to say "we have to do better." But the charter-school implementation at the center of education reform in New Orleans, according to critics, tends to pump up stats, reflecting improvements for an elite set of students while widely hurting the most disadvantaged, who leave the system entirely and are then no longer included in the data.

In many ways Puerto Rico had avoided accelerated forms of neoliberal privatization that have held sway in the states. Charter schools are just beginning to take root, albeit in the face of resistance; university tuition rates are relatively low; remnants of the regional health system in the form of Centros de Diagnóstico y Tratamiento (Centers for Diagnosis and Treatment, or CDTs) still exist; and the large unionized government workforce still dwarfs the private sector. The advent of María and the resulting severe crises have offered sudden opportunities for new private-sector-driven remedies that would have been difficult to implement previously.

Puerto Rico's government has long planned to close public schools, eliminate teaching jobs, and erode the school teachers' union. At first motivated by the increasing threat from the debt crisis, the plan is now being implemented in full force as the result of Hurricane María. In February 2018 Governor Rosselló announced his desire to clone the mainland United States' neoliberal plans for education, including a "school choice" voucher system and charter schools while also offering the backdoor reward of salary increases for teachers. With the policy's focus on charters and school-choice vouchers, the likely result is continued school closures. Of Puerto Rico's 1,100 schools, 244 have already been closed.

Keleher's position in Puerto Rico had been fraught with daily dramas about her legitimacy to be secretary of education, where her command of the Spanish language is constantly called into question. At one meeting with education department personnel, she openly admitted that as a native English speaker, she was merely translating her thoughts and not always very efficiently, which would account for their inability to understand her.[22] Although she speaks with a fairly competent approximation of an authentic island Puerto Rican accent, there are moments when her pronunciation has an unavoidable gringo tinge, which invokes either grudging acceptance or skeptical disapproval from the education workforce, the media, and public opinion. Perhaps even more problematic for Keleher is her $250,000 a year salary, one of the highest for a secretary of education position in the United States, inviting comparisons to FOMB president Natalie Jaresko, also an extravagantly compensated outsider.

The practice of extending outsized salaries to directors of major institutions or governmental departments has long been a staple of how neoliberalism rewards top-level executives, one of the keys to how its wealth redistribution benefits the corporate classes. The rationale of attracting "world-class" talent involves sometimes global searches that repeatedly have resulted in outsiders being brought into local situations with little understanding of the history and politics of the area. El Museo del Barrio in Spanish Harlem in New York is an oft-cited example, where a museum that was founded by and for local New York Latino residents has evolved into a global institution that has been importing directors from Mexico and Europe to run the institution for the last twenty years. Even police department chiefs are now de rigueur appointees from halfway across the country, as is also often the case with city university presidents, and so on.

But what makes Keleher's stint as education director particularly unsettling is her easy fit with Trump education secretary Betsy DeVos, whose family founded Amway and is among the more prominent Christian-right families of the United States.

Her brother, for example, is Erik Prince, who founded the mercenary military contracting firm Blackwater, which operated in the Middle East wars as a privatized force, one of whose members was convicted of first-degree murder in an incident that resulted in the killing of fourteen unarmed civilians in 2007.[23] DeVos has elicited continued criticism for her statements that public education is a dead-end system, that historically black colleges and universities were "real pioneers of public choice," that she favored more armed personnel in schools to prevent mass shootings, and that she agreed that the United States should pull out of the Paris climate change accord. She is the classic out-of-touch ultra-rich cabinet member that Trump has imposed on the American people in his blatant attempt to rule by oligarchy.

DeVos had been working very closely with both Keleher and Governor Rosselló to institute educational reforms, either directly or through Deputy Assistant Secretary Jason Botel.[24] DeVos's priorities were to allow multiple charter school authorizers—something that plagued Michigan, the state where DeVos had been chair of the RNC fundraising effort. The use of multiple authorizers can allow a poorly performing charter school to be more easily taken over by an authorizer—an entity approved by a local legislature that oversees a charter school's compliance with its contract—who may be less strict in its standards. New reforms also leave the door open for the expansion of online charter schools, a format that is easily abused. Lack of oversight and improperly substituting online instruction for traditional instruction can negatively impact students and devalue instructors' skills. The rush toward charter school solutions also ignores charters' many failures in the United States, including one in Philadelphia operated by a Puerto Rican diaspora organization called ASPIRA (a youth advocacy and education nonprofit organization whose name literally means "aspire"), which was closed because of corruption just weeks after a visit from Governor Rosselló, who later tweeted that it represented "an excellent charter school model."[25]

By early 2019 Keleher had opened the first charter school in Puerto Rico, a Boys and Girls Club–sponsored school in San Juan. She then announced that the proposal process was backlogged and rules for granting charters needed to be modified. Around the same time a company called Dealer Market Exchange announced it would be opening up a new online academy called DMX University that will train students in blockchain development in Puerto Rico. Meanwhile the island's storied university system struggles with disrepair, tuition increases, loss of faculties and departments, and a threatened loss of accreditation. Moreover, the teachers' union, Federación de Maestros de Puerto Rico, has continued to advocate for pay raises and better working conditions and filed a lawsuit against the implementation of charter schools as part of educational reform. Education in Puerto Rico will perhaps be its most crucial battleground going forward.

In April 2019 Keleher resigned as education secretary, citing "political" problems and the fact that she is a "game-changer" who had already implemented changes and that the system now needed someone who could "hold the course." She had arranged to remain as a consultant under the same $250,000 a year salary, but days after her resignation that contract was canceled. This was apparently related to questions raised by Keleher's connection to the law firm Hogan Marren Babbo & Rose, which offered legal counsel to charter school start-ups. The contact person for this firm is Jay Rosselló, Governor Ricardo Rosselló's brother, a fact that immediately sent Puerto Rico's local press into overdrive.[26]

THE COFINA DEAL:
RESTRUCTURING OR DEATH SENTENCE?

In October 2018 a bill passed Puerto Rico's legislature—without public hearings or discussion—that creates a crucial step toward the certification of what's called the COFINA Adjustment

Plan. COFINA is an acronym used to identify what can be translated into English as the Sales Tax Financing Corporation, a method for avoiding Puerto Rico's constitutional limits of issuing debt while covering operating costs for government agencies. COFINA was a strategy invented during the Acevedo Vilá administration in 2006, when GDB administrators employed it to circumnavigate legal limitations, making Puerto Rico a volatile investment with the possibility of a big payoff and especially attracting hedge and vulture funds. But it was those who came latest to the table, grouped together in what is called the COFINA Senior Bondholders Coalition, that stand to profit most from the adjustment plan's restructuring deal.[27]

Under the deal the majority (53.5 percent) of the funds collected from the 11.5 percent sales tax over the next forty years will be directed toward the COFINA bondholders' coffers, leaving only 46.5 percent of the sales tax revenue for the government of Puerto Rico and its people. The cuts in the value of the bonds were felt considerably more strongly by smaller and individual bondholders, including many local Puerto Rican investors, while the vulture funds will recover 93 percent of the nominal value of the bonds. Egregiously, five of the firms that will profit from this deal bought huge shares of the debt after prices dropped dramatically in the immediate aftermath of the hurricane, knowing that PROMESA would remain intact and that pressure was high to create debt restructuring while the island hopes for federal recovery money.

In fact, the COFINA debt restructuring deal was based in part on a fiscal plan created by the government and the Financial Advisory Authority (created to replace the failed GDB) in August. This plan assumed that $86 billion was "estimated to be invested in helping Puerto Rico recover and rebuild from Hurricane María."[28] Yet only $46 billion has been allocated, and by fall of 2018 only half of the $15 billion earmarked through FEMA had been spent. The delivery of any aid is complicated by the bureaucratic processes of releasing funds, the continued outbursts by Trump accusing the island of corrupt politicians misusing the money, the fact that much of it is in the form of loans, and that, in January 2019, the government shutdown created a backlog that would delay all government functions for months.

In effect, the plan would create an immediate profit windfall for hedge and vulture funds while sentencing Puerto Ricans to forty years of debt bondage because the restructuring itself mimics the mechanisms of capital appreciation bonds. In other words, the amount of debt will appreciate through the years of the restructuring deal, requiring Puerto Ricans ultimately to pay $33 billion on a principal of $17.5 billion.[29] Economists like Joseph Stiglitz and Martín Guzmán of Columbia University as well as Sergio Marxuach of Puerto Rico's Center for the New Economy have called for large parts of the debt to be forgiven as the only way for the economy to recover enough to create a semblance of economic development and, in that way, regain access to capital markets—the desired goal of PROMESA.

The final decision to certify the COFINA restructuring plan will go through the Title III courtroom of Laura Taylor Swain, who has already established a precedent for what will most likely be her decision. When she dismissed the lawsuits brought by UTIER and the Nonsecured Debtholders group over the validity of the FOMB and the naming of its officers under the Appointments Clause of the US Constitution, Taylor Swain basically justified any project put in place by the US Congress as legal—largely *because it says so*—by virtue of Puerto Rico's lack of incorporation into the fifty states. Despite the fact that Taylor Swain has spent much of her career protecting consumers, in a legal sense she has almost no choice but to rule to certify the agreement. This is notwithstanding the fact that, in mid-January 2019, a parade of witnesses besieged her courtroom, pleading with her to recognize the impossibility of Puerto Rico's economic plight and the patent unfairness of not only the COFINA deal but also the PROMESA mechanism created to enforce it in the first place.

While all this was going on, a special seven-night stand of Lin-Manuel Miranda's play *Hamilton* was being staged in San

Juan's Centro de Bellas Artes Luis A. Ferré, to be seen by hundreds of high rollers from the United States as well as most of the Democratic Hispanic Caucus, flown in from Washington during the government shutdown. In its breathless coverage the media was largely focused on the symbolism of staging the play there, most likely influenced by the expert public relations apparatus put together by Miranda's father, Luis. He had left his job at Mirram Group, a high-powered political consultancy firm in New York, to split his time between his role in Latino Victory Fund, an organization of Democratic PACs that was gearing up for massive fundraising for the 2020 presidential election, and the Flamboyan Arts Fund, a philanthropic fund designed to give grants to preserve arts and artists in Puerto Rico.

As hundreds demonstrated and marched outside Taylor Swain's courtroom and the island's leading legal minds, economists, and everyday citizens testified before her, it was telling that in all the major features that appeared in the *New York Times*, the *Washington Post*, the *New Yorker*, and the *Atlantic* there was not one mention of the COFINA deal. This is because since the beginning of the PROMESA process, the media and the functionaries of the US government have taken the debt and the sanctity of the municipal bond market as givens, leaving the only narrative to be written or recited about Puerto Rico as one of a well-intentioned mass of pseudo-citizens led astray by corrupt politicians and their own irresponsible ways. Enter Miranda's *Hamilton* to help create the illusion of hope in the face of the restructuring of PROMESA, which he once favored.[30] But would it just be a cover for a new financial regime that would further the island's subjugation to a slicker, more ravenous form of twenty-first-century colonialism?

CHAPTER 9

THE ART OF RESISTANCE

Homeless man on Calle Cerra, in the mural-driven San Juan art district. © Joseph Rodríguez

Santurce, a subdivision of San Juan just to the east of the tony Condado district, is Puerto Rico's urban core. Familiarly known as *Cangrejos*, meaning "crabs," it consisted of a small settlement surrounded by swampy mangroves that created a natural bridge for local crustaceans to roam around the land with the locals, who were largely black and poor. The hometown baseball team, called the *Cangrejeros*, or crabbers, have uniforms that combine the colors of the Brooklyn Dodgers and the design of the St. Louis Cardinals, and feature a pair of crabs perched on a baseball bat. Before spending all of his major league baseball career with the Pittsburgh Pirates, Roberto Clemente wore a Santurce Cangrejeros uniform.

On the western edge of Santurce sits the Centro de Bellas Artes, where Lin-Manuel Miranda's Puerto Rico staging of *Hamilton* was held in January 2019 after it was moved—allegedly due to security concerns—from the auditorium of the University of Puerto Rico in neighboring Rio Piedras. Bellas Artes was constructed at the urging of playwright Francisco Arriví and historian Ricardo Alegría in the 1970s as part of a new economic plan for Puerto Rico. A very local attempt at creating a space for performing arts to develop in all of Puerto Rico, the parallels between the Centro's urban spatial politics and those of New York's Lincoln Center on the Upper West Side of Manhattan are strangely compelling.

The playbook for Bellas Artes' construction echoed Robert Moses's attitude toward the people of San Juan Hill, which was the largely black and brown Latinx neighborhood that Lincoln Center displaced. As part of the land-clearing effort that occurred to make space for the Centro's construction, hundreds of poor and mostly black families were moved out of their Santurce neighborhood, which was near a bus stop on the Avenida Ponce de Leon known as Stop 22. This was an area frequented by practitioners of an autochthonous form of music known as *bomba y plena*, whose central figures, the bandleader Rafael Cortijo and vocalist Ismael Rivera, were symbols of pride and resistance for Puerto Rico's working class. The contemporary group Los Pleneros de la 21, which lives and thrives in New York, takes their name from their original neighborhood near bus stop 21, as those stops are known locally.

These days Santurce and one of its main thoroughfares, La Calle Loiza—which is about a mile or so from Centro de Bellas Artes—is experiencing social upheavals that are causing some to compare it to what's happening in places like Bushwick, Brooklyn. A confluence of visual and performing arts activity, accompanied by an explosion of trendy restaurants and clothing stores, has made the area around Calle Loiza a kind of hipster central in Puerto Rico. The hurricane devastated many poor and working-class neighborhoods like Barrio Machuchal, which surrounds the Calle Loiza hipster strip. It also inflicted heavy damage on the ironically named La Junta (discussed earlier in Chapter 7), a low-key burger and beer restaurant that hosted jazz nights and bomba and plena gatherings run by Héctor "Tito" Matos, one of the local scene's major figures; it has yet to reopen.

The politics surrounding Calle Loiza's resurgence and potential for displacing locals went into remission briefly after the hurricane, but it never really went away. The resurgence of interest in the arts in Puerto Rico is at the confluence of several factors, most of them having to do with real estate speculation and tourism. Although the US and global art establishment has largely ignored the classic Puerto Rican painters like Francisco Oller, José Campeche, and the more contemporary Rafael Tufiño, the island has invested considerably in two art museums— one in the southern city of Ponce and the other in Santurce. For much of the last twenty or so years there have been efforts to attract tourists with monthly open-house gallery nights in Old San Juan, a kind of natural staging ground for such activity. What's more, various galleries have sprung up in the metro area, attracting buyers from the mainland as well as a vibrant scene of locals. Even now speculators are swarming around a street in Santurce called Calle Cerra, home to a street-mural festival known as Santurce es Ley, which has been presaging "art-led gentrification" since the early 2010s.

Calle Cerra has become emblematic of trendy urban areas in Puerto Rico because of its early adoption of the postmodern urban-decay plus trendy street-art model that has characterized various cities in the United States. Beginning with the Downtown scene in Manhattan during the 1980s, which itself featured significant representation from Latinx artists and gallery owners who were ultimately overshadowed by white artists, the model of disinvestment, depopulation, and infrastructure decay has been codified as a de rigueur opportunity for real estate development. Calle Cerra's long period of decay stems from residents abandoning inner-city areas and the government's inability to reinvest in them, causing even more out-migration, crumbling buildings, and, post-María, the legendary potholes that have become so universal as to appear in lyrics by Bad Bunny, the island's pre-eminent *trapero* rapper. Capitalizing on the scarily enticing façade of bleak postindustrial detritus—the same ambience that fuels places like Bushwick, Brooklyn, and the Wynwood district of North Miami—is an Airbnb-organized mural tour, complete with a decadent $30 brunch at Latidos.

"There's a lack of responsibility from locals, who don't respect the history of the neighborhood," said Marina Reyes Franco, an art curator and historian who lives in San Juan. She was lamenting the Calle Cerra's transition from its status as the home of the music industry in Puerto Rico, a change that began accelerating a couple of years before María. In November 2015 the main branch of Discos Viera, whose ornate colonial architecture gave it the name La Catedral de la Música (the Cathedral of Music), was forced to close because of what its owner, Rafael Viera, called a fraudulent sale by Scotiabank for $100 million, despite what he said was a higher offer on his part.[1] The site of Viera Music is currently occupied by Latidos and its brunching tourists.

Calle Cerra is a site of intense creativity for Puerto Rican artists, who typically express strongly progressive sentiments along with biting sarcasm and a deep love for the island and its colonial reality. But it is also a vehicle for profit making by both local and outside investors. For example, the Santurce es

Ley event held in December of 2018 featured a mural depicting working-class Afro–Puerto Rican and Afro-Dominican women wearing hair rollers in a warm embrace, suggesting solidarity among women as well as an antidote to the continuing problem of anti-Dominican discrimination that affects all levels of Puerto Rican society. Also featured was a primitive roller-coaster installation called "Estamos Bien" (We're Okay), a kind of sarcastic echo of a Bad Bunny song of the same name that for many asserted *auto-gestión* (self-determination)—albeit in partying mode—that had become one of Puerto Rico's rallying cries.

Although the term had been in use for many years, auto-gestión had arisen to deal with the local and US governments' widespread inefficacy in repairing post-María damage in Puerto Rico. By saying, "Estamos Bien," Bad Bunny was asserting agency over passive victimhood. Yet with the sculpture, artist and musician Mark Rivera wanted to reactivate the indignation Puerto Ricans feel, signaling how much work still needed to be done. "Estamos Bien? In reality, corruption, the closing of schools, machista violence and femicide don't indicate that we're okay," he told local newspaper *Primera Hora*.[2] In this way, as had happened in New York's Lower East Side, Brooklyn's Bushwick, and San Francisco's Mission District, Puerto Rican/Latinx culture's vibrancy and engagement with arts and community creates an off-the-charts cool factor that irresistibly draws hipsters—both Anglos and middle-class Puerto Ricans— and pushes up commercial and residential rents while anchoring upscale restaurants and businesses.

Artists in Puerto Rico today are caught between trying to survive from their art, which is almost impossible to achieve outside of structures that cater to tourism and gentrifying forces, and producing art while finding other ways to support themselves, a strategy that opens up the possibility of making art of resistance. As is the case with most marginalized groups, the mere activity of producing art faithful to Puerto Rican culture and tradition carries with it a political component, just as seeking recognition counteracts the invisibility assigned to them by the exploitative mechanisms of colonial capital. Folkloric traditions like the music and dance associated with bomba and plena are an example of this, and it is not surprising that plena hand drums called *panderetas* are played at almost every demonstration organized by university students and union marches.

Plena was one of the things that helped me find my way back to what was really going on in Puerto Rico. It used to be that if you were Nuyorican like me, visits to the homeland were difficult because it wasn't always easy to convince Puerto Ricans that you were really Puerto Rican because of your accent, your clothes, or your lack of knowledge about the happenings and *chisme*, or gossip, on the island. This was hard for me to accept because New York Puerto Ricans are relentlessly nationalist, and it seems that about half of our cars have a Boricua flag or decal hanging from the rear-view mirror.

The classic anecdote about this was crystallized in a movie about Nuyorican poet Miguel Piñero. In it he admonishes a roomful of literary types for thumbing their noses at Spanglish. It was an assertion that being authentically Puerto Rican doesn't necessarily mean speaking perfect Spanish and that this kind of language policing had a lot to do with exclusionary tactics of the island's small white minority. The notion of being from *aquí* or *allá* (here or there) was subtly associated with whiter islanders who stayed and darker ones who left. Plena culture and spoken-word culture, which grew through out-migration and returning to the island, created what sociologist Juan Flores called "cultural remittances."[3] They hope to create a transnational Puerto Rican culture identity that doesn't need a physical territory to exist.

Because of a number of globalizing factors—like cable television, the internet, the post–2006 recession increase of migration back to the island from the United States, and the growth of urban culture through movements like reggaetón, spoken word, and the bomba y plena revival—Puerto Ricans and Diaspo-Ricans are bonding like they never have before.

Reggaetón and Latin trap are creating a kind of universal urban language for Puerto Ricans. Through them cultural exchange can be less of a translation and more a matter of sharing information. There's been a simultaneous explosion of interest in Nuyorican culture on the part of island Ricans and a new desire for mainland Puerto Ricans to dig deeper into their culture. Almost twenty years ago the Nuyorican Café opened in Old San Juan, echoing the famous spoken-word palace of the Lower East Side in New York. It created a space for urban-conscious poets reading off laptops and spouting *caserío* culture (the "urban" culture of the island's housing projects), as it was affected by the same kinds of broken-windows policing common in US cities.

The Vieques movement of the late 1990s and early 2000s not only united diaspora and island-based activists but also spoken-word poets from New York and San Juan. In 2005 a special issue of the *Hostos Review*, published by the Latin American Writers Institute at Hostos College, was dedicated to an *encuentro* (meeting) between Nuyorican and Puerto Rican poets and writers. It brought together New York poets like Mariposa (Maria Teresa Fernandez) and Willie Perdomo and island poets like Gallego and Guillermo Rebollo-Gil. In an act of mutual cultural remittance, the quintessential line from Mariposa's "Ode to DiaspoRican" was reversed. Whereas the New York poet insisted that she wasn't born in Puerto Rico and that Puerto Rico, instead, was born in her through ritual and ancestral memory, Gallego asserted that he wasn't born in New York and that New York was born in him. Gallego was eventually signed to a major label and had a small part in the reggaetón revolution of the 2000s alongside rappers like Tego Calderón, who constantly spoke out against racism on the island.

This spirit was also reflected in the Festival de la Palabra, a yearly event organized by Afro–Puerto Rican novelist and activist Mayra Santos-Febre in San Juan that was postponed in 2017 because of Hurricane María. Santos-Febre has long been interested in creating an atmosphere of literacy as empowerment. After María she immediately pushed the organization to instead visit schools with depleted supplies of books and do readings, regardless of whether the structures had roofs. There had been a sudden demand for books because of the lack of electricity, which had disabled phones, tablets, laptops, and televisions, and Santos-Febre stepped into the void. The organization eventually created an anthology called *Cuentos del Huracán*, and many of its stories focused on the anxiety and desperation of the days following the hurricane. Some of the authors who contributed stories wrote them in longhand with pens or, in one case, eyeliner.

The anthology was presented in March 2018 at an abbreviated version of the festival in the relatively new Conservatory of Music building, which was still struggling with electrical power issues. When Santos-Febre addressed the audience, she was nearly overcome with emotion. She spoke of the many nights she spent crying and then began to shed tears at the podium. "Nosotros somos una gente brava"—We are a brave people—she said unwaveringly, lending her sense of self as an Afro–Puerto Rican woman and the strength needed to bear those dual oppressions to a Puerto Rican people challenged like never before.

It was as if that storytelling narrative fueling plena musicians, with their versifying way of telling stories of everyday people, had a new kind of currency in pronouncements like those of Santos-Febre or even the emotion-inducing combativeness of Mayor Carmen Yulín Cruz. Plena is a living, breathing representation of the intersection between blacks and working-class Puerto Ricans that is antithetical to official narratives, which see "white" as the default when speaking of the working class. A plena revival on the island had predated the 2006 economic crisis, led by a new generation who wanted to demystify its folkloricism and practice it as a kind of new urban Latinx expression, parallel to the concurrent reggaetón explosion. Bands like Tito Matos's Viento de Agua—and their idea of open street *plenazos*, with practitioners learning right there on the streets—had fused with salsa nostalgia and representations of urban Afro–Puerto Ricanness to create hugely popular gatherings at places like El Balcón del Zumbador in Piñones and La Terraza de Bonanza in

Santurce. The latter space grew to attract throngs of not only locals but also well-heeled tourists in the mid-2010s.

Although these kinds of cultural production stem from somewhat traditional origins, there are many different hybrid cultural activities that combine aspects of Puerto Rican language, culture, and poetics with postmodern styles of graphic arts, video, and social media and internet technologies. The crossover between art and politics can happen just as easily in spaces like La Respuesta, a music/dance club located on La Calle Loiza that often has art exhibitions, as it does in a video of a song about the Cerro Maravilla killings called "Odio" by Ileana Cabra—also known as iLe—the sister of Calle 13 rapper René Perez Joglar, or Residente. The "Odio" video achingly detailed the violence and despair associated the incident that occurred forty years before, when Puerto Rico police shot and killed young independence activists, with the backdrop of trees stripped bare by Hurricane María.

"The hurricane was very raw, impactful, and it made us feel a lot of things strongly because we didn't have electricity, we didn't have water, and it made us question a lot of things," Ileana told me in a phone interview. "I think that Puerto Ricans, without realizing it, are shouting to be recognized, to shout out that we are here. I think that comes maybe [from] a repressed desire for, I don't know . . . independence. But we don't realize it yet."

The use of video for messaging and testimony after the hurricane extends widely—from the agitprop of Defend Puerto Rico, a collective of visual artists that includes contributors from both the island and the diaspora, to Gabriel Coss's promotional video of Lin-Manuel Miranda's return to perform *Hamilton* for the Puerto Rico tourism board, to Sofía Gallisá Muriente's collage video *B-roll*, which compiles footage used by the Department of Economic Development and Commerce to provide a "bird's eye view" of the island to entice investors and migrants lured by Laws 20 and 22.

Gallisá Muriente's point was that the "aerial view" these videos use doesn't diverge much from the perspective of the US military, whose targeting of the island for strategic use and experiments in surveillance is perhaps just another form of the same sort of *conquista*. In addition to her own voluminous mixed-media work, Gallisá Muriente is codirector of an Old San Juan–based non-profit organization called Beta Local, which tries to connect local artists with funding sources. "We have a situation where, in the last couple of years the Institute for Culture has experienced a 90 percent decrease in funding," she said in an interview.[4]

Hurricane María has put renewed attention on funding for Puerto Rican arts and culture, attracting philanthropy. However, Gallisá Muriente wonders how long it will last before the funding dries up. Through Beta Local she was able to acquire $350,000 in funding from major philanthropic organizations like the Hispanic Federation, the Andy Warhol Foundation for the Visual Arts, Red de Fundaciones de Puerto Rico, the Ford Foundation, and the Pollack-Krasner Foundation for "El Serrucho," or "The Saw," an emergency fund for cultural workers. "There's been quite a bit of money that comes in, and it seems like a lot of the motivation behind it is an attack on Trump," she said. "So some of us are thinking that in two years, we're not sure if it will still be there." By January of 2019 the funds for El Serrucho had already been used up.

Abstract painter Ivelisse Jiménez is one of the artists who found support from Beta Local. Hailing from the small mountain town Ciales, Jiménez credits her artistic formation with the schooling she received at the University of Puerto Rico, whose very existence as the central institution for Puerto Rican education is threatened by austerity cuts. She'd spent twenty years in New York between 1991 and 2011 getting her MFA and began to find herself going back and forth. That circular migration then become part of her identity. For the past decade she'd been living in Trujillo Alto, a mountainous suburb of San Juan with her partner, Teófilo Torres, one of the island's most renowned theater actors, on a piece of land the couple converted into a kind of old-school finca, or subsistence farm, with a menagerie of farm animals and spectacular views of the metropolitan area.

Hurricane María hit Jiménez particularly hard. She lost her studio, located on the property she shared with Torres, which held work she'd been creating for almost twenty years. She also lost her job at the Escuela de Artes Plásticas y Diseño (School of Visual Arts and Design) as the result of austerity cuts imposed by La Junta. Access to the Emergency Fund administered by Beta Local as well as other monies obtained from El Museo de Arte Contemporáneo was key in helping her survive the disaster.

"Everything is still uncertain these days," she told me in an interview.[5] "I survive day to day like most people. But I also feel a lot of energy and the need to keep working where I am. I feel a rootedness now that makes me think I won't leave the island despite the drastic and difficult circumstances as everything seems to be falling apart here." Jiménez feels that the island's precarious moment is exerting so much control and oppression over her that it becomes even more urgent to safeguard the Puerto Rican artist's capacity to think beyond the margins. "That's my form of resistance," she said.

ARTE E ACTIVISMO

In general Hurricane María decimated the gallery circuit in Puerto Rio. What was once thought of as a "gallery scene" no longer exists. Although some important galleries remain, many artists have been forced in several directions: the large-scale payoffs of making art for tourists, making art while working other jobs, or even making anonymous street art. The May Day disturbances of 2017, occurring when riot police flooded a peaceful demonstration with tear gas after some vandalism that occurred on the Banco Popular Building on the Milla de Oro of San Juan's Hato Rey financial district, compelled the government to implement a series of amendments to the penal code, one of which made painting something on public property punishable by three years in prison. Despite the increased risks, an anonymous group of artists calling themselves La Puerta, or "The Door," has been engaged in underground mural painting on prominent walls around San Juan.

Their first work was a painting of a black flag that hangs near Calle San Sebastián in Old San Juan. Ironically the work is so engaging that it has become a kind of tourist trap, with hundreds of people gathering to take selfies in front of it. The recasting of the colors of the Puerto Rican flag from red, white, and blue to black is claimed by the members of La Puerta themselves as an act of resistance, not mourning. A wall on the northern edge of Old San Juan, facing the entrance to the island's famous "hood," La Perla—a ramshackle barrio where the widely viewed video to the hit song "Despacito" was filmed—sports several paintings that announce the island's indignance. In one, a yawning, balding, and fattened capitalist sits framed by trees, one with what looks like a raven perched on a branch, picking at a pot of what looks like bonds or promissory notes. His image is part of a triptych formed by two slogans: "Promesa es Pobreza" (PROMESA Is Poverty) and "Welcome to the Oldest Colony."

The images convey the growing notion among the populace that the idea of the commonwealth has been shattered and Puerto Ricans can expect nothing but permanent austerity from the imposition of the FOMB. La Puerta, members of which give interviews wearing face-concealing masks or bandanas, is openly in favor of independence and claims that the ruling apparatus uses fear to dissuade the population from that option. On Route 17, near the Avenida Barbosa—ironically named after one of the early supporters of statehood—the group has painted a mural that passing drivers can see. It displays the message: "Puerto Rico, Cuándo Entenderés que Nos USAn," which means, "Puerto Rico, When Will You Understand That They Are Using Us," with the USA in capital letters.

Guerrilla artists usually make their living in a more conventional way, as is the case with a street theater group called Los Payasos Policías, who took their transnational act from Puerto Rico to New York to participate in the National Puerto Rican

Day Parade in 2017. The parade had been enveloped in controversy because it included freed political prisoner Oscar López
Rivera—who had been imprisoned for over thirty years and was
released in 2017—as an honored guest, inciting conservative elements to flood the media with denunciations of him as a "terrorist." Much of the pushback came from survivors of bombings
carried out by López Rivera's organization, the FALN, painting
him as a murderer. However, López Rivera had been an active
member of the FALN, but was found not guilty of directly participating in the bombings, and there is no evidence he participated in others, though he was found guilty of "seditious
conspiracy," essentially making him a political prisoner.

Los Payasos Policías, theater actors who dress as police in
an attempt to highlight absurdities and defuse confrontations
between demonstrators and authorities, are led in part by an activist named Israel Lugo. They made an appearance at the May
Day rally earlier that year, and in the aftermath, Lugo told me,
they had done their usual intervention of trying to convince the
police that they themselves were part of the working class and
that the colonial administration of Ricardo Rosselló was using
them. "We finished our presentation with the speech Charlie
Chaplin gives at the end of The Great Dictator, where he invites
the soldiers to join him," he told me in an interview, referring to
Chaplin's call in favor of democracy and against dictatorship.[6]

Lugo was astonished at the violence that eventually broke
out as well as the media's focus on the incidents of vandalism
perpetrated by young people wearing masks. That type of media
fascination has long been the case in Puerto Rico, going back to
the various violent incidents that have occurred during demonstrations at the university, outside Condado hotels, and on La
Milla de Oro. This narrative functions to stoke a kind of moral
panic that is used on the island to create monstros out of people
wearing clothing associated with anarchists and/or antifascists,
allowing the more conservative religious elements of the public
to scapegoat principled artists and radicals.[7] One of the manufactured menaces was Nina Droz, a six-foot-tall, heavily tattooed

thirty-seven-year-old veteran of Puerto Rico's punk-rock scene, who is currently being held in the Metropolitan Detention Center in Tallahassee, Florida. An art teacher, model, and one-time fire breather in an independent film, Droz seems to be in prison more because of the moral panic over an unusually tall woman responding to violence with violence: police found text messages on her phone in which she claimed to have punched a man in the face for abusing his dogs. Her hand was still in a cast when she was arrested and subsequently charged with conspiring to damage or destroy a building used in interstate commerce by means of fire.[8] Various witnesses claimed that she had tossed a liquid at the Banco Popular building, and police claimed that there were traces of a fire accelerant on her clothing and that a firestick used by circus performers to simulate breathing fire was found in her backpack. She pleaded guilty in July 2017 and was sentenced to three years in prison, which many consider a disproportionate sentence. She is the only person charged with a federal crime for that incident.

THE DIASPORA STRIKES BACK

Adrián "Viajero" Román, a visual artist based in New York, represents a widespread Nuyorican and diaspora perspective, having reconnected with his roots through visits with his family in the western town of San Sebastián. "In 2013 I traveled to Puerto Rico and noticed that some of my family and friends were leaving," he remarked at a panel I was on at El Museo del Barrio in New York in 2018. "In 2014 I realized it was getting worse." Román's observation was pretty common, particularly in regard to regions away from the crowded northeast "corridor" between San Juan and Rio Grande. "I wanted to bring awareness about the economic crisis by taking photos of all the houses that were being abandoned in towns like Lares. Digging deep into my family history allowed me to find other people who would open up with their stories."

Román's exhibition, called Exodus, focused on the uptick in migration that had been emerging long before revelations about the debt crisis and the onset of Hurricane María. With some reservations, he decided to allow one of the pieces, "De Aquí, De Allá," to become part of the permanent collection at the main Facebook office in New York, struggling with the decision because of his ambivalence about the social media giant. "I thought it would stand out from the other work they have and allow more people to understand what was going on in Puerto Rico," he said. In 2017 Román also organized an exhibit called CitiCien, in response to the hundredth anniversary of the Jones Act, which extended US citizenship to Puerto Ricans. Among the many artworks were numerous expressions of support for all three status options as well as the perpetual Puerto Rican ambivalence about their citizenship status.

When Hurricane Irma struck in early September of 2017 Román decided to hold a fundraiser in East Harlem. The date he chose, September 21, wound up being the day after Hurricane María hit. The event became an emotional gathering of people who wanted news of their relatives and friends on the island, which they wouldn't get for days or even weeks after the storm. "It turned into a place of healing," said Román. "We needed to share our stories and feelings. No one had spoken to their family."

After the storm Román revisited Puerto Rico to survey the damage and interact with the people. He made a painting depicting a small child waiting in line for gasoline. One branch of his family, from Rio Grande, saw their house completely destroyed. Then he came up with the idea to start a new series of works called PRtificats, a play on the word "artifacts." "As I was traveling around and helping people clean up their property, they were throwing away their items, cameras, toys, furniture because they were damaged," said Román. "I would ask them for these things because I'd often used found objects in my work. These artifacts told stories and held memories of their lives."

In June 2018 Román was concerned about the rumblings around the National Puerto Rican Day Parade, the first one to be held after the hurricane. The combination of the storm's aftermath and the continuing evolution of the FOMB's imposition of austerity measures was prompting some to wonder how there could be a mood of celebration in the usually raucous parade. Román decided to hold a candlelight vigil for those who felt strongly about not engaging in celebration, saying that he was inspired by a display that happened earlier in the month in San Juan in which Puerto Ricans reacted to the news that the number of dead resulting from the storm may have been as high as 4,645.

Starting in early June and climaxing at eleven in the morning on June 14, hundreds of Puerto Ricans came to the Capitolio building, the seat of the legislature and the scene of so many bitter protests over the last ten years. They brought pairs of shoes to represent the thousands of undercounted dead. Their indignation and mourning—exacerbated by the fact the government's official death toll was still only sixteen—was expressed, almost nine months after the storm, with shoes, placards naming the dead, and candles placed around the shoes. Reminiscent of the now-common altars constructed by inner-city residents to commemorate figures of the community who lost their lives under unjust circumstances, the mass display of shoes was etched into the memory of all Puerto Ricans and the diaspora as perhaps the island's greatest execution of performance art.

Almost as engaging as the display of shoes was an art project designed by Columbia University professor Frances Negrón Muntaner and visual artist Sarabel Santos Negrón called "Qué Valoras?" In February 2019 the two circulated six "pesos" via a "valor y cambio," or VyC machine, which resembles an ATM outfitted with a video recorder. The idea of the project is to engage Puerto Rican people to testify about what they value. The representation of historical figures in Puerto Rico's legacy hopes to add value to what people normally consider currency. In this batch of pesos the artists included renderings of

Ramón Emeterio Betances, Luisa Capetillo, Julia de Burgos, and Roberto Clemente. In a way these pesos recall Pedro Albizu Campos's ill-fated bonds for the Puerto Rico Republic and also reinforce the notion of currency as community and, perhaps, debt as a form of collective ownership and human solidarity.

COLLABORATION, DIRECT ACTION

Another prominent art-activist collaborative is AgitArte, a name drawn from the Soviet idea of agitprop—political propaganda delivered through popular media like literature, theater, and performance/visual art. It was founded by artistic director Jorge Díaz Ortiz, also known as DJ Cano Cangrejero. With roots in socialist organizing that go back to his 1990s days at Emerson College in Boston, Díaz and his collaborators, Dey Hernández Vázquez, Sugeily Rodríguez Lebrón, Tina Orlandini, José Hernández Díaz, and Javier Maldonado, use their base in Santurce, Casa Taller Cangrejera, as a platform for organizing and planning collective art actions and educational workshops. AgitArte has various manifestations, most notably Papel Machete, and they use an array of street-theater techniques, including puppetry and *cantastoria*, inspired by the radical politics of Bread and Puppet Theater and tools for activists such as their "When We Fight, We Win!" downloadable art kit. It is active on the island and in the United States, fusing efforts by local artists and the diaspora.

The art kit in particular features downloadable graphics reminiscent of the work of Lorenzo Homar. Homar is an extremely significant working-class artist whose family migrated from Puerto Rico to New York in 1928 and who took part in a Puerto Rico show in the 1960s featuring a series of "stamps" that tried to shift Puerto Rico's image from the dominant, tourist-friendly representations. The graphics in the art kit feature an intersectional array of activist issues, from environmental calls to protect bodies of water and beaches to anti-ICE and anti–charter school sloganeering. During the aftermath of Hurricane María AgitArte worked to distribute aid to devastated communities in Lares, Utuado, and urban Rio Piedras as well as to seamlessly interconnect with a network of Centros de Apoyo Mutuo (CAMs, Mutual Aid Centers). These are informal community centers that offer different kinds of support, from food to acupuncture treatments; they had been growing in size and scope in towns like Humacao and Caguas.

About a month after the hurricane I spoke with Díaz, who reiterated a concern many activists share: the alienation caused by the centralization of the FEMA aid efforts in the bunker-like Sheraton Hotel and Casino.[9] He set the tone for a narrative I would begin hearing again and again in my conversations with activists. "Because of this centralization, it has paralyzed most of the aid efforts, spotlighting what was already the local government's inefficiency," he said. "Because of this, we have tons of cargo and supplies sitting in the ports, but it's not distributed. It's very clear there are efforts to make sure aid is not getting to the people, and most of the significant efforts have come from self-organizing."

Díaz's words were part of a clarion call that artists and activists had begun to promote as the hurricane had laid bare the severity of problems they had been attempting to confront for years. Auto-gestión was slowly becoming a buzzword among islanders who had taken matters into their own hands following the storm, realizing, in the words of Díaz, that it was a moment "to rethink what Puerto Rico can be. We can't rebuild what Puerto Rico was. We have to build a new Puerto Rico." New York–based graphic artist Molly Crabapple, the daughter of influential Puerto Rican studies scholar Pedro Cabán, championed this new confluence between art and organizing.[10]

Crabapple traveled to Puerto Rico soon after the storm and created a series of sketches and drawings that immortalized Centros de Apoyo Mutuo in Humacao and Caguas. She told stories about community kitchens and new efforts at collective agriculture, and she documented an AgitArte cantastoria called

Solidarity for Survival and Liberation that featured the verse: "There are dead in the Fields / There are dead on the avenues / The government does not count the dead of María." Crabapple's intervention is just one example of how, just as *pleneros* told stories decades ago about the plight of dock workers in the southern city of Ponce, visual artists, theater activists, and musicians would tell the story of Puerto Rico's struggle to emerge intact.

Yet the politics of auto-gestión was wide open for appropriation by a number of different interests in the fractured landscape of Puerto Rican politics, which often pits the island's myriad municipalities against the central government in San Juan. In my conversation with Sofía Gallisá Muriente, for instance, she talked about a seminar she attended, sponsored by PARES, a left-leaning group of academics in Puerto Rico. In it Professor Carlos Pabón raised the question of who was talking about auto-gestión and how Puerto Rico could benefit from it. Pabón questioned whether auto-gestión of rural communities could be a valid model for urban spaces, where most Puerto Ricans actually live. Auto-gestión projects—like new agricultural strategies, solar energy delivery designed for small communities, and water distribution in rural areas—don't necessarily translate well for Puerto Rico's majority, who live near metro areas.

"There's been a lot of talk about municipalism," Gallisá Muriente mused, talking about how many island activists draw from a very valid movement in Spain. "But I wonder about it. . . . I think of how Casa Pueblo is sitting there in Adjuntas and is such a model in setting up solar energy for people, all the things they do for the community. But then at the same time they have this crazy mayor," she said, referring to the eccentric Adjuntas mayor Jaime Barlucea Maldonado, who Casa Pueblo's Arturo Massol said was behind his politically motivated summer 2018 arrest. "How does municipalism work there?" It's also not out of the question to imagine the translation of *auto-gestión* into entrepreneurship, an idea that came into focus early around the efforts of Chef José Andrés, an American of Spanish descent.

Andrés owns restaurants in seven different cities and created something called the World Central Kitchen, a nonprofit devoted to providing meals in the wake of natural disasters.

Chef José Andrés's latest project is the Mercado Little Spain, a cluster of small restaurants and tapas bars in an enclosed space in the new Hudson Yards neighborhood on the West Side of Manhattan. For $10 you can munch on a plate of slices of jamón serrano to tide you over from a labyrinth of high-end stores like Cartier, Coach, and Dior and climb around the smartphone-selfie structure called the Vessel, a temple of surveillance that evokes Jeremy Bentham's panopticon.[11]

If you believe that the project of neoliberalism is the erosion of the political state in favor of global capital, then entrepreneurialism might be the purest form of auto-gestión. Puerto Ricans have often prided themselves on self-sufficiency, especially those who live in rural areas. Much of the mythology around the construction of the jíbaro, for instance, relies on the notion of subsistence farming and the idea that Puerto Rican culture is largely a fusion between poor white Spanish subjects who fled the authority of the Spanish colonial state, escaped slaves and free blacks who followed the *cimarrón* model of neighboring Caribbean islands, and whatever remained of the Taíno culture of the interior. Although auto-gestión captures the very positive essence of that legacy, it is an idea that can also be co-opted by an ideology that promotes less government involvement in supporting the well-being of its citizens.

A recent article on a web magazine published on the Ritz Carlton Hotels site, written by New York Times staffer Mireya Navarro and called "The Autogestión of Puerto Rico," was hardly surprising. Featuring gourmet food truck entrepreneurs Yareli and Xoimar Mannig, agroecological farmer Elena Blamón, a solar panel cooperative, street puppeteers Agua, Sol y Sereno, and one of Puerto Rico's most celebrated painters, Antonio Martorell, the piece tried to educate elite travelers who might be considering a stay at the San Juan Ritz Carlton that the island was "coming back."

Navarro also wrote a *New York Times* piece in January 2019 describing Puerto Rico as the newspaper's number-one place to visit in 2019.[12] Navarro invokes the famous kite-flying panorama of an afternoon near El Morro, the fortress left by the Spanish colonists that has become one of Old San Juan's most famous landmarks, as well as the January 2019 "art installation of colorful umbrellas" on nearby Calle Fortaleza. She cites the Center for Responsible Travel's efforts to steer their affiliates toward new kinds of visitor-economy praxis: eco-tourism, voluntourism, agritourism. The accompanying photos use an aerial view, invoking a tourists' passion for the El Yunque National Rain Forest and another of my favorite sacred spots, the Cabo Rojo Lighthouse on the southwest coast. But the aerial view, with its origins in reconnaissance flights often used for military purposes, has been employed to promote Puerto Rico as a tourist destination. It immediately creates a perspective of both "discovery" and "conquest," this time by the consumer.

The enmeshing of recovery and appeals to tourism and agriculture is also expressed through nonprofit organizations like Para La Naturaleza, which has a scion of the Fonalledas family on its board. The Fonalledas own the behemoth shopping center Plaza Las Américas and have historically been supporters of the US Republican Party. In September 2018 they also partnered with the Starbucks Foundation to donate two million "disease resistance" coffee seeds to the island.

It was no surprise, then, that Lin-Manuel Miranda, whose smash-hit production, *Hamilton*, had captured the imagination of Americans in 2015 alluded to the importance of tourism in his plans to come to the island in January 2019 to "give back" to the island of his ancestors with a performance of his play. Coincidentally, in October 2018 Miranda and the Hispanic Federation—the nonprofit founded by his father, Luis Miranda—announced a partnership with Nespresso and Starbucks to invest millions of dollars in the regeneration of Puerto Rico's coffee industry in October. This was done despite accusations that Nespresso uses genetically modified seeds made by environmental villain Monsanto and had boasted about reviving coffee production in Sudan while being questioned for distributing coffee in single-serve aluminum pods that critics say are destroying the environment. The Mirandas would stage the play during a conveniently arranged visit by the Congressional Democratic Caucus, who would converge on El Teatro de Bellas Artes, creating yet another unique intersection between Puerto Rico's art and politics.

Working closely with "Discover Puerto Rico," the campaign launched by the Puerto Rico Tourism Company, the Mirandas participated in a video promoting the arrival of *Hamilton*. The video opens with an aerial shot of a San Juan area beach, cutting to a Jet Blue plane landing at Luis Muñoz Marín Airport. "This trip for me is really rediscovering Puerto Rico," Lin-Manuel says, smiling earnestly. "Rediscovering what makes it great." The plane-landing footage reminds me of the pattern suggested by Gallisá Muriente's critique of the intersection between tourist and military videos.

The idea of Miranda's "return" to the island—a kind of reverse Great Migration scenario from the 1950s—as a "rediscovery" is an unapologetic reminder of how the word *discovery* whitewashes the violent and at times genocidal process begun by Columbus when he arrived in the Caribbean in 1492. Nuyoricans often use the logic of rediscovery when reflecting on their own identities via trips to the island, usually during childhood. It was part of my childhood, a crucial moment of reconnection with culture, language, and tradition, and, even beyond that, the visceral encounter with tropical landscape, smells, and, of course, the enveloping ocean. That Miranda's experience was probably different—his family has considerable presence in the professional and entrepreneurial class of his hometown Vega Alta, whereas mine mostly left the areas where my grandfathers ran subsistence farms—may account for a difference in our worldviews, but the theme is the same. In my extended interviews with salsa hero Willie Colón, for instance, he stressed the importance of childhood visits to the island with his formation as an artist. Going back to Puerto Rico to visit, a privilege not all in the diaspora enjoy, allows a full-featured US/islander identity to evolve and permits one to escape the antagonistic relationship usually associated with disaffections between diaspora and Boricua.

The video shows Miranda with his father, the camera following the two pulling their luggage through the Jet Blue terminal, the first new building constructed after the airport was privatized in 2013. But there was more than the simple relatableness of this prodigal-son narrative, returning to stage his award-winning musical about the life of Alexander Hamilton. It was the culmination of a series of philanthropic gestures that Miranda had undertaken post-María—million-dollar donations to local artists and a major reconstruction of the UPR theater where the work would be staged. The performances of the play, which were well received by fans and members of the Puerto Rico cultural elite, along with the controversy around them served to obscure two ancillary activities taking place: a visit from several congressional Democrats, including those attending an annual meeting of Bold PAC, an appendage of the Congressional Hispanic Caucus, as well as the hearings in PROMESA's Title III court, presided over by Judge Laura Taylor Swain, which would approve a deal for restructuring COFINA debt that was strongly criticized as a windfall for vulture fund holders of those bonds.

Congressional Democrats—some of whom voted for PROMESA in 2016—attended a series of informational meetings about issues facing the island in addition to being invited to see a performance of *Hamilton*. Right-wing outlets like the *Washington Examiner* and the *Daily Caller* accused the Democrats of abandoning Congress in the middle of a shutdown and, without proof, insisted that corporate sponsors like Verizon were present in the Bold PAC functions and the Old San Juan mingling activities. These reports were in turn picked up by *Vox* and San Juan's liberal *NotiCel* website.[13] Although those particular accusations were possibly speculative overreach, the perception that this was primarily a fundraising opportunity was hard to avoid given the involvement of Latino Victory, a PAC founded by actress Eva Longoria and now helmed by Luis Miranda.

The mainstream US press had been on the *Hamilton* bandwagon from the start, offering little criticism of an ostensibly historical play based on the work of a single historian, Ron Chernow. Despite ample evidence that Hamilton was not an underprivileged immigrant, as he is painted in the play—in fact, he was propped up by the Nevis elite that had employed him as an accountant for transactions that included participation in the slave trade—Miranda was celebrated for using a neoliberal "rags to riches" narrative to champion the idea that immigrants "get the job done." The fact that Hamilton's marriage tied him to one of the largest slave-owning families in New York, the Schuylers, was also glossed over. Although the play was notable on Broadway for featuring a diverse cast, there is not a single *character* of African American descent in the play, which is set in New York during a time when an estimated 15 percent of New York's population were slaves or freed Africans.[14]

Even the *New York Times* covered Miranda's prodigal-son narrative as the play's opening night approached, describing his family's connection to Vega Alta, a town west of San Juan. Miranda's family had a presence in the town for decades as entrepreneurs and small-business owners, a fact that distinguishes him from the vast majority of the Puerto Rican diaspora in the United States, which is largely descended from landless peasant jíbaros who are forced to work undesirable jobs. The feature story describes a photo op of Miranda planting coffee beans supplied by Nespresso.[15] It also goes into detail about the Miranda family's philanthropy, stating that they have given more than $4.6 million to nonprofits while raising $43 million for the Hispanic Federation, which has been criticized for its hegemonic influence on funding for New York Latinx community organizations and advocacy groups.[16]

For *Hamilton*'s run in Puerto Rico, three thousand tickets were available at $5,000 apiece, with another ten thousand to be sold at $10, while another batch of tickets would be included in tour packages sold by Discover Puerto Rico. The production also spent $1 million repairing the theater at University of Puerto Rico's Rio Piedras campus. All the profits from the show were redistributed to the island's art foundations through something called the Flamboyan Arts Foundation, an arm of the ten-year-old Flamboyan Foundation, whose main office is in Washington, DC. Founded by the husband-and-wife team Vadim Nikitine and Kristin Ehrgood, Flamboyan has a seemingly benign agenda of funding educational nonprofits, which is Ehrgood's focus, with Nikitine reinvesting profits from his real estate interests, which include shopping centers, mixed-use projects, hotels, and mini-warehouses.

The phenomenon of *Hamilton* in Puerto Rico is largely derived from its success in the United States, its association with the Obama administration—who can forget the moment on the White House lawn in 2016 when Lin-Manuel invited Obama to freestyle?—and its syncretic trick of casting nontraditional people of color to somehow usurp the racial identity of America's founding fathers and perform a kind of glorious revolution. Some authors have pointed to the resuscitation of Hamilton as wresting away the progressive narrative from the Old Left's agrarian hero, Thomas Jefferson, to the founding father who created the centralized banking system of the United States and set the stage for American Empire. Regardless, on the island the divide was between liberal elites, who saw the liberatory strength of Miranda's identity-politics sorcery, and the skeptical working class–radical student coalition, which had provided the most resistance to the austerity projects that began under Governor Fortuño and questioned the Mirandas' intentions.

In November 2017, when he came to the University of Puerto Rico to announce plans for the production, Miranda was confronted with students who rushed the stage while holding a sign that said, "Our lives are not your theater." Given mainstream Puerto Ricans' dismissiveness of radical idealistic youth, the public's sympathy largely remained with the Mirandas, who had already been involved in post-hurricane fundraising through their platform, UNIDOS (whose name is remarkably similar to Unidos por Puerto Rico, the organization run by Governor Rosselló's wife, Beatriz).

By the time Miranda had appeared on *CBS This Morning* with David Begnaud, the tide was beginning to change. Even as Miranda now favored forgiving an unspecified portion of the debt because squeezing Puerto Rican students who were going to "make [Puerto Rico] great again" was not the answer, the chorus of anti-*Hamilton* sentiment had been growing among many on Puerto Rico's left. They recognized the contradiction between celebrating the United States' War of Independence and the same nation's hundred-plus years' colonial control of Puerto Rico. One opinion writer in the socialist weekly *Claridad* sarcastically joked, "Bringing *Hamilton* to Puerto Rico after María is as if the United States went to Hiroshima or Nagasaki with a musical celebrating the life of Harry S. Truman to collect funds for those affected by the radiation."[17]

But then something odd happened. HEEND, a union representing nonfaculty workers at the University of Puerto Rico, sent the Mirandas a letter explaining that because they were engaged in an ongoing battle with the administration due to the austerity measures imposed by the Junta, tensions between the union and the administration were considerable. They continued, "We warn you about the situation we find ourselves in and the possibility that a major-scale conflict might arise that could affect your presentation."[18] Unsurprisingly, the Mirandas took this as a threat.

Within a week the Mirandas regretfully announced the withdrawal of the play from the University of Puerto Rico. Instead, it would be performed at the Teatro de Bellas Artes in Santurce. The withdrawal was couched in language like not "compromising" on "security," even citing the history of police interventions on the campus of the university, which had created an official policy prohibiting them from intervening, a policy that the PRPD had been violated as recently as the student strikes of 2010 and 2011.[19] However, the real reason for the change, orchestrated with the cooperation and input of Governor Rosselló, seems to have been revealed in a *New Yorker* feature on *Hamilton* in Puerto Rico. It discussed Luis Miranda's response when encountering UPR students after a production meeting:

> One of them says, "Oh, yeah, we have dedicated entire classes to discuss if this is good for the University of Puerto Rico or not." He blanched. "I'm listening to this discussion, and I'm thinking, Is this for real? I remember looking at one of the kids and saying, 'You know what? We made the right decision to come to Puerto Rico. We made the wrong decision of going to the U.P.R. theatre.'"[20]

The elder Miranda was clearly trapped in the logic of neoliberal philanthropy. According to Luis, his and his son's generous monetary contribution to the university exempted him from any political criticism, despite clear evidence that there was an awareness among students and the public that the Mirandas had supported the austerity-inducing PROMESA. Not only that, but through various organizations—like the Mirram Group consulting firm, the Hamilton Campaign Network, and the Latino Victory Fund—the Mirandas were centrally involved in fundraising and political consulting for centrist Democrats who had participated directly in creating the debt-restructuring legislation. Luis Miranda—and perhaps Lin-Manuel as well—expected that the latter's vague statements favoring debt relief (something that even Trump had suggested soon after the hurricane) would shield them from any criticism for presenting *Hamilton* in Puerto Rico.

Yet in the end one needs to ask: What exactly is *Hamilton* celebrating, and what does it have to do with Puerto Rico? Is it celebrating an American Revolution that came about in part because of the colonists' fear that England was planning to eliminate slavery in the colonies?[21] Is it celebrating a vehicle that purports to provide a model for young people of color to imagine themselves as part of a revolution that denied their ancestors

freedom? How does one make that argument on a stage provided by a population that has come to realize that their island-
nation is and has been a colony of that same United States
since 1898 and that it is destined to repay a massive amount of
debt plus interest to a small coterie of Wall Street bankers and
vulture-fund moguls?

Suppose we set aside the contradictions we can find in Alexander Hamilton's aristocratic elitism and his dubious involvement in abolitionism while living in a slave-holding family and
engaging in slave transactions, as well as his involvement in the
negotiations for the horrendous three-fifths compromise in the
US Constitution, which would count slaves as three-fifths of a
person. When ignoring these facts, his most salient contribution to the United States and its ability to project power around
the world was his nationalization of individual states' debt from
the Revolutionary War. By absorbing the states' debt, the federal
government provided temporary relief while asserting a centralized power that would continue to this day. At odds with both
James Madison and Thomas Jefferson, Hamilton centralized
the nascent power of the new independent United States of
America by concentrating fiscal power in the hands of an elite
core of powerful investors. Barack Obama praised this development for its role in producing a "business culture" that created
"a prosperity that's unmatched in human history."[22]

But Hamilton did more than just consolidate the national
debt that created a centralized apparatus of financial power
that became synonymous with the essence, goals, and consolidation of political power in the Constitution. He also created
a central element of American development that haunts Puerto
Rico to this day: he institutionalized the true nature of power
in the United States as the ability of its banking class to engage in debt speculation. Not only that, he successfully argued
against Madison that all creditors be rewarded at face value
of their original investment, which favored speculators who invested in the war debt when the bonds were at their lowest
value. Long before the advent of late-twentieth-century Wall

Street decadence, Hamilton, by empowering speculators who hoarded debts at their low point, gambling on full repayment in the future, set the stage for the vultures who would ultimately descend on Puerto Rico.

Hamilton's run in Puerto Rico concluded on January 27, 2019. There Lin-Manuel Miranda draped himself in the Puerto Rican flag, performing a gesture that has stirred Puerto Ricans for so many years because of its legacy as part of the Spanish-speaking Caribbean's attempts to wrest itself from Spain, its banning for decades via the Gag Law, and its use as a symbol for an imaginary nation still denied by US colonialism. It was widely seen as a moment of catharsis both for him and an island weary of devastation and crisis. A little over two weeks later—at a panel held at the New York City Bar Association featuring activist lawyers representing demands for investigating the debt, worker's interests, decolonization, and one member of La Junta—an audience member asked how the COFINA debt-restructuring deal turned out to be a windfall for vulture-fund speculators at the expense of the original bondholders, many of whom were Puerto Rico residents.

"I've been doing this for nearly thirty years," said FOMB member Arthur González, putting away the notes he referred to for the two-hour-plus talk. "I understand the complaint—someone buys the bond at twenty cents on the dollar and gets a recovery of sixty cents on the dollar and you say how can that be? Essentially that's what the law is. You're allowed a claim on the face amount of the debt. Unless you act in some improper way during the bankruptcy that may push you to the back of the line, at the end of the day the person who made the $100 loan and the same person standing next to him that paid ten cents for another $100 claim, both have the same rights from the US Bankruptcy Code to collect based on the $100 amount for each. . . . That is the law that exists. At the end of the day it is the law that dictates that."[23]

CHAPTER 10

FANTASY'S END

Rural resident crossing a bridge in Utuado. © Joseph Rodríguez

The twin disasters of 2017—the imposition of a Fiscal Oversight and Management Board and Hurricane María—dealt an undeniable death blow to Puerto Rico's illusion of being a prosperous, democratically governed, sunny Caribbean island outpost of the United States. The fantasy that, as an unincorporated territory, Puerto Rico had the best of both worlds—pseudo-statehood and illusory autonomy—was finally over. As the grim reality became more obvious every day, with increasing out-migration, the erosion of the health care system, an uptick in violent crime, and the almost-daily torrent of news about debt restructuring imposed from above and politics increasingly affected by corruption, Puerto Ricans faced an increasingly uncertain future.

Some would rather spruce up the tattered façade of that fantasy with another one. The two-headed NPP leadership continued its split-personality political line, with Governor Ricardo Rosselló, a member of the Democratic Party, threatening to sue the Trump administration if it tries to take funds earmarked for Puerto Rico to build a border wall, while Resident Commissioner Jenniffer González remained steadfastly loyal to Trump's policies. Both, significantly, touted consultations with Representative Rob Bishop, who no longer even had control over the House Committee on Natural Resources—having ceded that position to Representative Raúl Grijalva after the 2018 midterms—about paving a path for statehood through the intermediate step of "incorporated territory." Although some legal scholars feel that Puerto Rico is already a de facto incorporated territory—a status that, historically at least, has been a significant step closer to statehood—formal recognition of such a status would distance it from its illusory commonwealth status as well as independence but might create a situation in which Puerto Ricans would pay income taxes without voting representation in Congress.

In general, Washington's stance toward Puerto Rico has remained essentially unchanged since the hurricane. There is almost no discussion inside the Beltway of anything pertaining to Puerto Rico, with the exception of Representative Nydia Velásquez and others' criticism of Trump's inadequate response to María as the subject of a potential House investigation. Puerto Rico's most vocal advocate on the House floor, Representative Luis Gutiérrez, left office in January 2019, and no one picked up the slack, even after the celebrated visit of the Hispanic Congressional Caucus to see the performances of *Hamilton* in Puerto Rico.

While there has been some Congressional criticism of the COFINA deal by Nydia Velásquez, Elizabeth Warren, Raúl Grijalva, and Darren Soto, it's been muted. One wonders how something that was splashed all over the pages of the United States' most prominent financial media outlets is not on the political radar. The *Wall Street Journal* breezily reported the deal as an almost deserved windfall for vulture-fund bondholders, who swooped in to buy massive amounts of bonds in the wake of Hurricane María.[1] "The wagers paid off this week," *WSJ* reporter Anthony Scurria's text concluded. "When Judge Laura Taylor Swain approved the settlement from a courtroom in San Juan, a stark illustration of how sophisticated players can turn profits through financial engineering even when borrowers can't or won't pay everything they owe." While the deal was understandably trashed by "junior" bondholders like Oppenheimer Funds, which took the brunt of the haircut, it was welcomed by Cristian Sobrino, Junta liaison to Governor Rosselló, who called it a "critical step in the fiscal rehabilitation of Puerto Rico."

Business as usual in Puerto Rico is really the only lens through which the United States views the island. "Puerto Rico is Open for Business," is perhaps the most repeated post-María slogan. Its ten-year recession has been conveniently forgotten, and now that COFINA had been restructured and some $6 billion was on a legal path to be annulled because of violations of Puerto Rico's constitution regarding its debt limit, the island would be left to pick up the pieces. This would happen despite the fact that restructuring was based on "fantasized" revenues that didn't account for the impacts of continued out-migration and loss of jobs and income that would be filling the COFINA sales-tax coffers.

The unrealistic predictions the Puerto Rico government made in the fiscal plans they submitted hinged on several dubious assumptions: that Puerto Rico's economy would grow in the coming years, despite the standard tendency of postdisaster economies to show negative economic growth (something Puerto Rico was already experiencing after Section 936 tax abatements were phased out) for up to fifteen years, and that out-migration would decrease, though worsening conditions made it more likely that out-migration would remain steady or even accelerate.[2] In a study sponsored by Puerto Rico nonprofit Esapacios Abiertos and published in January 2018, Columbia University economists Pablo Gluzmann, Martín Guzmán, and Joseph Stiglitz were very clear: the government fiscal plan was not in line with debt-sustainability requirements. Instead, the debt should be substantially reduced—more so than the token $6 billion of annulled GO debt—and a feasible economic growth plan must be devised.[3]

In written testimony given to the House Committee on Natural Resources in May, Columbia University economist Martín Guzmán asserted that instead of rewriting fiscal plans and moving toward a sensible debt restructuring, the current plan will leave a legacy of debt and risk for Puerto Rico. He also criticized the "generosity" of the COFINA deal to its bondholders, which could not be sustained unless the reduction of the rest of the debt came to at least 85 percent. "The outcome of the political game among the Board, the government of Puerto Rico, the U.S. Congress, and the bondholders over disaster relief funds is contrary to the interests of Puerto Rican citizens," he concluded. "Those who bought COFINA bonds in the months that followed Hurricane María have made massive profits at the expense of the future of Puerto Rico's economy. In fact, with this deal, COFINA bondholders will be among the main beneficiaries of the effects that the federal relief will have on the island's economy."[4]

Unfortunately, with COFINA and PREPA deals officially approved, government officials seemingly powerless, disaster capitalism in full bloom under Trump, and the essential structure of the colonial relationship between the United States and Puerto Rico, which is a finely tuned mechanism that returns profits back to the mainland, unchanged, any improvement in fiscal terms seems well out of reach. Trump himself continued to tweet disparaging critiques of the Puerto Rico government's corruption (not entirely untrue) while claiming, in an outrageous lie, that Puerto Rico has already received $91 billion in aid, when in fact Puerto Rico had been promised only $45 billion, of which it had received only about $20 billion, with only $1.5 billion directly related to reconstructing the island.[5]

Because no real help is forthcoming from the United States outside of private philanthropy, the nonprofit industrial complex, a well-meaning diaspora, and a handful of Congresspeople, what are Puerto Ricans to do? Left with no other alternatives, they either migrate to the mainland or continue to struggle and maintain a strong cultural presence that enhances an already well-developed notion of national core identity. This identity continues to evolve as we move forward into an era of intersectional politics—particularly evidenced by a growing feminist movement—that seems to be emerging in the United States and the rest of the world. For Puerto Rico the way forward lies not so much in engaging with the politics of optimism represented by a neoliberal spin of the concept of auto-gestión and hopeful entertainment like Hamilton but rather to turn the sudden onset of widespread pessimism into an organized resistance.[6]

ACTIVISM AND CRISIS

One of the major fronts of activism in Puerto Rico now is a campaign called Auditoría Ya!, or "Audit Now." It is the political arm of the Frente Ciudadano por la Auditoría de la Deuda (Citizen Front for the Audit of the Debt). Led by human rights attorney Eva Prados and law professor Luis José Torres Ascencio, the group is in constant motion, promoting workshops and teach-ins to understand how the debt was accumulated, what can be learned from forensically analyzing the debt, and the revelations that much of the debt could be considered illegal as an argument for reducing it. The Frente advocates for canceling the entirety of Puerto Rico's debt because of disclosures about the, at best, irregularities and, at worst, outright illegalities in how the debt was accumulated. These come from their own investigations, some of which established that bond emissions that were made to pay the structural deficit should be considered illegal going back to transactions made in 2007, years before the massive 2014 emission.

But one of the most important shifts the Frente is making is its attempts to forge links with international movements against austerity measures to collect debt. In this way they hope to unite Puerto Rico with a global struggle against debt, one that in Europe has created movements like Spain's Podemos, a working-class movement born out of labor struggle and that country's mortgage crisis as well as the election of Barcelona mayor Ada Colau, a founding member of the Plataforma de Afectados por la Hipoteca (Platform for People Affected by Mortgages), whose preferred tactic was occupying offending banks. In early December 2018 the group sponsored a summit in conjunction with the international Committee for the Abolition of Illegitimate Debt, which brought together island and diaspora Puerto Ricans to discuss not only Puerto Rico's debt but also the struggles of other countries in Latin America, Europe, and the Global South.

Although Puerto Rico has long suffered from being estranged from the rest of Latin America as well as Europe by virtue of US colonial control of its information discourse, it retains a core community of legal professionals and academics who continue to engage in global dialog. The CADTM (Committee for the Abolition of Illegitimate Debt) conference put forward an array of speakers from Europe, the Caribbean, and the rest of Latin

America, all of whom insisted that individual cases of debtor nations—or, in Puerto Rico's case, colonies—were made stronger in solidarity with similarly exploited countries.

The predominant analysis around Puerto Rico's debt in media and political circles suggested one of the central ideas in David Graeber's *Debt: The First 5,000 Years*: that the commonsense narrative of capitalist democracies is that debts must be paid as a kind of universal moral principle. But what if, as CADTM leader Eric Toussaint suggested, there is strong evidence that a debt is illegitimate or illegal? Would there be room to assert that there would be no absolute obligation to pay it? In Toussaint's brief speech at the conference's opening panel he alluded to the world's history of eliminating debts. Long before the nineteenth-century European debt-forgiving jubilees were the 1762 BC debt cancellations in Babylon's Code of Hammurabi, in which tablets where debts were recorded were smashed; the Jewish book of Jubilees, which called for a canceling of debts every fifty years; and the Seisachtheia reforms mandated by the Athenian poet and lawmaker Solon, who decided in sixth-century BC that Athens had been plagued with too much serfdom and slavery, which were imposed when an individual could not pay back the creditor.

Solon's reforms also created limits on the amount of property that individuals could own to prevent the excessive accumulation of land as property. It is not surprising that his reforms are credited with putting Greece on the path to democracy as its period of warlords waned. At the conference Touissant reminded the gathering that the debt Puerto Rico owed could be categorized as odious because it was accumulated against the interest of Puerto Ricans and the process of accumulation involved the creditors' awareness of its odiousness, or at least their failure to prove lack of such knowledge. Modern antidebt movements in countries on the periphery of the Eurozone were created around citizen debt audits, and although mainstream media commentaries try to celebrate those countries' "return" to the capital markets, the story is not as rosy as it seems.

Take Greece, for example, a country with which Puerto Rico is often compared. Although the good news might be that, as the mainstream media would suggest, "the bailouts (also called rescue packages) are over," and Greece's dependency on the European Union and the IMF has lessened, its people's fortunes are in disarray.[7] The economy might be growing, but household income is down by 33 percent, most of the jobs are low paying and short term in nature, not permanent, and the imposition of pension cuts and tax increases has not ended.[8] The implications for Puerto Rico are clear: this is what happened to Greece after only eight years of IMF intervention—what will happen when Puerto Rico is, per the COFINA deal, obligated to repay a restructured debt for at least forty years, ten years over the constitutional limit of thirty years for debt repayment?

Other speakers, like Camile Chalmers, reminded attendees of the historical extraction of debt from Haiti, its "debt of independence," the "severance payment" it wound up paying to France for over 150 years after its revolutionary war of independence ended. One wonders if the COFINA debt deal will be the model for a perpetual debt restructuring that could hold Puerto Rico in debt repayment mechanisms for over a century as well, long after it is deemed eligible to return to the capital markets.

Human rights lawyer Natasha Lycia Ora Bannan painted a picture of Puerto Rico searching to restore social justice in the midst of a seemingly never-ending future of stagnating underdevelopment accompanied and enabled by institutionalized governmental corruption. "I haven't come to talk about the crisis, but the solutions that we need to formulate," she said. "It's the people that are saying that the debt is illegitimate, not the government. Odious debt is most often connected to a regime, rather than individual transactions, and this is a regime looking to impose austerity when it has preached equality for so long."

Law professor and scholar Efraín Rivera Ramos recalled his activism in the 1980s when the US government intercepted hundreds of Haitians in their desperate attempts to reach the US mainland and sent them to be held in a detention center in Ponce. The Caribbean context is so important and particularly relevant in view of the anti-American disturbances in Port Au Prince that took place in early 2019, spurred by economic crisis, perceived government corruption, and disenchantment with the global nonprofits that have failed in their attempts to rebuild Haiti nine-plus years after its calamitous earthquake.

Rivera Ramos felt strongly about how important it was for Puerto Ricans to be aware that there are various crises plaguing the island simultaneously: a fiscal crisis (the debt), an economic crisis (the economy), and a democratic crisis, in which the government has devolved into an apparatus that only serves to exacerbate previously existing colonial domination and control. He also stressed that Puerto Rico must connect its struggle to the one against financial capital around the world and engage in international solidarity. Further, though he is a practicing lawyer, Ramos asserted that the colonial problem wouldn't be solved in the courts and that somehow academics, the media, and the forces in the streets must find a new synergy.

Still, the actions being taken in the case seeking to invalidate $6 billion in debt seem to show part of the process of PROMESA working. The lawsuit filed by the FOMB and the Unsecured Creditors Committee of Puerto Rico has built on some of the claims in the COFINA legislation that challenged the legality of at least parts of the debt. In a cumulative effect it is slowly being revealed that the Constitution of Puerto Rico was violated in several ways by several different actors. Where the Junta once scoffed at the idea of illegality, the tables are turned, and they are now active participants in litigation that seeks to prove that. The logic is fairly simple: If a government constitution has a balanced-budget clause, the government shouldn't be in bankruptcy.

If $6 billion is declared illegal and Puerto Rico winds up not having to pay, it's not something to dismiss lightly. But the way this is playing out seems to take the focus off the rest of the $72 billion (plus $49 billion in pension obligations) that weighs over the next several decades of Puerto Rico's future. If it's true—that according to a debt-sustainability plan included in the Junta-certified fiscal plan, the most Puerto Rico can pay over the next thirty years is $4 billion—where does that leave the people? If, as the same report says, of the $16 billion in revenues raised by taxes $14 billion will be consumed by COFINA and its debt, where do we go?

"I believe we're going to be back here in five years doing another Title III process," said SEIU attorney Alvin Velazquez. "Martín Guzmán was right when he said 90 percent of the debt should be eliminated. We're going to be doing Title III squared if not."

One dizzyingly sunny and warm day a few months after María I went to visit one of the Centros de Apoyo Mutuo (CAMs) that had been gaining strength around the island. These were basically food kitchens retrofitted as political organizing workshops, group-encounter sessions aimed at consciousness raising as well as mental health therapy, small-scale art and poetry festivals, and centers of resistance. One of the staples of the Centros is the Comedores Sociales de Puerto Rico project, which had been going on for about five years. The Comedores grew out of the UPR strikes of 2010–2011. The university protests had generated a politics centered around protesting tuition increases, and a new generation of leadership, including Giovanni Roberto, who met me at the Centro. Roberto had been a rare champion of poor and working-class students at UPR, a traditionally middle-class milieu, and had solidified the idea that direct action was the most effective way for people's immediate needs be addressed.

Roberto and his post-UPR strike comrades were intent on emulating 1970s radicals like the Young Lords, a New York Puerto Rican militant activist group who had modeled themselves after the Black Panthers. Both of those groups engaged with poor communities by combining free breakfast programs with dialoguing about radical politics. So, almost as an homage, the Comedores movement came to focus on the theme of food, which is obviously political in many ways, from its production to its consumption. He and his allies felt that sharing food would lead to sharing ideas and feeding minds and, from there, a political consciousness could be built. As for traditional political discourse, Roberto was fed up with reading the mainstream press every day and reacting to its outrage-inducing formula. There was no need to engage with political status debates because "we wanted to build an independent movement, not a movement for independence." Roberto was alluding to the left's general disenchantment with the Puerto Rico Independence Party, whose role in keeping island politics focused only on status has prevented new political ideas from growing.

The CAMs wanted to move away from street protest as the center of a left strategy. Roberto mentioned discarding the mode of the *pregoneo*, or the street-crying, about injustice the way the traditional left has pursued in direct action. He was echoing in a way former Occupy activist Micah White, who contended in his book *The End of Protest: A New Playbook for Revolution* that street protest was a kind of dead end, a revelation that was a breath of fresh air for some and heresy for others. Roberto felt that working within horizontalism—a strategy pioneered by the Zapatistas that gained strength in Europe, and was employed in the UPR strikes of 2010 and 2011—should be a continuing strategy. His organizational theory focused on engaging in the complex tasks of effectively deploying committed radicals turned kitchen volunteers. For post-María Puerto Rico, this was the real work of revolution. "We're dealing with a population that is politicizing itself for the first time," he said.

In the months after the hurricane the CAMs saw an explosion of mental health issues, including stress and depression. Much of their work centers around administering acupuncture to local residents, which they promote as a remedy for insomnia, diabetes, arthritis, and drug addictions. Interactions with law enforcement are minimal and subdued, despite many UPR organizers' fiery history during the Fortuño administration. The

CAMs' stated goal is not confrontational demands over tuition increases but rather a kind of anarchic form of auto-gestión, which strives for dignity through survival. Their kitchen shelves are bursting with donations, jammed with cans of red Goya beans, Barilla pasta and spaghetti, tomato sauce, and oatmeal. Participants skewed younger in age, with some exceptions, and most are feminist advocates like Emilú Fernos, who insisted that much work needed to be done for women to be considered equal. "Machismo and patriarchy are really imbued in women as well as men," she admitted. "There's quite a bit of decolonization to be done so people will realize I can use a hammer as well as the men can."

People who had long been involved in left organizing saw the rapid deterioration of Puerto Ricans' faith in the government as a welcome realization of a bad situation that had been going on for years. "Every crisis is an opportunity," said Roberto. "Things were getting really bad even before the hurricane, but now . . . if we can take advantage of this opportunity, I'd give us five or ten years and we can really begin to construct something that you can say is an alternative."

The CAM movement has expanded to ten cities and remains a significant force, but it's possible the extreme locality that defines it might be too disconnected to create the movement Puerto Rico needs. The opposition between rural and urban areas—a gap that not only marks differences between wealth, education, and professional skills but also a different idea of cultural politics—seems to re-emerge. However, to be fair, there are CAMs in relatively urban towns like Caguas and Rio Piedras.

David Galarza, a veteran Brooklyn-based activist in issues that involve both stateside and island Puerto Ricans, thinks that smaller-scale organizations like the CAMs represent the best possible vision for the future of Puerto Rico. "The nonprofits do solid work and have a strong political message, but it's very top-bottom in terms of organization," he said in an interview in New York. Galarza had met Roberto in 2011 when he was on a trip with fellow UPR activists who decided to visit the scene at

Occupy Wall Street. "When I look at the work that Casa Pueblo and the Comedores and AgitArte are doing, for the most part that speaks at a higher volume for independence than any time we're marching in front of the UN waving our flag," he admitted.

One of the most crucial areas of contention in post-hurricane Puerto Rico has emerged as federal appropriation moneys are being funneled into what are called Community Development Block Grant–Disaster Recovery (CDBG-DR) funds. Reminiscent of the Urban Empowerment Zones created in the 1980s and 1990s to provide investment opportunities for private capital in underdeveloped urban areas in major US cities, these "opportunity zones" seem potentially devised to formalize investment opportunities to blunt perceptions of disaster capitalism. Although some of this money will be earmarked for infrastructure redevelopment, most of the appropriations will fall into the housing category.

Because real estate is such a contentious issue and displacement and out-migration are very much in play, the impact on Puerto Rico will be huge. Even before the grants, which will eventually amount to almost $20 billion, were designated to be available for opportunity zones, Puerto Ricans were having a difficult time accessing federal grants through FEMA and other organizations because many lacked titles to prove ownership of their own homes. Record keeping of real estate transactions is notoriously erratic in Puerto Rico, something that stems from many local municipalities' sporadic rate of incorporation.

One area already cited for political abuse is the preferential zonings of coastal communities to be designated for evacuation due to possible flooding in future storms. A poor area like San Juan's Cayo Martín Peña, for instance, could be deemed to be susceptible to floods, discriminating against that poor community while allowing wealthy communities like Condado to escape evacuation orders. Puerto Rico representative Manuel

Natal Albelo was even stronger in his criticism. "They are buying up property in Old San Juan and other areas to create a new floor for real estate prices," he said in a phone interview. "They aren't just buying up property, but they are contributing to local candidates here in Puerto Rico. They've already influenced the changing of condominium rules to allow short-term rentals."[9]

Natal Albelo complains that billionaire migrant Marc Curry has bought a home in San Juan as well as the online news service *NotiCel*, which recently ran a report that Curry had staged a fundraiser for conservative Republican US representative Sean Duffy, who is one of the intellectual authors of PROMESA.[10] "People think La Junta is simply there to confirm or reject plans and budgets, but they are intervening in numerous aspects of public policies," said Natal Albelo. "It's become a front for lobbying so that people now say, 'Why should I spend all my money on fifty different legislators when I can do it directly with a junta of six or seven people?'"

The redistribution of real estate in Puerto Rico—taking it out of the hands of locals and putting it in the hands of outside interests—is one of the most threatening aspects of post-María outside-investment patterns. Ariadna Godreau-Aubert is a human rights lawyer who lives in metro San Juan and had long contended with local government and law enforcement to protect the rights of demonstrating teachers' unions, students, and construction workers. Within a month of Hurricane María Godreau-Aubert started a nonprofit organization called Ayuda Legal Puerto Rico, specifically designed to aid Puerto Ricans facing unjust outcomes in disputes over eviction, foreclosure, and applying for federal disaster relief from FEMA. She is particularly anxious over the potentially stacked-against-the-people nature of how CDBG-DR funds are disbursed, particularly as so many are being administered through HUD, which is run by an unqualified Trump appointee, Dr. Ben Carson.

"We are experiencing a housing crisis that obviously began before the hurricane but has been exacerbated," said Godreau-Aubert. "We have seventeen thousand homes in foreclosure process and an additional two thousand which are in federal court because banks here sell the debt to creditors in the mainland United States who then have the right to present complaints in federal court."[11] While the banks were slowly returning to business as usual in issuing mortgages—there had been some reports that for a period of time they were strongly preferring home purchases in cash—the idea was not necessarily to provide homes for displaced people but to issue more loans that may go into foreclosure, representing another opportunity through home resale or outsourcing the debt.

"The problem with the majority of the money coming from the CDBG-DR grants is that for the most part [an organization or investor] needs a $10 million line of credit to get them," Godreau-Aubert said. "So the recuperation being subsidized is limited to those who can invest at that level." The much-publicized invasion of Puerto Rico by crypto-currency blockchain types has grown increasingly blatant in a political and economic climate that caters so exclusively to the wealthy. Locals notice people dressed like hipsters wandering around, and the streets associated with the so-called opportunity zones for investment have inordinate amounts of advertisements for blockchain currency speculation. "But they're not the real problem," said Godreau-Aubert. "Once they realize that the infrastructure is not working, streetlights out, etcetera, it doesn't go with the vibe they're trying to create and they move."

Godreau-Aubert welcomes alliances with the diaspora, like the one she has made with the New York–based social justice organization Latino Justice, but she is not happy with the perception that the diaspora's recovery efforts are seemingly inseparable from the agenda of the Democratic Party. Local community organizations are beginning to question whether the money they are receiving from diaspora sources is linked to Democratic Party loyalty. This is because most of the major philanthropical organizations share revenue streams with party loyalists. Although Mayor Carmen Yulín Cruz has often been connected to mainstream Democrats, it should be noted that she became the Bernie Sanders point person for Puerto Rico soon after he announced his candidacy for presidency in early 2019.

As for the future, Godreau-Aubert is unsatisfied with the success of efforts for the Puerto Rican people to mobilize. She confesses to giving a speech at the University of New Hampshire a few months after María and assuring people that this was the moment when progressive movements were coming together. "The groups that were pushing from the left have existed for decades and they had become further validated by the apparent reality that the government was nonexistent, corrupt, and was only there to repress free expression," she said. "But I don't think we've grown, and we need to analyze why that is. Maybe the way we're framing the issues isn't working. Maybe we've been too abstract. The people out there who lost their roofs don't care about mobilizing over the debt. They lost their roof—it's something real."[12]

PUERTO RICO'S FUTURE:
CONCRETE ACTION AND GUT FEELINGS

A narrative often heard in diaspora circles is the fear of a flood of Puerto Ricans leaving Puerto Rico and an influx of outsiders coming in to replace them. Because gentrification of Latinx neighborhoods in New York and other major cities is so prevalent, it can be easy to make the jump to speculate that island Puerto Ricans themselves are being forced out of their homeland. The example of Hawaii is often raised when we talk about doomsday scenarios like this. Imagine the cities and beaches of San Juan metro clogged with US tourists, many of whom have decided to buy up that little house in Ocean Park or even a country ranch in Trujillo Alto—something that is already happening on a small scale—to the point where you could spend a whole day, as you might in a place like Maui, driving and walking and sunning and going out to dinner, without seeing a single Puerto Rican! What would that look like? How could we possibly imagine something like that?

The depopulation of the island is already on its way. As Frances Negrón Muntaner brilliantly muses in her essay "The Emptying Island: Puerto Rican Expulsion in Post-María Time," there might be something inevitable about it.[13] After all, the "overpopulation" of Puerto Rico has been an issue of American colonialism since the United States took over in 1898. From the attempts to universally implement birth control on the island during the age of eugenics to the "common wisdom" that Puerto Rico's population was too dense to sustain an agriculturally based economy, the island has been perceived to have a population "problem."[14] And it fits perfectly into the cycle of postindustrial capitalism: disinvestment, decline, and depopulation preceding new development and expansion. In the sixteenth century white Spaniards were leaving the island for Peru in such large numbers that the Spanish crown had to find new ways to encourage new white settlement. Now it seems to be the opposite.

Or does it?

Will the Bitcoin bros and billionaire tax evaders prevail? Will hedge-fund billionaire John Paulson really be spending more time in his Condado Vanderbilt Hotel now that he's become an empty nester? After the tumult of early 2019, when the COFINA deal was pushed through and the Second Circuit case in Boston decided that the Junta was invalid because its officers were named in violation of the Appointments Clause of the Constitution, there was a feeling that the future was more uncertain than ever. Perhaps an opportunity had presented itself.

The case, brought on behalf of the UTIER union, which represents workers at PREPA, temporarily had the effect of making the Junta's future uncertain. "With this decision, La Junta is weakened, and in ninety days Trump will have to name new people, who will then have to be confirmed in the Senate and that will mean more transparency in the process," said Rolando Emmanuelli, a lawyer for the plaintiff, electrical energy utility union UTIER. "Trump would have had to name new members in September anyway according to the PROMESA law, and who even knows if Trump will be in office by that time."[15]

As far as the decline of government in Puerto Rico, Emmanuelli thinks the public has been slowly assimilating awareness of the situation, but the real problem will occur when the gubernatorial campaigns begin in 2020. "The candidates will make promises everyone knows they can't fulfill because they have no agency. Their role has become purely decorative. The future of Puerto Rico is approaching a crossroads, and we're going to have to go to battle. I think we are on the verge of many, rapid changes."

With its lack of full citizenship rights, colonial underdevelopment, and history of racialization and neglect, Puerto Rico represents the living, breathing bodies of oppressed peoples trying to find a path to the freedom that was denied centuries ago when the United States and Latin America secured their freedom from European colonization. It has been used up in its role as a staging ground on the periphery of US capitalism and fallen into a postindustrial economic nightmare where debt is a promise more sacred for bondholders than the promises made by government to voters. As part of its colonial formation, Puerto Rico has inherited a battered psyche that feels the language of debt and repayment resonate with the moral lessons imposed on them by a supposedly benevolent Christianity, subjected to servitude in honor of ancient moral conceptions of guilt.

As a colonial territory of the United States, some Puerto Ricans have tried to believe that America's unrelenting assertion of exceptionalism somehow applies to them. Perhaps it was the luckiest of circumstances that allowed the United States to retain Puerto Rico as a colony so it could be rescued from the wretched conditions that exist in neighboring islands in the Caribbean. By this logic Puerto Ricans, through their ability to integrate themselves into the American project, could fuse with American exceptionalism, become part of that self-delusion, and chase the final unification of its lone star with the fifty others that represent the full citizenship of the Stars and Stripes.

It's true that, as a part of America, Puerto Rico is exceptional, but not in the way colonial apologists would like. Puerto Rico is a colonial exception to the rules of industry, trade, and finance that allowed moneyed interests in the United States to produce profits that would have been impossible without exploiting a people it considered inferior. And now Puerto Ricans have been left to endure an extended period of suffering that amounts to the quiet violence of a long but intimate relationship.

Yet in some ways, as I reflect, I find that what is happening in Puerto Rico is not all that different from what has been happening in Flint and Detroit in Michigan, the Lower Ninth Ward of New Orleans, the Central Valley of California, or Camden, New Jersey. And, earlier, the ghost towns of the Southwest and the factory towns of Upstate New York, used up and left to slowly disintegrate in the harsh winds of American capitalism. In yet another sense Puerto Ricans are very much in tune with the subjection of US citizens of the 99 percent. As we head into this century's third decade, the "freedom" to take on the "risk" of inventing ourselves in the constantly shifting gig economy rings hollow, as most of us are branded as indebted subjects in a permanent debt crisis.

At this point it seems there's nothing more American than to be in the red, underwater, under substantial debt. Maybe we're all colonized now—by student loans, credit card debts, and adjustable rate mortgages. We all have reason to join the resistance. Puerto Rico is, then, in a privileged position by virtue of our growing skepticism of the American Dream, one that was never really granted to us, that grows ever new tentacles of corruption, where human bodies are just vessels for capital expansion, feeding on themselves and betraying sacred human trusts. By being both on the inside of pseudo-citizenship and outside of sovereignty, Puerto Ricans have a unique incentive to explore new ways to get free.

It doesn't matter that we might like Coldplay, as Residente once rapped in an early Calle 13 hit, or that we are born and inhabit the cities of late capitalism, like I was and did, leaving our plantain-stained skin on streets that were never paved with gold. We have transformed our surroundings into a tropical simulacrum everywhere we go, making a borderless, imaginary nation that doesn't need a physical territory or the ceremonial prize of a sovereign state: a seat in the UN General Assembly. In the end we may not have sovereignty on paper, but we have it in our hearts, and we are not going to beg anyone in Washington to cut us a break. We are not going to play quid-pro-quo politics and line the revolving door's pockets.

Bottom line: Congress can't save Puerto Rico. Only Puerto Ricans can. And despite the fact that Puerto Ricans on the island can't vote for president and don't have voting representation in Congress, leading some to suggest that the diaspora should somehow carry the water for them, Puerto Ricans have plenty of power. They showed it in the Lares Rebellion of 1868. They showed it despite those who died in the police massacre in Ponce in 1937. They showed it by pressuring the US Navy out of Vieques in 2001. They showed it when they stood up to Luis Fortuño's Republican austerity and mano dura in 2011, long before anyone was paying attention. While I embrace my US *familia* for doing what they have to do, it seems to me the diaspora should spend more time reaching out to people who actually live on the island and ask what they need us to do.

What should Puerto Rico's status be, after all this? Statehood—even the most recent proposal offered by Florida Representative Darren Soto, with strange bedfellow, the Trump-supporting Resident Commissioner Jenniffer González—is a pipe dream, and being part of the commonwealth means being a territory to be exploited by the United States. The only redeeming value of commonwealth status is its ability to consolidate a national cultural identity, which is what most Puerto Ricans feel is essential. The only choice, then, is to continue agitating for a full and fair citizens' debt audit to vastly reduce—or even eliminate—the debt and to advocate for independence with reparations, combining self-determination with social justice.

Independence with reparations was an idea put forth by legal scholar Pedro Malavet in 2002 and then dropped. The increased enforcement of debt enslavement of underdeveloped countries has blunted talk of reparations among many aggrieved constituencies to the point where it is rhetorically almost impossible. Reparations is the exact opposite of what the ruling rich states have on their agenda when it comes to the Global South, despite its reappearance as an early campaign issue raised by Democratic candidates like Julián Castro and Elizabeth Warren. Yet as the United States has not fully recovered from the 2008 recession and continues to pursue an agenda of public-sector cost cutting, the federal government may find transfer payments for entitlement programs that Puerto Rico is owed to be an untenable economic burden. This might make the US government amenable to negotiating reparations as a cheaper alternative to decades of paying for the US safety net to cover Puerto Ricans.

Of course, independence can be a scary prospect. There is not really an organized conception of what a free and fair economy would look like in the Caribbean today. The decline of the Pink Tide in Latin America has left us with a standoff between new rightist (either moderate or authoritarian) governments and increasingly under-siege, defensive, and freedom-restricting left authoritarianism. There are so many staggering questions: What economic system do you opt for? Who do you put in charge to run a "democratic socialist" government? What is the endgame of globalized capital? Have social democratic states failed because they have retained capitalism as their operative economic system?

We can decolonize, but it's still possible that decolonization can leave us with the same exploitative structures in place in the political and economic systems. To make Puerto Rico a vanguardist state, a new dynamic power in the Caribbean, it needs to develop an innovative economic system that seeks to democratize workplace decisions, take advantage of relationships with local Caribbean economies, make social justice issues a central part of the state ideology, focus on funding health care and cultural production, encourage bilingualism, create new self-sustaining agricultural models, and revise its nationalist ideology to include a pan-Caribbean Afro-diasporic vision. Violence against women, which has reached unacceptable levels, and reactionary proposals to roll back LGBTQ rights must be strongly opposed.

As both Puerto Rico and the United States gear up for the 2020 election campaigns, which will decide whether Trump remains in power and whether Puerto Ricans vote out the pro-statehood government of Ricardo Rosselló, the political landscape remains unsettled. It remains to be seen how much worse Trump's appointees in Puerto Rico will be. With Democrats in charge of the House, the political orientation of the junta could change slightly. But Trump has been clear about his disdain for Puerto Rico, typically using a twisted "left" argument—that the government is largely corrupt, which is actually close to the truth—to further racialize the Puerto Rican people and deny it necessary recovery aid. Meanwhile San Juan mayor Yulín Cruz has announced she will run for governor in what may become a reimagined Popular Democratic Party while simultaneously advocating for Bernie Sanders's campaign. A new political party called Victoria Ciudadana has been formed to explicitly advocate for decolonization without affiliating itself with a particular status position. Victoria Ciudadana is being led by Alexandra Lúgaro, who won an impressive 11 percent of the vote as a small-party candidate in 2016 and is collaborating with Representative Manuel Natal Albelo and Worker's Party governor candidate Rafael Bernabe.

In many ways we're on our way. What remains to be accomplished is a careful, fair process of decolonization. Of course, decolonization means many things to many people. And the situation of Puerto Rico in the current world situation is extremely precarious. I'm only certain of one thing: Puerto Ricans must struggle harder than ever before to create their destiny, protect themselves from being buffeted by the whims of the United States, and dispel the historic fantasy that we are a free people.

EPILOGUE

Just as midnight was about to strike, marking the first hours
of July 25, 2019, thousands of protestors were celebrating
at the barricades set up in front of the governor's mansion
on the corner of Cristo and Fortaleza streets in Old San Juan.
After twelve straight days of intense, joyful, tear gas–dodging
protest, a surge of Puerto Rican people power had successfully
pressured Governor Ricardo Rosselló to resign after the leak of
a series of private smartphone chats with his subordinates that
revealed strong evidence of corruption as well as an ugly streak
of racist, sexist, and homophobic behavior.

The date was an important one: on July 25, 1952, then-Governor
Luis Muñoz Marín celebrated the signing of the constitution
that would begin Puerto Rico's existence as a "commonwealth,"
a fictitious autonomous status that obscured the fact that it remained subject to the plenary powers of Congress. In marking
that date as a new era for Puerto Rico, Governor Muñoz Marín
was, in effect, erasing the memory of the US Navy's landing in
the town of Guánica in 1898 that began US colonial rule.

But now, Puerto Ricans have taken to the streets and re-
claimed that date for a new purpose—seizing control of their
political destiny. What has happened on the streets of Old San
Juan and distant west coast and mountain towns on the island
has been a stunning, hauntingly beautiful display of political and
cultural solidarity. For decades, islanders invoked the *"Despierta
Boricua"* slogan, and now, that long-augured awakening is here.
It allows islanders to say things like *"ya no es el mismo país"*
(it's no longer the same country) and revel in the revolutionary

awareness that *"somos más, y no temenos miedo"* (there are more of us than them, and we are not afraid).

Personally, I'm overjoyed. I have some friends out there singing, dancing salsa, doing yoga, banging kitchen pots, shaking their butts to nasty reggaetón mixes, generally taking their years of resisting increasing austerity to the streets, and, for a couple weeks at least, it seemed to work. The people had not only forced Ricky to resign, but also created the sense of urgency needed to continue to overturn the United States' neoliberal-colonial project, which they hoped to replace with new leaders and a sense of collectivist politics.

The staggering diversity of the demonstrators, straddling age groups, political orientations, and social class, reflected a widespread disaffection with Rosselló's handling of the aftermath of Hurricane María, as well as his administration's ineffectual, if not cynical, attempts to curb the austerity measures imposed by La Junta. The vulgar and entitled frat-boy nature of the governor's chat with his associates, conducted on Telegram—a smartphone app that has a spotty history of security leaks—revealed a group of entitled men who identified political enemies; insulted them, usually through misogynistic and homophobic name-calling; and targeted them for revenge through the use of armies of internet trolls and other forms of intimidation. They showed that Rosselló's government was more interested in protecting its power through a vicious strain of public relations than actually helping the Puerto Rican people in the aftermath of Hurricane María.

The most damaging revelations concerned a lobbyist, Elías Sánchez Sifonte, a longtime personal friend of Rosselló's (he was the best man at Sánchez's wedding) who was his campaign director and original, nonvoting representative on the fiscal oversight and management board. The 889-page chat was published by the Centro de Periodismo Investigativo (CPI), and a subsequent report by CPI revealed that Sánchez intimidated government officials to approve contracts from clients he represented, at higher rates than those who properly submitted requests for proposal bids, and that Rosselló had been warned various times about this behavior. Other revelations showed that La Junta had also been aware of Sánchez's questionable activities and done nothing.

Rosselló's behavior, both through active participation in the insults and his silence or lack of criticism of his aides when they engaged in the same, was devastating for Puerto Ricans who were still suffering from the psychological damage of the storm. It triggered the dormant anxiety of those unable to reach their relatives for days—of those who, having lived through months without electricity or hot water, feared for their family's future on an island that was experiencing a complete infrastructural and economic collapse. It revived memories of the embarrassing Whitefish Energy scandal over a contract to restore fallen power lines, and a government that insisted that there were only thirty-six people who died from the hurricane when, in fact, according to a study funded by the Harvard T. H. Chan School of Public Health, there were as many as 4,645.[1]

Perhaps what was most important about the fall of Ricardo Rosselló was how it served as evidence that the Puerto Rican people are ready to reject the two-party system represented by the Popular Democratic Party and the New Progressive Party. They understand that corruption has been a constant over several decades and that both parties are implicated; they no longer seem to be willing to choose the lesser of two evils. At the same time, several new, promising political movements that have been coalescing for many years have emerged, signaling a strong possibility of change.

One of those movements, Victoria Ciudadana, has been working toward reform since it was launched in March 2019. The group has focused on protesting against the austerity measures of the Fiscal Oversight and Management Board, such as job and pension cuts, the privatization of public institutions and utilities, and budget cuts to the University of Puerto Rico and various cultural centers. They have also called for a constitutional assembly that would allow citizens to discuss new proposals for decolonization that could be directly presented to the US Congress.

At the moment, Victoria Ciudadana is a big-tent affair, openly encouraging pro-statehood and pro-independence supporters to join in the discussion, as well as those who favor a new form of free association with the US that would remove Congress's plenary powers. Its central figures are Rafael Bernabe, Alexandra Lúgaro, Manuel Natal Albelo, and Ana Irma Rivera-Lassen, a feminist activist and human rights lawyer. Lúgaro and Bernabe were opponents in the 2016 elections, where Lúgaro had a much better showing, garnering 11.25 percent of the vote, the highest by an independent candidate for decades. Natal, who resigned from the PDP in 2017, had been a target of the chats for his years of posting videos on Facebook detailing the corrupt practices of public relations czar Edwin Miranda.

Victoria Ciudadana has opened its doors to members of all political parties and could be an incubator for a serious third-party challenge. It has tried hard not to close itself off to anyone because of party affiliation, has avoided endorsing socialism despite choosing a logo that closely resembles the Venezuelan Socialist Party, and is focused on three goals to create a new political consensus: 1) rescue public institutions, 2) social, economic, environmental, and fiscal reconstruction, and 3) decolonization.

One of the most arresting and dynamic aspects of this new Puerto Rican political mobilization has been its intersectional character. The demonstrators clearly recognized that they were being ruled and exploited by an elite privileged class, exemplified by Rosselló's inner circle of lighter-skinned men who engaged in corruption schemes and influence peddling. They not only built their movement around resisting structural inequality, but also worked to construct a new kind of nationalism that was inclusive of working-class, feminist, and queer people and their agendas. A crew of motorcyclists called to action by a social-media influencer called El Rey Charlie twice flocked to San Juan after stopping in various public housing projects, called *residenciales*, the crucibles for the creation of reggaetón music. A committed group of radical feminists, Colectiva Feminista en Contrucción, who have long been clamoring for Rosselló to acknowledge that there is a crisis of violence against women in Puerto Rico, was a major force in quickly organizing protests and *cacerolazos*—nightly pot-banging that allowed people to demonstrate in their home communities.

LGBT and queer activists played an important role, increasingly asserting a public presence and articulating an antipatriarchal narrative in the face of the island's somewhat painful transition from Roman Catholic social conservatism. The Puerto Rican people's mobilization was filled with queer (spelled "cuir" on the island) symbols and activities. One of most iconic images from the massive, 1,000,000-people–plus march on July 22 was out pop idol Ricky Martin waving a huge rainbow flag while riding a flatbed truck. Drag queens were present during speeches by Martin, Residente, and his sister Ileana Pérez (Ile) at an earlier protest at the Capitolio, as well as a staging of La Renuncia Ball, a full-on drag queen ball featuring voguing performers.

But the most spectacular and transgressive of the *cuir* interventions in Puerto Rico's fortnight of protest was El Perreo Combativo, a competitive dance-off that featured twerking contestants on the steps of Old San Juan's most cherished Catholic cathedral. They left no doubt that Puerto Rico's new political freedom could not happen without free sexual expression. They showed how the bodies of women, racialized people, and queer people could symbolize a new kind of collective common good.

Perhaps the worst thing about the Rosselló chat scandal is that it serves to corroborate President Trump's continuing accusations that Puerto Rico's government is corrupt and cannot be trusted with the federal funds that Trump has been denying it. The removal of Rosselló and the ensuing power struggle within his pro-statehood, ironically named New Progressive Party have deeply wounded Puerto Rico's democratic system of governance. The game of musical chairs to determine Rosselló's successor is just a distraction from a dark reality: Puerto Rico's government had already been reduced to a shell of itself by La Junta.

Since the investigations of corruption and wrongdoing in Puerto Rico are all led by the US Department of Justice and not by Rosselló's own ineffectual anticorruption board, it seems convenient that the governor's ruin serves Trump's racist agenda, as well as the Wall Street financial sector's quest for advantageous settlements through a board with no government to block it. Wall Street and Washington chimed in quickly after Rosselló announced his resignation, apparently thrilled with the way things turned out. The *Wall Street Journal* published an editorial, "Puerto Rico's Political Meltdown," that was a virtual rewrite of former IMF honcho Anne Kreuger's 2015 report about Puerto Rico, which claimed that wages and benefits on the island were too high. "Puerto Rico's main problem is democratic socialism, and Mr. Rosselló is typical of a political class that buys votes with handouts," the editorial proclaimed.[2]

The focus on Puerto Rico's government corruption not only serve to divert attention away from a possible power-grab by the board, but also serves to give Trump—who has repeatedly lied about the amount of aid Washington has sent to the island—and Congress justification for delaying or micro-managing further aid to Puerto Rico. It demonizes Puerto Rico's government as being uniquely guilty of the corruption and influence peddling that is essentially the Trump style of government, where cabinet appointments are given to those best positioned to take advantage of granting contracts to their closest business associates with impunity.

Recent US history has been rife with pay-to-play and influence peddling corruption scandals, from Enron to the spectacular malfeasance of Congressman Tom DeLay. Democratic mayors Rod Blagojevich (Chicago) and Ray Nagin (New Orleans) are symptomatic of an American political system that grows increasingly corrupt in the wake of the 2010 Citizens United Supreme Court ruling. In addition, the complex political trolling machine used by the Rosselló government is business as

usual for right-wing Republicans and white supremacists, and
the FBI doesn't seem to be investigating it efficiently enough to
provoke the release of a chat storm that could bring down most
of the government.

The events in Puerto Rico made me wonder why the Puerto
Rican people-power movement doesn't get replicated in the
United States, with an arguably far worse government in charge.
There are several factors. As many as 45 percent of Puerto Ricans live below the poverty line, trying to keep their heads above
water in an increasingly precarious economic situation. Puerto
Ricans are also reminded daily of being colonial subjects, which
has been their reality for over five hundred years, and their second-class citizenship leads them to question with even more
urgency the existing political structure. When Trump says, dis-
gustingly, that he is the best thing that ever happened to Puerto
Rico, it's not all that different from what islanders have been
hearing from the United States since being subjugated in 1898.
That lack of inclusion, and the unmasking of racist indifference
by the United States after the hurricane, creates a kind of inherent character of resistance.

The Puerto Rican resistance is part socialist, with many
roots in labor and student groups as well as the openly socialist
Colectiva Feminista, which tries to ground feminism in the revolutionary subject of a racialized woman. But it's also a kind of
unprecedented millennial nationalism, where subaltern groups
come together in an alternative universe that's a ready-made
constituency for something that looks like Occupy Wall Street,
except it's several times more inclusive. And it's been building
for years, since the 2010 protests at least, when students I interviewed breathlessly described their horizontalism and the democratic assembly decision-making they learned from Spain's
indignados months before Occupy.

Puerto Ricans have suffered much since the terrible twin
blows of Hurricane María and the imposition of La Junta, but it
seems these twin tragedies have been the impetus to allow them
to see through the one hundred–plus years of colonial fantasy.

They have been granted the vision to see, en masse, the connection between the corrupt political class that has ruled them for centuries and the neoliberal agenda of its colonial master. They are a people that no longer wants to settle for the lesser of two evils. They are ready to embark on a bold new experiment that might allow them, for the first time, to truly construct their political future.

New York
August 1, 2019

ACKNOWLEDGMENTS

My motivation for writing this book came from so many different places. I was born in New York and maintain the profile of a typical first-generation Nuyorican: a halting deployment of the Spanish language, the tendency to view Puerto Rico as a tourist, and a lack of familiarity with local politics and customs. But when my parents moved back to the island in the 1990s, I was able to solidify my ties to the island through regular visits and eventually connect with many new friends and colleagues through my journalistic work and personal life. Out of this came a desire to break the isleño/diaspora binary and find ways to write a coherent narrative about the Puerto Rican experience that builds a bridge between the two.

Beginning in 2011, when the *Nation* assigned me to write a long feature about the US DOJ's investigation of the Puerto Rico Police Department, I began to make strong connections among Puerto Ricans actively involved in politics, economic analysis, journalism, and the arts. I began to understand the repercussions from the economic recession that begin in 2006 as a result of phasing out Section 936 of the IRS tax code, and I felt the need to look beyond status politics—the endless debate over whether Puerto Rico should remain a "commonwealth," petition for statehood, or negotiate its independence from the United States. By 2014 it became clear to me that Puerto Rico's economic crisis was about to explode, and I began to successfully place articles about that in *Jacobin*, the *Nation*, and the *Guardian*.

By the summer of 2017 I decided that the media had not adequately addressed the story of Puerto Rico, instead portraying its economic crisis as one that mostly affected US investors in the municipal bond markets, not the people on the island itself. The coverage of the congressional legislation known as PROMESA was also inadequately characterized as something that would "save" Puerto Rico from a bankruptcy crisis rather than what it was: a tool for debt collection that would severely limit Puerto Rico's autonomy and the integrity of its democracy.

Just a couple of months after I finished the proposal for this book, Hurricane María struck Puerto Rico with all of its terrible force. The storm and its aftermath revealed all of the flimsily concealed crises in Puerto Rico and, through President Trump's unacceptable response, the callous indifference the US government is capable of displaying toward the island because of its colonial power. The enormous and almost unspeakable tragedy of the storm also instantly created a much larger market for this book, one I hope can lead to a positive reevaluation of Puerto Rico's situation and to launch a conversation to help construct a vision for its future.

You would not be holding a copy of *Fantasy Island* in your hands without the incredible support and steadfast belief in my vision provided by my editor, Katy O'Donnell, and my agent, Edward Maxwell. Thanks to Remy Cawley for her precise, fine-tuned edits. I'm also so happy to recognize the entire Bold Type Books/Hachette Group team who have shown so much energy and faith to help make this book a success: Brooke Parsons, Jocelyn Pedro, and Miguel Cervantes.

I am extremely appreciative of Joseph Rodríguez, who graciously contributed several brilliantly executed black-and-white photos for the chapter openings of this book and with whom I've collaborated by providing text for two breathtaking photo essays published in the *New York Times*.

I'd like to send a shout-out of solidarity to Shey Rivera Ríos, whose 2017 art installation *Fantasy Island* inspired the name of this book.

I would not be Puerto Rican nor Nuyorican if it weren't for my parents and extended family. My father, Zoilo Morales, passed away in 2013 and is survived by my mother, María, and my sister, Marisa. My parents both come from very large families: some branches never left the island, others have returned, and others are spread across the United States, from New York to Florida, Texas, Colorado, and beyond. I collectively salute them here.

Fantasy Island would not have been possible without all of the immortal cultural and political giants who make up our collective identity as Puerto Ricans. I want to acknowledge my foundational muses from the 1970s, like the Young Lords, the Nuyorican Poets, and the giants of bugalú, salsa, and Latin jazz—Maelo Rivera, Rafael Tufiño, Eddie Palmieri, Lorenzo Homar, Adál Maldonado, Eddie Figueroa. And praise heroines like Antonia Pantoja, Evelina López Antonetty, Iris Morales, Rita Moreno, Miriam Colón, Lolita Lebrón, Luisa Capetillo, Julia de Burgos, Sylvia Rivera. Also, I have a debt to Puerto Rican political prisoners, and regarding elected officials, compromised or not, I thank you for representing.

To all editors/gatekeepers who nurtured my work and found my perspective on Puerto Rico, Puerto Ricans, and Nuyoricans fit to print: Roane Carey, Neil De Mause, Karen Durbin, Annette Fuentes, Richard Goldstein, Shawn Gude, Andrew Hsiao, Lisa Kennedy, Julia Lobbia, Katrina vanden Heuvel, Sandra Lilley, Jarrett Murphy, Nuria Net-Costas, Colette Perold, Evette Porter, Constance Rosenblum, Dominic Rushe, Matthew Rothschild, Simon Vozick-Levinson, and Vanessa Williams.

To colleagues in academia who embraced my teaching, writing, and speaking at Puerto Rican and Latino studies departments at several New York–area universities: Jillian Báez, Luis Barrios, Cristina Beltrán, Eduardo Bonilla-Silva, Yarimar Bonilla, Arnaldo Cruz-Malavé, Arlene Dávila, Arcadio Díaz Quiñones, Ana Dopico, Juan Flores, Alyshia Gálvez, Gabriel Haslip-Viera, Miriam Jiménez-Román, José Luis Morín, Frances Negrón Muntaner, Marisol Negrón, Tomás Uruyoán Noel, Suzanne Oboler, María Pérez y González, Vanessa Pérez Rosario, Marlene Ramírez Cancio, Ian Seda-Irizarry, and Andrés Torres.

Thanks to the brilliant and passionate people who helped me reconnect to Puerto Rican–ness on the island: Judith Berkan, Ismael Cancel, Luis Fernando "Peri" Coss, Gabriel Coss, Ivelisse Jiménez, Héctor "Tito" Matos, Carla Minet, Ileana Pérez Joglar, Neetlje von Marissing Juan Llonsi Martínez, Prima y Franky, Argeo Quiñones, Mariana Reyes, Laura Rivera, Giovanni Roberto, Alexandra Rosa, Mayra Santos Febre, Oscar Serrano, Ana Teresa Toro, and Teófilo Torres.

It would be impossible to do my best work without the support, cajoling, needling, and friendship of people like Vanessa Arce, Greyzia Baptista, Lara Bello, Ulla Berg, Rubén Blades, Saulo Colón, Esperanza Cortés, Carina del Valle Schorske, Rebio Díaz, David Galarza, Matthew and Malinda Galindo, Camila Gelpí, Andrea Gordillo, Libertad Guerra, Victor Hernández Cruz, Adriana Hurtado, Maite Junco, Esperanza León, Phillip and Lila Levin, Bill Lipton, Monxo López, Felipe Luciano, Miguel Luciano, Jorge Matos, Mickey Meléndez, Efraín Molina, Mario Murillo, Michael Pribich, William Ramírez, Yasmín Ramírez, Rubén Reyes, Draco Rosa, Juan Sánchez, Ray Santisteban, Macdara Vallely, and Bryan Vargas.

In memoriam I would like to extend a special recognition to one of the giants of Puerto Rican/Nuyorican politics and policy analysis who passed away in May 2017, Ángelo Falcón.

I am also deeply grateful to Lidia Hernández Tapia for her endless wit, insight, support, and patience.

NOTES

INTRODUCTION

1. United States Census Bureau, QuickFacts, Puerto Rico, www.census
.gov/quickfacts/pr.
2. Danny Vinik, "How Trump Favored Texas over Puerto Rico," *Politico,* March 27, 2018.
3. Juan R. Torruella, "The Insular Cases: The Establishment of a Regime of Political Apartheid," *Revista Jurídica Universidad de Puerto Rico* 77, no. 1 (2008).
4. Rafael Hernández's 1929 song "Lamento Borincano" told the story of a subsistence farmer whose fortunes collapsed as a result of the Great Depression in the United States.
5. Peter James Hudson, *Bankers and Empire: How Wall Street Colonized the Caribbean* (Chicago: University of Chicago Press, 2017); Cedric Robinson, *Black Marxism: The Making of the Black Radical Tradition* (Chapel Hill: University of North Carolina Press 1983, 2000).

CHAPTER 1. A BRIEF HISTORY OF
US COLONIALISM IN PUERTO RICO

1. Neal Thompson, "Ship's Sinking Remains Mystery: After 100 Years, Naval Scholars Disagree on *Maine,*" *Baltimore Sun,* October 12, 2018.
2. Matthew Karp, *This Vast Southern Empire* (Cambridge, MA: Harvard University Press, 2016).
3. Edgardo Meléndez, "Citizenship and the Alien Exclusion in the Insular Cases: Puerto Ricans in the Periphery of American Empire," *Centro Journal* 25, no. 1 (Spring 2013): 106–145.
4. Ibid.
5. *Congressional Record,* 1914, 6718–6720.
6. Harry Franqui-Rivera, "National Mythologies: U.S. Citizenship for the People of Puerto Rico and Military Service," *Memorias: Revista Digital de Historia y Arqueología Desde el Caribe,* no. 21 (September/December 2013): 5–21.

7. Harry Franqui-Rivera, "So a New Day Has Dawned for Porto Rico's Jíbaro: Military Service, Manhood and Self-Government During World War I," *Latino Studies* 13, no. 2 (January 2015): 185–206.

8. Anthony M. Stevens-Arroyo, "The Catholic Worldview in the Political Philosophy of Pedro Albizu Campos," *U.S. Catholic Historian* 20, no. 4 (Fall 2002): 53–73; Marisa Rosado, *Pedro Albizu Campos: Las Llamas de Aurora, Un Acercamiento a su Biografía* (San Juan: Editores Corripio, 1991).

9. Margaret Power, "Nationalism in a Colonized Nation: The Nationalist Party and Puerto Rico," *Memorias: Revista Digital de Historia y Arqueología Desde el Caribe Colombiano* 10, no. 20 (August 2013), and "Discurso por el Dr. Pedro Albizu Campos," *Nacionalismo Enarbola la Bandera de la Raza en Lares* (Partido Nacional de Puerto Rico, 1971).

10. Guzmán Manolo, *Gay Hegemony/Latino Homosexualities* (London: Routledge, 2005); Federico Ribes Tovar, *Albizu Campos: El Revolucionario* (New York: Ultra Books, 1971).

11. Power, "Nationalism in a Colonized Nation"; Ovidio Dávila, "Los Bonos del Partido Nacionalista Para la Reconsitución de la República de Puerto Rico (1930)," *Revista de Institutio Cultura Puertorriqueña* 6, no. 11 (2005).

12. Pedro Cabán, "Puerto Rico, Colonialism In," *Latin American, Caribbean, and U.S. Latino Studies Faculty Scholarship* 19 (2005).

13. Dianne Lourdes Dick, "U.S. Tax Imperialism in Puerto Rico," *American University Law Review* 65, no. 1 (2015).

14. Iris Ofelia López, *Matters of Choice: Puerto Rican Women's Struggle for Reproductive Freedom* (New Brunswick, NJ: Rutgers University Press, 2008).

15. Laura Briggs, "The Politics of Sterilization," in *Reproducing Empire: Race, Sex, Science, and U.S. Imperialism in Puerto Rico* (Berkeley: University of California Press, 2002).

16. César Ayala and Rafael Bernabe, *Puerto Rico and the American Century: A History Since 1898* (Chapel Hill: University of North Carolina Press, 2007).

CHAPTER 2. CLEAR AND PRESENT DANGER:
PRELUDE TO THE CRISIS

1. James L. Dietz, *Economic History of Puerto Rico: Institutional Change and Capitalist Development* (Princeton, NJ: Princeton University Press, 1986).

2. Kimberley Phillips-Fein, *Fear City: New York's Fiscal Crisis and the Rise of Austerity Politics* (New York: Henry Holt, 2017).

3. Sam Roberts, "Infamous 'Drop Dead' Was Never Said by Ford," *New York Times*, December 28, 2006.

4. N. R. Kleinfield, "Hanging On in the 'Muni' Market," *New York Times*, November 29, 1987.

5. Dietz, *Economic History of Puerto Rico*.

6. César Ayala and Rafael Bernabe, *Puerto Rico and the American Century: A History Since 1898* (Chapel Hill: University of North Carolina Press, 2007).

7. Stephen J. Lubben. "Puerto Rico and the Bankruptcy Clause," *American Bankruptcy Law Journal* 88, no. 4 (Fall 2014): 553–578.

8. Paula Chakravartty and Denise Ferreira da Silva, "Accumulation, Dispossession and Debt: The Racial Logic of Global Capitalism—An Introduction," *American Quarterly* 64, no. 3 (September 2012): 361–386.

9. Vijay Prashad, *The Darker Nations: A People's History of the Third World* (London: New Press, 2008).

CHAPTER 3. THE *DIABLO* IN DERIVATIVES: BORROWING TO MEET BASIC NEEDS

1. David Harvey, *A Brief History of Neoliberalism* (Oxford: Oxford University Press, 2005).

2. James L. Dietz, *Puerto Rico: Negotiating Development and Change* (Boulder, CO: Lynne Rienner Publishers, 2003).

3. Maurizio Lazzarato, "The Making of the Indebted Man—An Essay on the Neoliberal Condition," trans. Joshua David Jordan, Semiotext(e) Intervention Series, 2011.

4. Petra Rivera-Rideau, *Remixing Reggaetón* (Durham, NC: Duke University Press, 2015).

5. David Kaplan, "End of Tax Break Could Endanger Puerto Rico's Economy," *Bond Buyer*, August 9, 1996.

6. Gillian Tett, *Fool's Gold: How the Bold Dream of a Small Tribe at J.P. Morgan Was Corrupted by Wall Street Greed and Unleashed a Catastrophe* (New York: Free Press, 2009).

7. Robert Kuttner, "The Alarming Parallels Between 1927 and 2007," *American Prospect*, February 12, 2012.

8. James Heintz and Radhika Balakrishnan, "Debt, Power, and Crisis: Social Stratification and the Inequitable Governance of Financial Markets," *American Quarterly* 64, no. 3 (September 2012): 387–410.

9. David R. Martin, "Back Story on Puerto Rico's Debt Crisis," *The Hill*, September 4, 2015.

10. Michael Casey, "Governor Sila Maria Calderon's Success in Puerto Rico Rides on Tax Credits," *Wall Street Journal*, December 26, 2000.

11. Governor Anibal Acevedo Vilá, interview with author, San Juan, July 2018.

12. "Informe Final Sobre la Investigación de los Sucesos Ocurridos en el Municipio de Hormigueros el 23 de septiembre de 2005 Donde Resultó Muerto el Ciudadano Filiberto Ojeda Ríos," San Juan, March 31, 2011, revision September 22, 2011.

13. Leonardo Aldridge, "Governor Has Suspicions About Irregularities in the Death of Ojeda-Rios," Associated Press, September 25, 2005.

14. "A Review of the September 2005 Shooting Incident Involving the Federal Bureau of Investigation and Filiberto Ojeda Ríos," Office of the Inspector General, August 2006.

15. Adam Cohen, "The Strange Case of an Imprisoned Alabama Governor" *New York Times*, September 10, 2007. Also see Scott Horton, in various posts on the *Harper's* blog in 2006.

16. "An Investigation into the Removal of Nine U.S. Attorneys General in 2006," U.S. Department of Justice, September 2008.

17. Carrie Johnson, "Karl Rove Had a Bigger Role in 2006 Removal of U.S. Attorneys," *Seattle Times*, July 31, 2009.

18. Senator Eduardo Bhatia, phone interview with author, September 6, 2011.

19. Kirk Semple, "U.S. Issues Indictment of Governor of Puerto Rico," *New York Times*, March 28, 2008.

20. Testimony of Attorney Linda Backiel, speaking on behalf of her client, Michelle Padrón Gaulthier, May 2, 2011, Río Piedras, Puerto Rico, cited in "Island of Impunity: Puerto Rico's Outlaw Police Force," American Civil Liberties Union, June 2012.

21. Ed Morales, "Puerto Rico's Policing Crisis," *The Nation*, December 26, 2011.

22. Rachel Hiskes, interview with author, San Juan, July 2011.

23. Carmen Yulín Cruz, phone interview with author, July 2011.

24. Interview, WLII-DT Univision, Puerto Rico, July 1, 2010.

25. "Luis Fortuño Justifica las Acciones de la Policía Ayer en el Capitolio," *Primera Hora*, July 1, 2010.

26. William Ramírez, interview with author, ACLU Puerto Rico office, San Juan, July 2011.

27. Adriana Mulero, interview with author, New Brunswick, NJ, October 1, 2011.

28. "Ley 7 Fue Adversa Para la Economía," *Primera Hora*, April 19, 2011.

29. Lauren Sieben, "Students Resume Protests Against Fees at U. of Puerto Rico," *Chronicle of Higher Education*, February 8, 2011.

30. "PPD: Fortuño Enriquece a su Pana con El Gasoducto," *NotiCel*, July 29, 2012.

31. "A Casa Blanca Polémica por el Gasoducto," *Periódico La Perla*, October 5, 2011.

32. Ely Acevedo Denis, "Bufete Agradecido le da Trabajo a Fortuño en Washington, D.C.," *NotiCel*, January 24, 2013.

CHAPTER 4. BOND EMISSIONS, CORRUPTION, AND BETRAYAL: HOW TWO GOVERNMENTS FAILED PUERTO RICO

1. "Pirates of the Caribbean: How Santander's Revolving Door with Puerto Rico's Development Bank Exacerbated a Fiscal Catastrophe for the Puerto Rican People," Hedge Clippers, in collaboration with Committee for Better Banks, December 15, 2015.

2. "Puerto Rico's Payday Loans," Refund America Project, June 30, 2016.

3. "Scooping and Tossing Puerto Rico's Future," Refund America Project, August 31, 2016.

4. Mary Childs and Michelle Kaske, "Puerto Rico Distress Spells Wall Street Opportunity: Muni Credit," *Bloomberg*, November 12, 2013.

5. Hedge Clippers, "The Antonio Weiss Files: Vultures, Bribes and Conflicts of Interest in Puerto Rico," *Hedge Papers* 21, September 24, 2015; "Hedge Funds Are Muscling into Munis," *Wall Street Journal*, November 11, 2013; and "Puerto Rico Distress Spells Wall Street Opportunity: Muni Credit," *Bloomberg News*, November 12, 2013.

6. Michael Corkery and Matt Wirtz, "Hedge Funds Are Muscling into Munis," *Wall Street Journal*, November 11, 2013.

7. Ben White, "Warren Wins on Weiss Nomination," *Politico*, January 12, 2015.

8. "Banks Pitch Possible Puerto Rico Bond Offers," *Financial Times*, January 22, 2014.

9. Michael Corkery and Mary Williams Walsh, "Puerto Rico Gets a Break with Rates on Its Bonds," *New York Times*, March 10, 2014.

10. Mike Cherney and Matt Wirtz, "Puerto Rico Hires Millstein Affiliate to Study Debt," *Wall Street Journal*, March 5, 2014.

11. "Puerto Rico Finance Arm Hires Restructuring Lawyers: Government Development Bank for Puerto Rico Hires Cleary Gottlieb Steen & Hamilton," *Wall Street Journal*, April 7, 2014.

12. Luis Valentín Ortiz, "Puerto Rico's Fiscal Control Board: Parallel Government Full of Lawyers and Consultants," Puerto Rico Center for Investigative Journalism, August 1, 2018.

13. Bond Offering, Commonwealth of Puerto Rico, General Obligation Bonds of 2014, March 11, 2014.

14. "Wall Street and the Financial Crisis: Anatomy of a Financial Collapse," Majority and Minority Staff Report, Permanent Subcommittee of Investigations, US Senate, April 13, 2011.

15. Juan Aponte, interview with author, San Juan, August 2014.

16. Federal Reserve Bank of New York, "An Update on the Competitiveness of Puerto Rico's Economy," July 31, 2014.

17. 2015 Puerto Rico Investment Summit press release, *Business Wire*, February 12, 2015.

18. Nathaniel Parish Flannery, "Will Puerto Rico Find a Way to Survive Its Debt Crisis?" *Forbes*, June 1, 2017.

19. Don Reisenger, "The Average American Household Has $8,284 in Credit Card Debt," *Fortune*, December 10, 2018.

20. Anne O. Krueger, Ranjit Tea, and Andrew Wolfe, "Puerto Rico: A Way Forward," commissioned by the Government of Puerto Rico, June 29, 2015.

21. Ed Morales, "How Hedge and Vulture Funds Have Exploited Puerto Rico's Debt Crisis," *The Nation*, July 21, 2015.

22. "Pirates of the Caribbean."

23. Joel Cintrón Arbasetti, "The Trajectory of Hedge Funds Found in Puerto Rico," Center for Investigative Journalism, Puerto Rico, July 15, 2015.

24. "Gundlach Sees Puerto Rico Like Mortgages in 2008 Crisis," *Bloomberg News*, May 4, 2015.

25. A bundler is a kind of super-fundraiser who bundles together contributions in blocks of hundreds of thousands of dollars, wielding significant influence in a campaign and commanding the possibility of increased access once the candidate is elected.

26. Michael D. Shear and Gardiner Harris, "With High-Profile Help, Obama Plots Life after Presidency," *New York Times*, August 16, 2015.

27. Mike Spector, "Avenue Capital's Investor in Chief: He's Prescient, He's Well-Connected. Just Don't Call Marc Lasry a 'Vulture,'" *Wall Street Journal*, March 27, 2010.

28. Jackie Calmes, "Clinton Supports Obama at New York Fundraisers," *New York Times*, June 4, 2012.

29. Matthew Goldstein and Steve Eder, "For Clintons, a Hedge Fund in the Family," *New York Times*, March 22, 2015.

30. Matt Wirtz and Aaron Kuriloff, "Mutual Funds Are Front and Center in Puerto Rico Talks," *Wall Street Journal*, July 19, 2016.

31. "Avenue's Lasry Sees No Puerto Rico Debt Payments for 2–3 Years," Reuters, November 15, 2017.

32. Danny Vinik, "Obama's Radical Proposal for Puerto Rico's Debt," *Politico*, October 23, 2015.

33. Eric Lipton and Michael Corkery, "Puerto Rico's Prosperous D.C. Power Couple," *New York Times*, April 12, 2016.

34. "Addressing Puerto Rico's Economic and Fiscal Crisis and Creating a Path to Recovery: Roadmap for Congressional Action," U.S. Department of the Treasury, November 3, 2015.

35. Natasha Lycia Ora Bannan, "Puerto Rico's Odious Debt: The Economic Crisis of Colonialism," *CUNY Law Review* 19, no. 2 (2017).

36. Ed Morales, "Puerto Rico's Soaring Cost of Living, from Giant Electric Bills to $5 Cornflakes," *The Guardian*, July 12, 2015.

37. "Antonio Weiss, Lazard Freres and the Puerto Rico Crisis," Hedge Clippers, September 24, 2015.

38. Plenary Panel Center for Puerto Rican Studies Puerto Rico Summit, Silberman School of Social Work Auditorium, New York, April 22, 2016.

39. Acevedo Vilá interview.

40. *Limtiaco, Attorney General of Guam v. Camacho, Governor of Guam,* Supreme Court, January 8, 2007–March 27, 2007.

41. Heather Long, "'Hamilton' Creator Urges Congress to Help Puerto Rico," *CNN Business*, March 15, 2016.

42. Bob Menendez, "National Sea Grant College Program Amendments Act of 2015," floor speech, Congressional Record, vol. 162, no. 105 (Washington, DC: Government Publishing Office, June 29, 2016).

CHAPTER 5. PROMESA = *POBREZA*

1. Rolando Emmanuelli Jiménez and Yasmín Colón, *PROMESA: Puerto Rico Oversight Management and Economic Stability Act* (Editorial del Derecho y Del Revés, 2016).

2. Deborah Isadora Kobes, "Out of Control? Local Democracy Failure and Fiscal Control Boards," PhD Thesis, M.I.T., Cambridge, MA, September 2009.

3. Ibid.

4. Sonali Kohli, "Modern-Day Segregation in Public Schools," *Atlantic*, November 18, 2014.

5. Kobes, "Out of Control?"

6. "The Silent Expansion of Fiscal Control Boards," Center for Investigative Journalism, Puerto Rico, June 1, 2017.

7. Eric Scorsone, "Municipal Emergency Laws: Background and Guide to State-Based Approaches," Working Paper, Mercatus Center, George Mason University, July 2014.

8. Maurice Carroll, "Badillo Assails Became Leaflets," *New York Times*, August 30, 1973.

9. "Starr's 'Shrinkage' Plan for City Slums Is Denounced," *New York Times*, February 11, 1976.

10. Mauritzio Lazarrato, "The Making of the Indebted Man: An Essay on the Neoliberal Condition," translated by Joshua David Jordan, *Semiotext(e)* Intervention Series (2011).

11. John Eligon, "A Question of Environmental Racism in Flint," *New York Times*, January 21, 2016.

12. Robert Parry, "How Ukraine's Finance Chief Got Rich," *Consortium News*, November 15 2015.

13. Bernat Tort, phone interview with author, April 2017.

14. Jeff Nussbaum, "The Night New York Saved Itself from Bankruptcy" *New Yorker*, October 16, 2015.

15. Ed Morales, "Students Are Now Leading the Resistance to Austerity in Puerto Rico," *The Nation*, April 27, 2017.

16. Ed Morales, "Puerto Rico's Political and Economic Crisis Deepens," *The Nation*, May 24, 2017.

17. Ibid.

18. "Bhatia Demanda al Gobernador Para Que Entregue el Presupuesto," *NotiCel*, May 4, 2017.

19. Luis J. Valentín Ortiz and Joel Cintrón Arbasetti, "Emails Expose Federal Government Influence Over Puerto Rico's Fiscal Board," Puerto Rico Center for Investigative Journalism, November 28, 2018.

CHAPTER 6. STATUS UPDATE?

1. Manuel Maldonado Denis, *Puerto Rico: A Socio-Historic Interpretation* (New York: Random House, 1972).

2. Ivonne Acosta-Lespier, "The Smith Act Goes to San Juan: *La Mordaza* 1948–1957," from *Puerto Rico under Colonial Rule: Political Persecution and the Quest for Human Rights*, ed. Ramón Bosue-Pérez and José Javier Colón Morera (Albany: State University of New York Press, 2006).

3. Ramón Bosque Pérez and José Javier Colón Morera, *Las carpetas: Persecución política y derechos civiles en Puerto Rico Centro para la Investigacion y Promocion de los Derechos Civiles* (San Juan, 1997).

4. William Steif, "Puerto Rico's Watergate," *Progressive*, October 1992.

5. Barceló originally published a pamphlet called "La Estadidad Para Los Pobres," which was translated into English and published in 1978.

6. Eli Rosenberg, "A Brief History of Rep. Don Young's Incendiary Remarks (All Right, It's a Long History)," *Washington Post*, February 28, 2018.

7. Chris Mooney, "Treasure Island," *American Prospect*, December 19, 2001.

8. DeLay's conviction was reversed in 2014.

9. Scott Powers, "Stephanie Murphy Gets Former Puerto Rico Official Kenneth McClintock's Backing," *Florida Politics*, November 1, 2016.

10. Chris Mooney, "Status Anxiety in San Juan: Left-Wing Advocates of Puerto Rican Statehood Come under Fire from All Sides," *Lingua Franca* 11, no. 3 (April 2001).

11. Sheryl Gay Stolberg, "Latinos Gain Political Muscle, and Fundraisers Show How," *New York Times*, March 7, 2013.

12. Avi Zenilman and Ben Smith, "The Obama Campaign's Unsung Hero," *Politico*, May 12, 2008.

13. Aníbal Acevedo Vilá, interview with author, August 2018.

14. Tim Vandenack, "U.S. Rep Bishop Gets $110,000 in Donations, $20,200 of It from Puerto Rico," *Standard-Examiner*, April 18, 2017.

CHAPTER 7. HURRICANE MARÍA DESTROYS THE COMMONWEALTH FANTASY

1. Charley E. Wilson, Phillip M. Singer, Melissa S. Creary, and Scott L. Greer, "Quantifying Inequities in US Federal Response to Hurricane Disaster in Texas and Florida Compared with Puerto Rico," *BMJ Global Health*, January 2019.

2. Ed Morales, "In Puerto Rico, Disconnection and Grace Under Pressure," *The Nation*, October 13, 2017.

3. "Mortality in Puerto Rico After Hurricane Maria," *New England Journal of Medicine*, July 12, 2018.

4. Frances Robles, Kenan Davis, Sheri Fink, and Sarah Almuktahar, "Official Toll in Puerto Rico: 64. Actual Deaths May Be 1,052," *New York Times*, December 9, 2017.

5. Danny Vinik, "How Trump Favored Texas Over Puerto Rico," *Politico*, March 27, 2018.

6. A report in the Associated Press, "Urgently Needed Tarps Delayed by Failed $30m FEMA Contract," November 28, 2017, described how a company named Bronze Star LLC, which had no experience in tarp distribution, failed to deliver any of the five hundred thousand tarps for which they were contracted.

7. Lizette Alvarez and Abby Goudnough, "Puerto Ricans Brace for Crisis in Health Care," *New York Times*, August 2, 2015.

8. "Puerto Rico Health Care Infrastructure Assessment," The Urban Institute, January 2017.

9. Jessica M. Mulligan, *Unmanageable Care: An Ethnography of Health Care Privatization in Puerto Rico* (New York: New York University Press, 2014).

10. Ibid.

11. Valeria Pelet, "Puerto Rico's Invisible Health Crisis," *Atlantic*, September 3, 2016.

12. John D. Sutter, "'The Maria Generation': Young People Are Dying and Suffering on an Island with a Highly Uncertain Future," CNN, September 17, 2018.

13. John D. Sutter and Sergio Hernández, "Exodus from Puerto Rico: A Visual Guide," CNN, February 21, 2018; Edwin Meléndez and Jennifer Hinojosa, "Estimates of Post-Hurricane Maria Exodus from Puerto Rico," research brief, October 2017.

CHAPTER 8. THE TRUMP FACTOR:
VULTURES, LOBBYISTS, AND DISASTER CAPITALISM

1. Naomi Klein, *The Shock Doctrine: The Rise of Disaster Capitalism* (London: Random House of Canada, 2007).

2. Donna Borak, Martin Salvidge, and Greg Wallace, "How Whitefish Landed Puerto Rico's $300 Million Power Contract," CNN Business, October 29, 2017.

3. Christopher Helman, "Is That $300 Million Puerto Rico Power Contract 'Whitefishgate' or Just a Red Herring?" *Forbes*, November 3, 2017; Ken Klipperstein, "300M Puerto Rico Recovery Contract Awarded to Tiny Utility Company Linked to Major Trump Donor," *Daily Beast*, October 24, 2017.

4. Steven Musfon, Jack Gillum, Aaron C. Davis, and Arelis R. Hernández, "Small Montana Firm Lands Puerto Rico's Biggest Contract to Get the Power Back On," *Washington Post*, October 23, 2017.

5. Yanira Hernández Cabiya, "Puerto Rico Government Signs Third Multimillion-Dollar Contract to Reestablish Electric Grid," *Caribbean Business*, October 20, 2017.

6. Ramos, who was fired because he had become "a distraction," claimed six months later in a radio interview that Rosselló knew about the Whitefish process every step of the way because they were in constant daily communication. Frances Robles, "CEO of Puerto Rico Power Authority Resigns," *New York Times*, November 17, 2017; "Ricardo Ramos: El Gobernador Sabía lo que Estábamos Haciendo," *Primera Hora*, May 2, 2018.

7. Andrew G. Biggs, Arthur J. Gonzalez, Ana J. Matosantos, and David Skeel, "Privatize Puerto Rico's Power: It Would Reduce the Cost of Living and Spur Economic Growth," *Wall Street Journal*, June 29, 2017.

8. Cathy Kunkel and Tom Sanzillo, "Privatization Bill Will Not Solve Puerto Rico's Electricity Crisis," Institute for Energy Economics and Financial Analysis, April 2018.

9. "Republican Senators Quietly Pushed Privatization of Puerto Rico's Power Utility," *Centro de Periodismo Investigativo*, December 1, 2018.

10. Yarimar Bonilla, "For Investors, Puerto Rico Is a Fantasy Blank Slate," *Nation*, February 28, 2018.

11. "Retail Choice Will Not Bring Down Puerto Rico's High Electricity Rates," Institute for Energy Economics and Financial Analysis, August 23, 2018.

12. Omar Alfonso, "Something Happened in Arroyo Barril," Centro de Periodismo Investigativo de Puerto Rico, March 2, 2016.

13. "Electricity Prices to Rise If the AES Fades Out," *El Nuevo Día*, July 15, 2017.

14. "Arturo Massol Denuncia Detención Ilegal de la Policía," *El Nuevo Día*, July 29, 2018.

15. Mark Bittman, "Is Natural Gas Clean?" *New York Times*, September 24, 2013.

16. Julian Dibbell, "The Decline and Fall of an Ultra Rich Online Gaming Empire," *Wired*, November 24, 2008.

17. Neil Strauss, "Brock Pierce: The Hippie King of Cryptocurrency," *Rolling Stone*, July 26, 2018.

18. Footage of remarks by Brock Pierce at "Restart" event, San Juan, March 2018.

19. Steven Mufson, "Bitcoin's Popularity Has a Downside: It's an Energy Glutton That Could Hurt Earth's Climate, Study Finds," *Washington Post*, January 20, 2019.

20. Jesse Baron, "How Puerto Rico Became the Newest Tax Haven for the Super-Rich," *GQ*, December 6, 2018.

21. Andrea Gabor, "The Myth of the New Orleans School Makeover," *New York Times*, August 22, 2015.

22. "Keleher discute con maestros durante taller de capacitación," *NotiCel*, March 9, 2018.

23. Tom Jackman and Spencer S. Hsu, "Blackwater Security Guard Convicted in 2007 Iraqi Civilian Massacre at Third U.S. Trial," *Washington Post*, December 19, 2018.

24. Rachel M. Cohen, "Betsy DeVos Is Helping Puerto Rico Re-Imagine Its School System. That Has People Deeply Worried," *The Intercept*, February 22, 2018.

25. Ricardo Rosselló, Tweet, February 16, 2018, 5:36 PM, translation mine.

26. "Ties of Puerto Rico Governor's Brother to Ex-Education Chief's Firm Questioned," *Caribbean Business*, April 5, 2019.

27. Abner Dennis and Kevin O'Connor, "The COFINA Agreement, Parts 1&2," *LittleSis*, November 12–20, 2018.

28. Fiscal Plan for Puerto Rico, August 20, 2018, Revision.

29. Kate Aronoff, "Vulture Funds Stand to Make Millions in the Wake of Hurricane María," *The Intercept*, September 20, 2018.

30. Lin-Manuel Miranda, "Give Puerto Rico Its Chance to Thrive," *New York Times*, March 28, 2016.

CHAPTER 9. THE ART OF RESISTANCE

1. Laura M. Quitero, "Desahuacian la 'Catedral de la Música," *Noti-Cel*, November 20, 2015.

2. "Santurce Es Ley: Las Calles de San Juan se pintan de Arte Urbano," *Primera Hora*, December 14, 2018.

3. Juan Flores, *The Diaspora Strikes Back: Caribeño Tales of Learning and Turning* (New York: Routledge, 2008).

4. Sofía Gallisá Muriente, phone interview with author, February 2019.

5. Ivelisse Jiménez, email interview with author, February 2019.

6. Israel Lugo, telephone interview with author, May 2017.

7. Yarimar Bonilla, "El conejo de todos males," *El Nuevo Día*, October 24, 2018, in English: "Bad Bunny, Good Scapegoat: How 'El Conejo Malo' Is Stirring a 'Moral Panic' in Post-Hurricane Puerto Rico," *Billboard*, November 13, 2018.

8. Molly Crabapple, "Trial by Fire: How Nina Droz Franco Became a Face of Puerto Rican Resistance," *The Baffler*, June 2018.

9. Jorge Díaz Ortiz, phone interview with author, September 2017.

10. See "Puerto Rico's DIY Disaster Relief," *NYR Daily*, November 17, 2017; "Puerto Rico Sketchbook: There Are Dead in the Fields," *Paris Review*, December 18, 2017.

11. Sopan Deb, "Following Outcry, Hudson Yards Tweaks Policy Over Use of Vessel Pictures," *New York Times*, March 19, 2019.

12. Mireya Navarro, "Why Puerto Rico Is No. 1 on Our Places to Go List: Recovering from Hurricane María, in 2019 the Island Represents So Many Fragile Spots Around the Globe," *New York Times*, January 9, 2019.

13. Aaron Ruper, "Why the White House Is Attacking Democrats for Travelling to Puerto Rico, Explained: With Some Help from Fox News," *Vox*, January 17, 2019.

14. Lyra Monteiro, "Race-Conscious Casting and the Erasure of the Black Past in Lin-Manuel Miranda's *Hamilton*," *Pubic Historian* 38, no 1 (February 2016): 89–98.

15. Michael Paulson, "Lin Manuel-Miranda's Passion for Puerto Rico," *New York Times*, December 26, 2018; Marc Gunther, "The Good, the Bad and the Ugly: Sustainability at Nespresso," *The Guardian*, May 27, 2015.

16. Angelo Falcón, "The Hispanic Federation-Luis Miranda Connection: Undermining the Agenda of a Latino Community Institution," National Institute for Latino Policy, July 10, 2014.

NOTES TO CHAPTER 10

17. Rafah Acevedo, "No Hacer Fila Para *Hamilton*: Es una PROMESA?" *Claridad*, November 20, 2018.

18. "La HEEND Advierte que la Presentación de 'Hamilton' en la UPR Podría Afectarse," *El Nuevo Día*, November 29, 2018.

19. David Smith, "*Hamilton* in Puerto Rico: A Joyful Homecoming . . . but Complicated," *The Guardian*, January 11, 2019.

20. Michael Schulman "What *Hamilton* in San Juan Means to Puerto Rico," *New Yorker*, January 17, 2019,

21. Gerald Horne, *The Counter-Revolution of 1776: Slave Resistance and the Origins of the United States of America* (New York: New York University Press, 2014).

22. Paul Street, "Miranda, Obama, and Hamilton: An Orwellian Ménage a Trois for the Neoliberal Age," *Counterpunch*, June 14, 2016.

23. "PROMESA Two Years Out: Are We Closer to a Solution?" Panel at New York Law City Bar Association, February 12, 2019.

CHAPTER 10. FANTASY'S END

1. Andrew Scurria, "Hedge Funds Bask in Puerto Rico Bond Deal," *Wall Street Journal*, February 20, 2019.

2. Omaya Sosa Pascual and Luis J. Valentín Ortiz, "The Fantasy of the Fiscal Plan for Puerto Rico," *Centro de Periodismo Investigativo*, February 20, 2018.

3. Pablo Gluzmann, Martín Guzmán, and Joseph E. Stiglitz, "An Analysis of Puerto Rico's Debt Relief Needs to Restore Debt Sustainability," Commissioned by Espacios Abiertos, January 2018.

4. "Written Testimony by Martín Guzmán, Non-Resident Senior Fellow for Fiscal Policy, Espacios Abiertos," submitted to Committee of Natural Resources of the United States House of Representatives, May 2, 2019.

5. José Delgado, "Trump Insiste en Alegar Falsamente que Puerto Rico ha Recibido $91 billion," *El Nuevo Día*, May 6, 2019.

6. Rocío Zambrana, "Colonial Debts," in *Una Proposición Modesta: Puerto Rico a Prueba*, ed. Sara Nadal-Melisó (Barcelona: Allora & Calzadilla, 2018).

7. Milan Schreuer and Niki Kitsantonis, "Greece Prepares to Stagger Back from Debt Crisis, the End of Bailouts in Sight," *New York Times*, June 21, 2018.

8. Ibid.

9. Manuel Natal Albelo, phone interview with author, March 2019.

10. Damaris Suárez, "Congressman Who Delivered the PROMESA Bill Holds Fundraiser in Puerto Rico," *NotiCel*, February 18, 2017.

11. Ariadna Godreau-Aubert, phone interview with author, February 2019.

12. Ibid.

13. Hemispheric Institute, February 2019.

14. Simon Rottenberg, "The Problem of Over-Population of Puerto Rico," *Caribbean Quarterly* 2 (1952).

15. Rolando Emmanuelli, email interview with author, February 2019.

EPILOGUE

1. Nishant Kishore, Domingo Marqués, Ayesha Mahmud, et al., "Mortality in Puerto Rico After Hurricane María," *New England Journal of Medicine* 379, no. 2 (July 12, 2018), www.nejm.org/doi/full/10.1056/NEJMsa1803972.

2. "Puerto Rico's Political Meltdown," *Wall Street Journal*, July 25, 2019, www.wsj.com/articles/puerto-ricos-political-meltdown-11564010349.

INDEX

ABOUT THE AUTHOR

Lidia Hernández Tapia

Ed Morales is a journalist who has investigated New York City electoral politics, police brutality, street gangs, grassroots activists, and the Latino arts and music scene. His work has appeared in *Rolling Stone*, the *New York Times*, *Miami Herald*, *San Francisco Examiner*, the *Los Angeles Times*, the *Guardian*, *Jacobin*, and the *Nation*. Morales has also appeared on CNN, *Hispanics Today*, *Urban Latino*, HBO Latino, CNN Español, WNBC-TV's *Visiones*, WABC's *Tiempo*, BBC television and radio, and the *Fox Morning News* in Washington, DC. He has lectured at Bowdoin College, Vanderbilt University, University of New Mexico, West Chester College in Pennsylvania, Columbia University, Hunter College, Wooster College of Ohio, New York University, and the University of Connecticut. Ed Morales is currently an adjunct professor at Columbia University's Center for the Study of Ethnicity and Race and occasionally appears as a host on WBAI-FM. He lives in New York City.